Facts on Aging in Canada

Compiled by

The Office of Gerontological Studies
McMaster University

Gail Elliot
With the Assistance of
Melanie Hunt and Kim Hutchison

1996

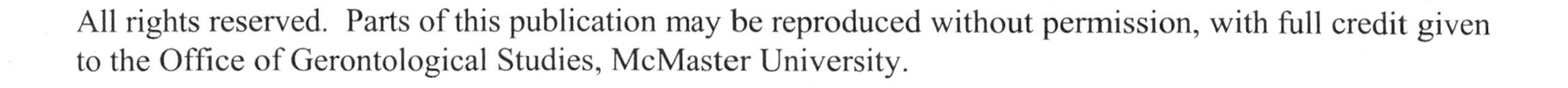

This fact book was prepared by Gail Elliot, with the assistance of Melanie Hunt and Kim Hutchison, at the Office of Gerontological Studies, McMaster University. Editorial consultation was provided by Dr. Carolyn Rosenthal. Dr. Ellen Ryan offered valuable support and encouragement, particularly in the early stages of this project. The assistance of Martha Schumovitch, Derek Lapierre, Jennifer Aarden and Kim Lizotte is also acknowledged. Thanks is also extended to Derek Sardo, of Rolling Thunder Online, Hamilton, Ontario, who was instrumental in getting this book ready for print.

The Ministry of Citizenship and Human Resources Development Canada provided summer student assistance for this project.

A special thanks is extended to McMaster's Educational Centre for Aging and Health (ECAH) for the generous financial support they have provided in the production of this publication. The Faculty of Health Sciences established the Educational Centre for Aging and Health at McMaster University in 1987 with funding from the Ontario government through the Ministry of Colleges and Universities.

Printed and bound at McMaster University, Hamilton, Ontario, Canada.
ISBN 0-920603-09-2

Index

Section B. Social Support and Contributions (Cont'd)

Section C. Cultural Characteristics

Section C. Cultural Characteristics (Cont'd)

Section D. Housing

Section E. Education

Section F. Leisure

Section F. Leisure (Cont'd)

Section G. Labour Force

Section H. Income

Section H. Income Sources and Distribution (Cont'd)

Section I. Retirement

Section J. Health Status and Quality of Life (Cont'd)

Section K. Health Care

By the year 2031, it is expected that 20% of Canada's population will be over the age of 65 - which is estimated to be more than 8 million seniors.

Statistics Canada, Profile of Canada's Seniors, 1994

According to the 1991 General Social Survey, 45% of Canadians over the age of 65 received a flu shot.

Health Status of Canadians, General Social Survey, 1991

In the adult Canadian population, 4% (762,000 persons) have a hearing problem which is not overcome with an aid, while 2% (405,000) have an uncorrected sight problem.

Health Status of Canadians, General Social Survey, 1991

PROLOGUE

Gerontologists are dedicated to refuting the myths and stereotypes of aging that permeate our society. We believe that it is important for both the young and old to understand the characteristics of our aging population and to develop realistic ideas about the later years of life. Furthermore, the facts of aging are not only critical for understanding our older population but they are also necessary for making plans that will meet the needs of an aging society.

A look at the demographic profile of our population can contribute a great deal to our understanding of the 65 and over age group. Demography is a macro level science of population dynamics which "focuses on large and broad statistical groups within and across populations " (Woodruff and Birren, 1983). The three factors that determine the make-up of the population are fertility, mortality and migration (immigration/emigration). Fertility is an important variable in understanding the size of population cohorts. If we look at how many people are born in a certain time period, for example 1900 to 1910, when many of the old-old elderly were born, we then have a basis for both understanding and projections. For example, the people in this cohort are now in their 80's or 90's, have survived war, depression, the introduction of an incredible change in technology and, generally, have experienced similar historical events. The numbers and proportions of any age group can be tracked over time and existing figures can be used to determine estimates for the future simply by taking mortality and immigration/emigration rates and projections into consideration. Although each group of individuals born in a particular time period is exposed to the same national trends and social and economic conditions, it is important to recognize that each individual will experience these conditions from a different economic, cultural, health and socio-psychological perspective. The data presented in this fact book provide the macro perspective and should therefore be used to describe groups of people rather than individuals.

This Fact Book might be considered a macro level overview of groups of individuals who are riding the "cohort highway." This information will be particularly useful to educators, researchers, planners, practitioners, students and seniors. These data can be used to simply present "facts on aging" or they can be used to develop insight and interpretations about the older population of today and tomorrow. For example, if we know about the health status of the 65-69 age group today we can try to project the health status of this same group in 10 or 20 years from now. This can help us to plan for their health, financial, and, possibly, their housing needs in the years to come.

It has become a well known fact that the demographic profile of our population is changing. Although some claim that we are not prepared for an aging society it is important to note that demographers and population planners have known about the increasing numbers and proportion of the 65 and over age group for many years. For example, Statistics Canada reports that 5.1 % of Canada's population was over the age of 65 in 1901 compared to 7.8% in 1951 and 11.6 % in 1991 and a projected 14.6% in 2011 (Statistics Canada, 1991). This type of broad-based demographic data helps to lay the groundwork in the development of social and economic policy. However, the numbers and proportions of older age groups alone are not sufficient if one wants to understand the many variables that attempt to describe the aging population. A comprehensive analysis includes such variables as marital status, living arrangements, economic security, labour force participation, health status, mortality rates, support networks, educationalattainment and leisure lifestyle. It is important to look at national studies that focus on these types of variables that contribute to our understanding of aging and older adults.

OUR OBJECTIVE

Before embarking on the development of this publication a small survey was conducted to determine the types of information that would be most useful to educators, researchers, planners, practitioners, students and seniors. Since there were so many areas of interest expressed we decided to include as many details as possible but limit it to a Canadian, rather than provincial, perspective. Our intent is therefore to provide a Canadian overview rather than an exhaustive set of tables that would exhibit provincial and/or regional variations.

The purpose of this fact book on aging is to provide a reference tool for those who want to easily access current data about our older population. Most of the information refers to the 65 and over age group. However, there are full population breakdowns for topic areas that are enriched by age group comparisons. Unfortunately, not all surveys use the 65 and over age group as their base for data collection and/or reporting. Therefore we were limited to the amount and type of information that was available to us. Generally, however, we have used the 65 and over age group as our focus.

THE FORMAT

A standardized format has been adopted in the preparation of this document for ease of understanding and application. We have accessed a wide variety of resources that have used a large sample base in data collection. In some cases we have presented the information in table form precisely as it was in the original source. In other cases we have pulled the data from raw figures, and then condensed it into the selected categories. Generally, the data in the tables are depicted in graphic form on the adjacent page, unless the tables were too inclusive in their information for transcription into graphic form. We hope this method of formatting will assist educators with presentations. We encourage you to make copies and overheads, but ask that complete referencing and full credit be clearly cited. If you have questions about any of the specific details please refer to the source reference for clarification.

Explanatory text has not been provided in this publication. When we started this project we fully intended to write summary statements about the data but after working on the text it occurred to us that the tables and graphs speak for themselves.

In a fast-paced world there is an ever-increasing need to have current information upon which to base critical decisions. The data in this publication will provide factual details required by individuals working in the field of aging. It is our hope that these data will promote the facts of aging, contribute to the development of positive attitudes towards aging and facilitate the development of policies that will contribute to quality of life in the later years.

Demographics

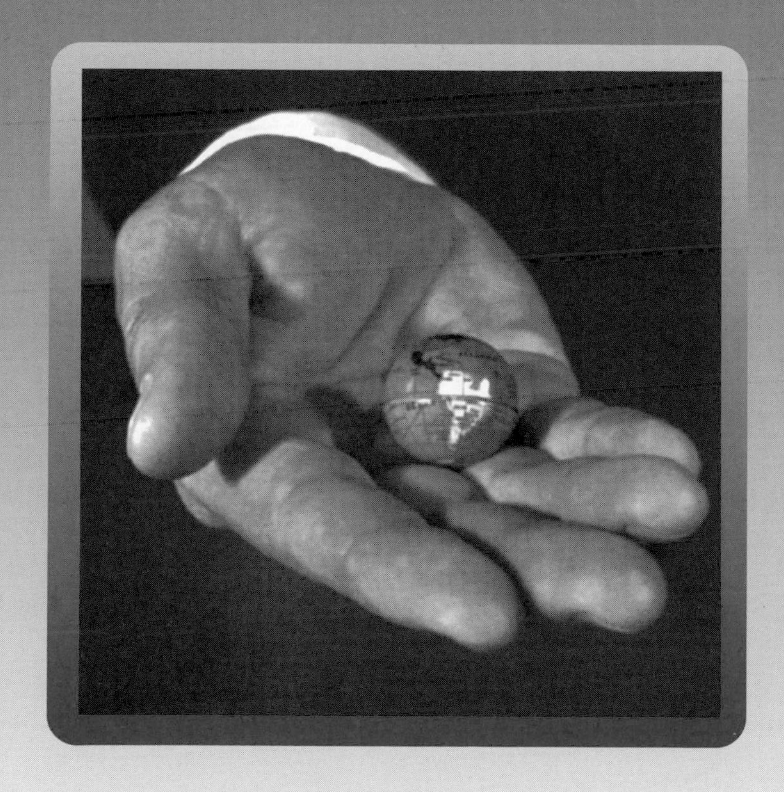

A.1: *Population aging: Proportion of population aged 65+ in selected regions of the world, (actuals for 1950-1990 and projected for 2025)*

	1950 (%)	1970 (%)	1990 (%)	2025 (%)
More Developed Regions	7.6	9.6	12.1	19.0
Less Developed Regions	3.8	3.7	4.5	8.0
Africa	3.2	3.1	3.0	4.1
Latin America	3.3	3.9	4.8	8.6
North America	8.1	9.6	12.5	19.9
Asia	4.0	4.0	5.0	9.6
Europe	8.7	11.4	13.4	20.1
Oceania	7.5	7.3	9.0	13.9
USSR	6.1	7.4	9.6	14.8
World	5.1	5.4	6.2	9.7

Statistics Canada Definitions:

Less Developed Regions - includes Africa, Latin America, some countries of South and East Asia other than Japan, and Oceania (as stated below).

More Developed Regions - includes North America, Japan, Europe, the USSR, Australia, and New Zealand.

Oceania - includes islands of the Pacific Ocean (e.g., Melanesia, Micronesia and Polynesia).

Source: Statistics Canada. Population Ageing and the Elderly. Ottawa, 1993 (1991 Census of Canada; Cat. No. 91-533E, p109).

Proportion of Population Aged 65+
By Selected Geographic Regions
(Actuals for 1950-1990 and Projected for 2025)

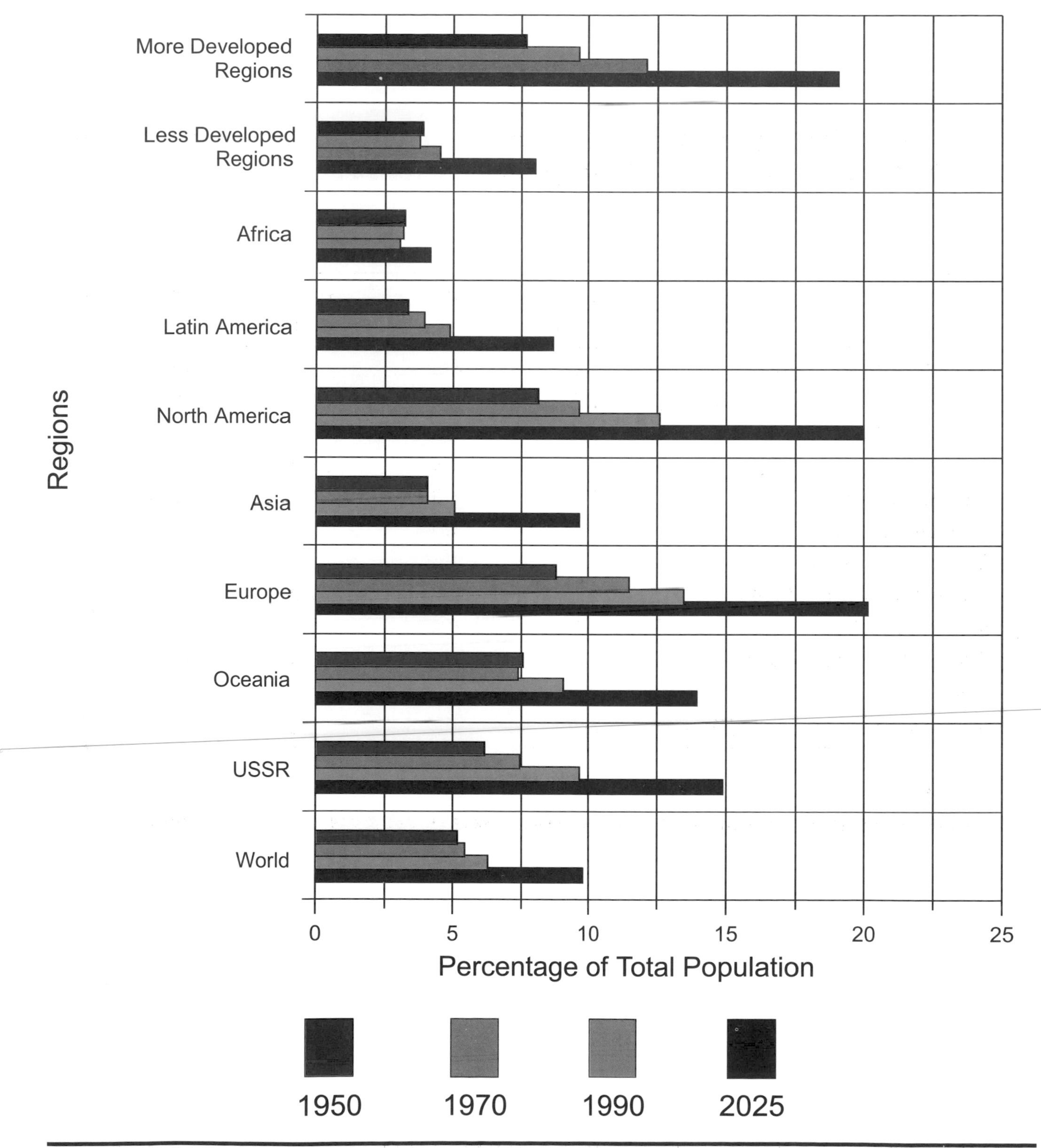

Source: *Statistics Canada. Population Ageing and the Elderly. Ottawa, 1993.*

A.2: Population aging (65+) in Canada, by provinces and territories, (estimated for 1951-1991 and projected for 2011)

	1951 (%)	1971 (%)	1991 (%)	2011 (%)
Newfoundland (NFL)	6.5	6.2	9.7	15.1
Prince Edward Island (PEI)	9.9	1.0	13.2	16.3
Nova Scotia (NS)	8.5	9.2	12.6	15.5
New Brunswick (NB)	7.6	8.6	12.2	16.0
Quebec (QUE)	5.7	6.9	11.2	15.3
Ontario (ONT)	8.7	8.4	11.7	14.3
Manitoba (MAN)	8.4	9.6	13.4	14.3
Saskatchewan (SASK)	8.1	10.2	14.2	14.5
Alberta (ALB)	7.1	7.3	9.1	12.4
British Columbia (BC)	10.8	9.4	12.9	15.4
Yukon	5.1	2.8	4.0	9.6
Northwest Territories (NWT)	2.7	2.2	2.8	6.6
Canada	7.8	8.1	11.6	14.6

Source: Statistics Canada. Population Ageing and the Elderly. Ottawa, 1993 (1991 Census of Canada; Cat. No. 91-533E, p48).

Population Aging (65+)
Provinces, Territories & Canada

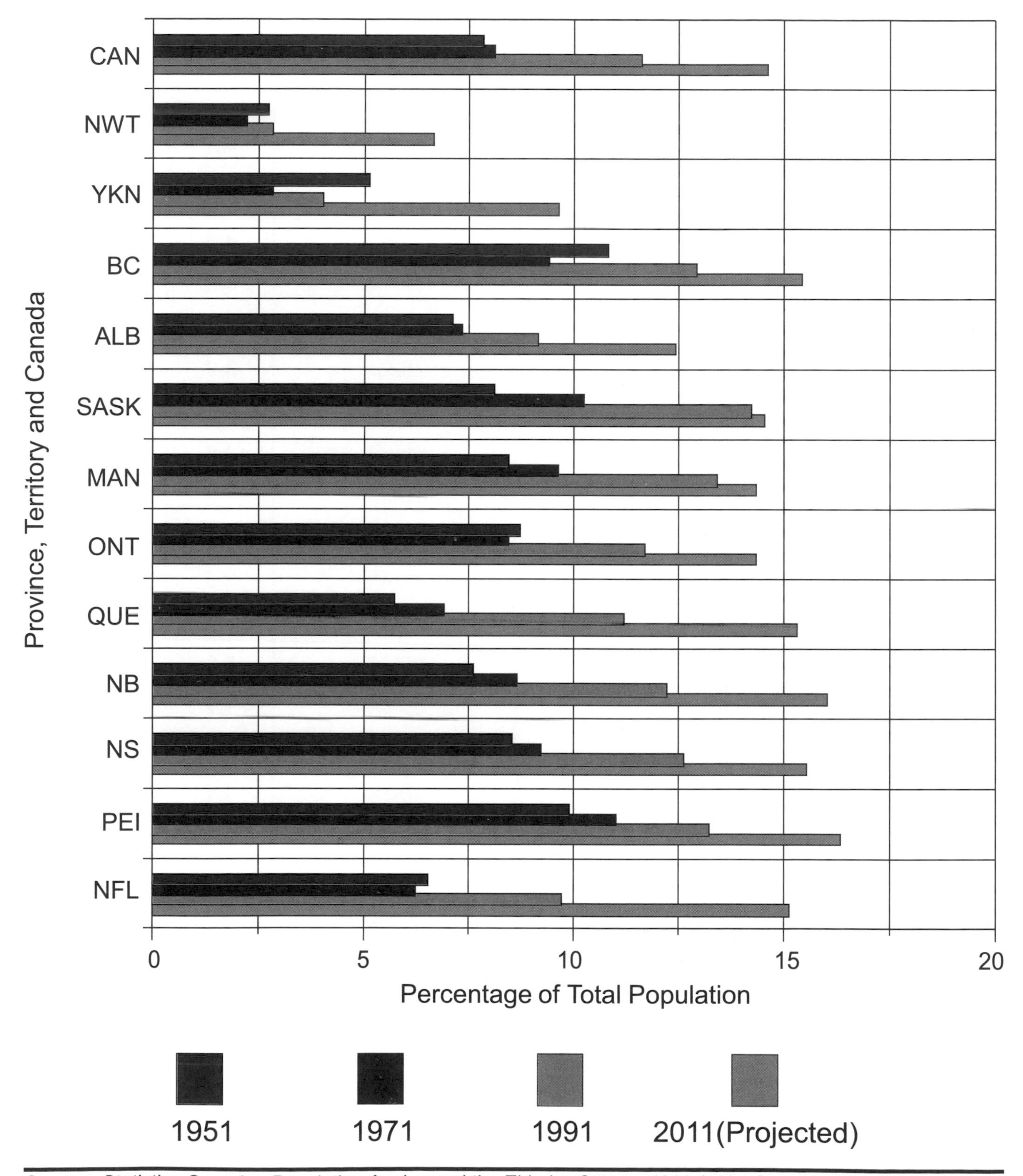

Source: Statistics Canada. Population Ageing and the Elderly. Ottawa, 1993 (1991 Census of Canada).

A.3: Canada's population pyramids, 1951 and 1991

MALES Age Group	1951 (%)	1991 (%)	FEMALES Age Group	1951 (%)	1991 (%)
0-4	6.3	3.6	0-4	6.0	3.4
5-9	5.1	3.6	5-9	4.9	3.4
10-14	4.1	3.5	10-14	4.0	3.4
15-19	3.8	3.5	15-19	3.8	3.3
20-24	3.8	3.6	20-24	3.9	3.6
25-29	3.9	4.3	25-29	4.1	4.4
30-34	3.7	4.5	30-34	3.8	4.6
35-39	3.6	4.2	35-39	3.5	4.2
40-44	3.2	3.8	40-44	3.0	3.8
45-49	2.8	3.0	45-49	2.5	3.0
50-54	2.4	2.4	50-54	2.3	2.4
55-59	2.1	2.2	55-59	2.0	2.3
60-64	1.9	2.1	60-64	1.7	2.2
65-69	1.6	1.8	65-69	1.5	2.1
70-74	1.1	1.3	70-74	1.1	1.7
75-79	0.7	1.3	75-79	0.7	1.3
80-84	0.3	0.5	80-84	0.4	0.9
85-89	0.1	0.2	85-89	0.2	0.5
90+	0.04	0.01	90+	0.05	0.3

Source: Statistics Canada. Population Ageing and the Elderly. Ottawa, 1993 (1991 Census of Canada; Cat.No. 91-533E, p111).

Canada.s Population Pyramid, 1951

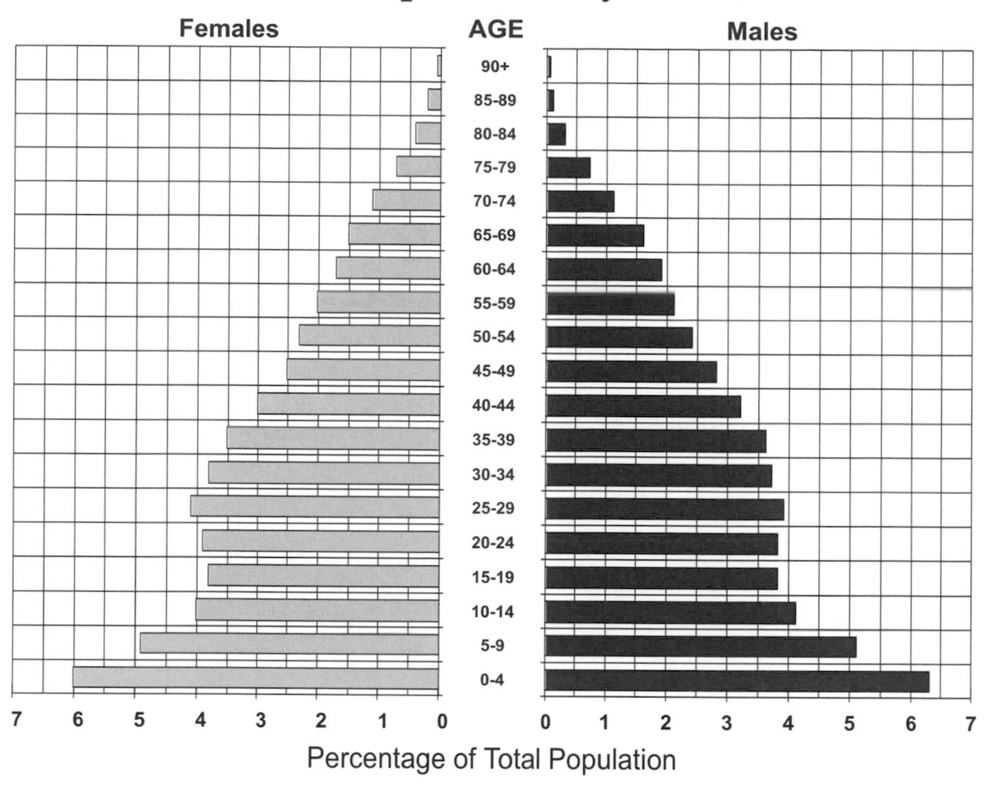

Canada.s Population Pyramid, 1991

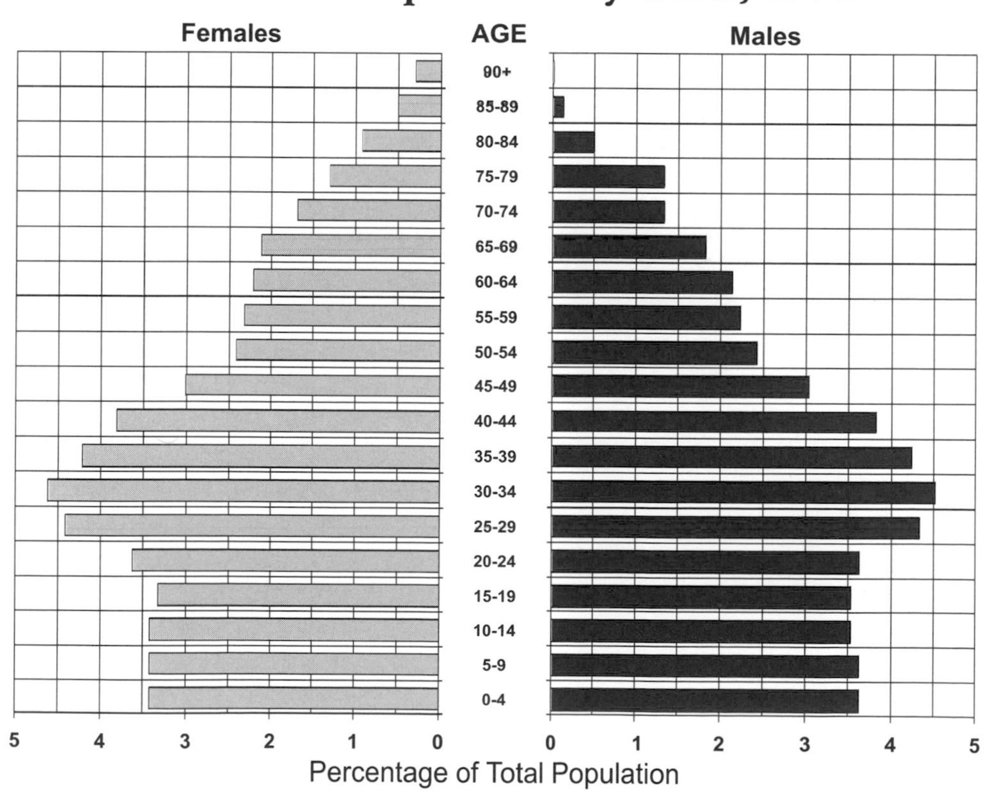

Source: Statistics Canada. Population Ageing and the Elderly. Ottawa, 1993.

A.4: Growth of Canada's population aged 65+, 1951-2031

Age Group	1951 (%)	1971 (%)	1991 (%)	2011 (%)	2031 (%)
65+	7.8	8.1	11.6	14.6	22.7
65-69	3.1	2.9	3.9	4.5	6.4
70-74	2.2	2.1	3.0	3.3	5.8
75-79	1.3	1.5	2.3	2.6	4.5
80-84	0.7	0.9	1.4	2.0	3.2
85+	0.4	0.6	1.0	2.1	2.8

Note: Discrepancies among totals within each column are due to rounding in the original source.

Source: Statistics Canada. Population Ageing and the Elderly. Ottawa, 1993 (1991 Census of Canada; Cat.No. 91-533E, p110).

Growth of Population Aged 65+
Canada, 1951-2031

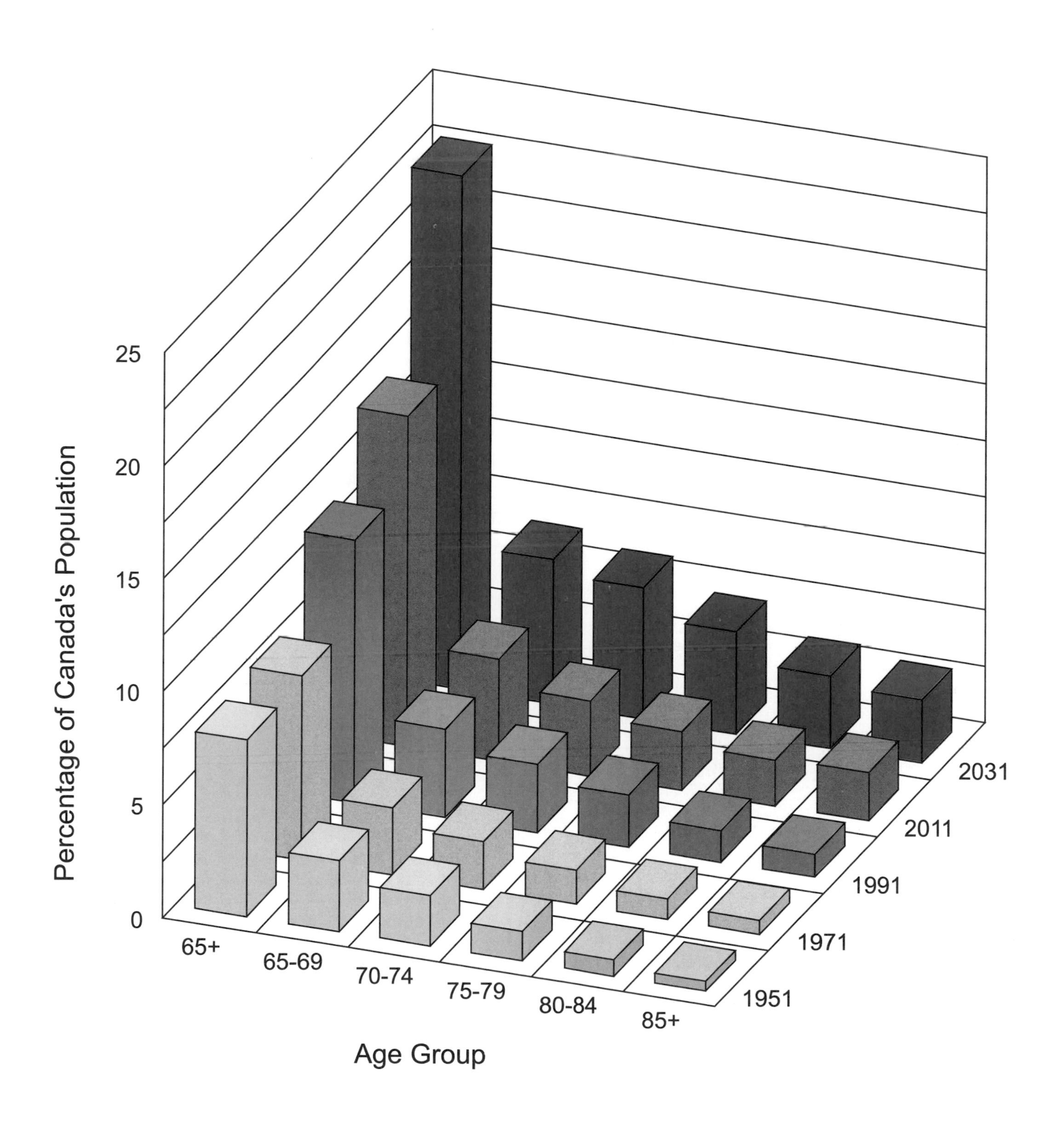

Source: *Statistics Canada. Population Ageing and the Elderly. Ottawa, 1993.*

A.5: Life expectancy of Canadians, 1920-1991

Males

Year of Birth	Expected remaining years of life at:			
	Birth	65 Years	75 Years	85 Years
1920-22	58.8	13.0	7.6	4.1
1930-32	60.0	13.0	7.6	4.1
1940-42	63.0	12.8	7.5	4.1
1950-52	66.4	13.3	7.9	4.3
1960-62	68.4	13.6	8.2	4.6
1970-72	69.4	13.8	8.5	5.0
1980-82	71.9	14.6	9.0	5.2
1989-91	73.9	15.4	9.4	5.2

Females

Year of Birth	Expected remaining years of life at:			
	Birth	65 Years	75 Years	85 Years
1920-22	60.6	13.6	8.0	4.3
1930-32	62.1	13.7	8.0	4.4
1940-42	66.3	14.1	8.2	4.1
1950-52	70.9	15.0	8.8	4.7
1960-62	74.3	16.1	9.5	5.0
1970-72	76.5	17.6	10.7	5.9
1980-82	79.1	18.9	11.9	6.6
1989-91	80.5	19.6	12.3	6.7

Source: Statistics Canada. J.A. Norland. Focus on Canada - Profile of Canada's Seniors. Ottawa, 1994 (Cat. No. 96-312E, p 58).

Life Expectancy, By Age
1920 - 1991

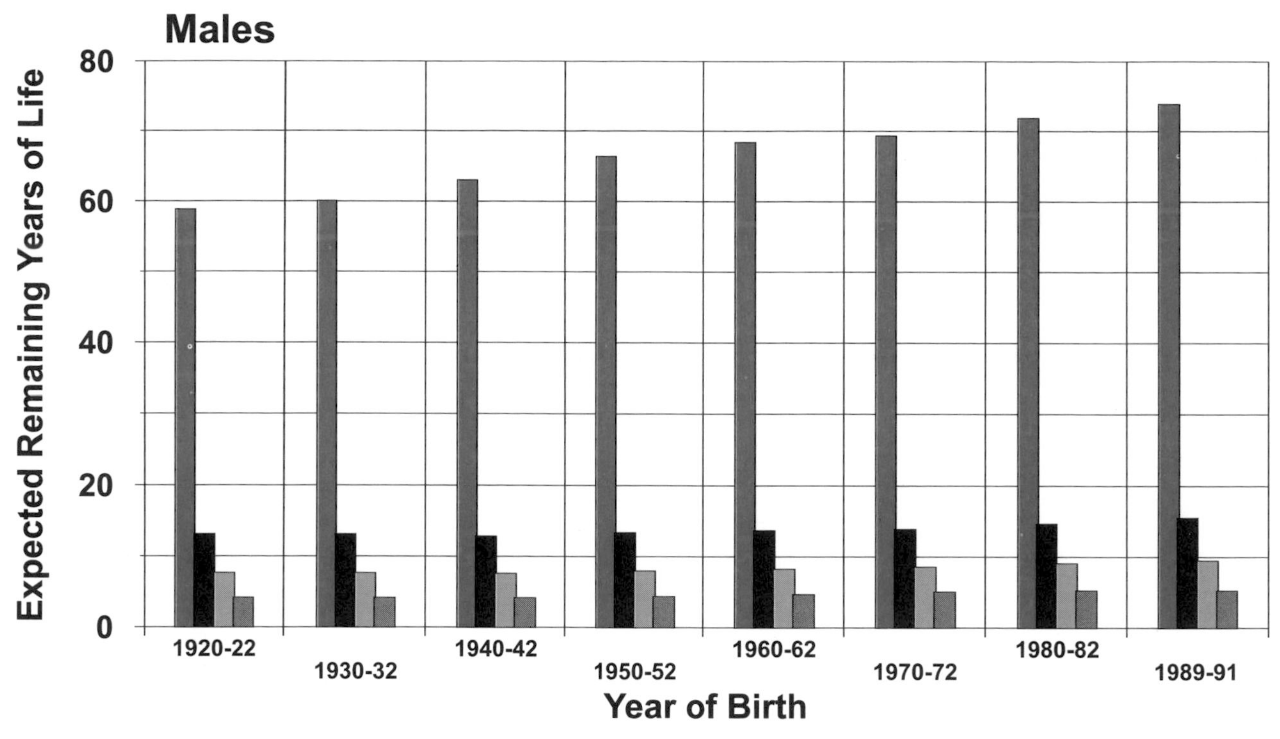

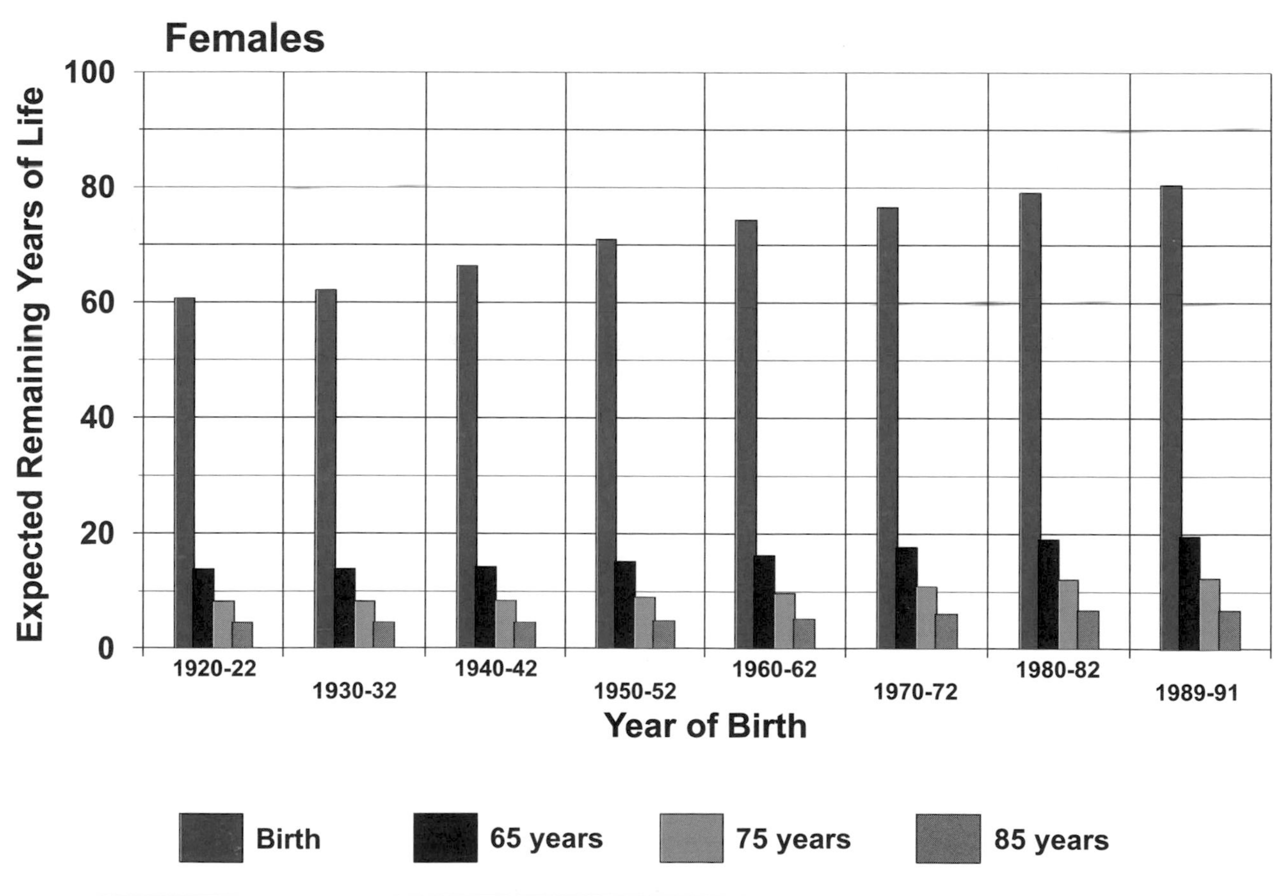

Birth | 65 years | 75 years | 85 years

Source: *Statistics Canada. J.A. Norland. Focus on Canada - Profile of Canada's Seniors. Ottawa, 1994.*

A.6: Canadian gender ratios, by age group, 1911-1991 and projected for 2031

Age Group	1911	1951	1991	2031
All Ages	112.9	102.4	97.2	95.5
65+	103.6	103.1	72.3	72.4
65-74	105.5	107.9	81.6	85.4
75-84	101.7	96.6	65.6	67.2
85+	90.4	76.3	43.8	41.7

Statistics Canada Definition:

Gender ratio - The number of males per 100 females.

Source: Statistics Canada. J.A. Norland. Focus on Canada - Profile of Canada's Seniors. Ottawa, 1994 (Cat. No. 96-312E, p89).

Gender Ratios, Population Aged 65+
By Age Group, Canada, 1911-2031

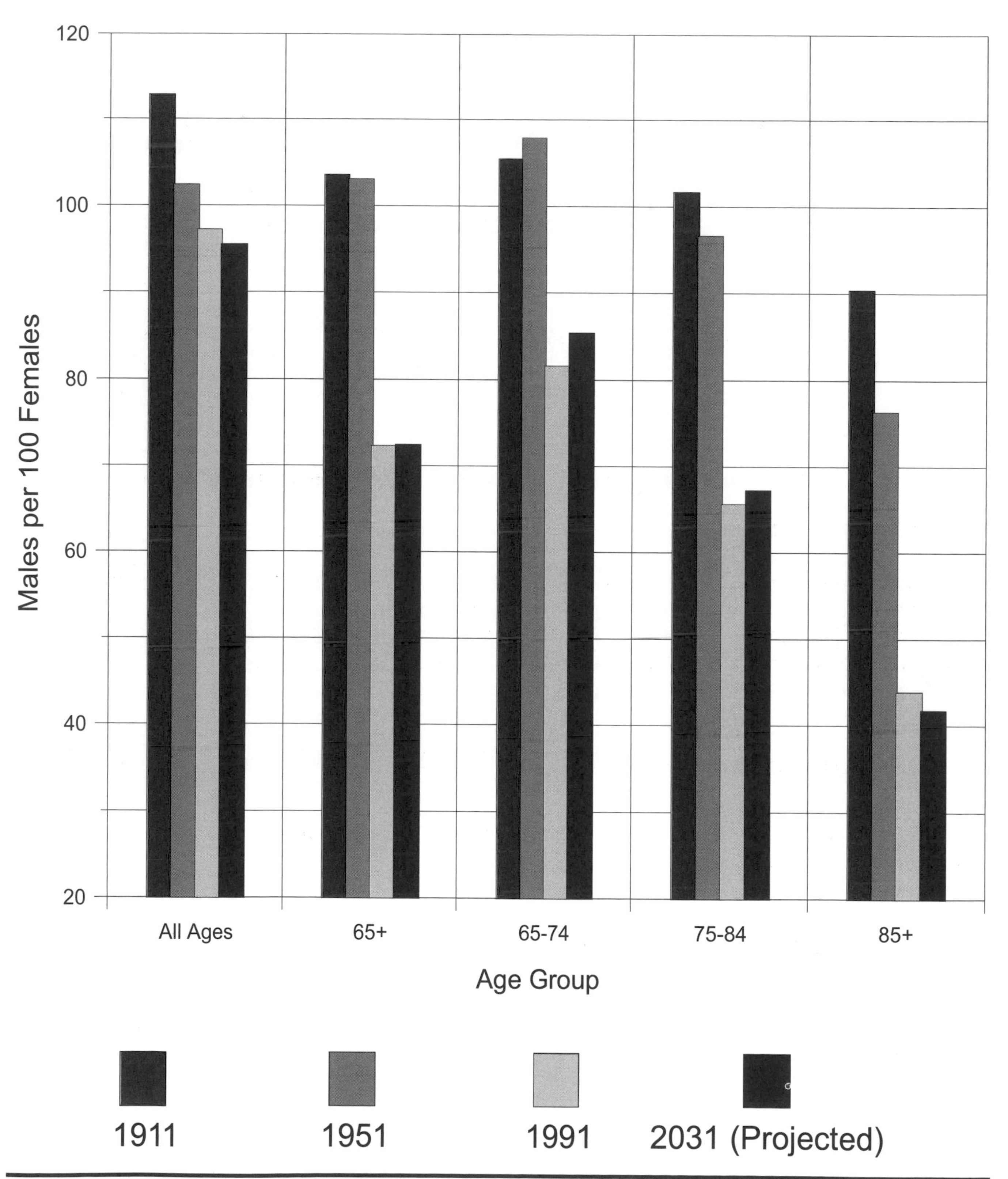

Source: Statistics Canada. J.A. Norland. Focus on Canada - Profile of Canada's Seniors. Ottawa, 1994.

A.7: Age and old-age dependency ratios, Canada, 1961-1991

Year	Age Dependency	Old-age Dependency
1961	87.0	14.3
1971	77.8	14.4
1981	60.8	15.6
1991	57.7	18.3

Statistics Canada Defintions:

Age dependency ratio - The ratio of the number of persons in economically dependent parts of the population to the number in economically productive parts. Generally this means comparing the number of children (0-17 yrs) and seniors (65+) to the number of persons working (18-64 yrs). The Age Dependency Ratio is usually expressed as the number of children and elderly per 100 population of working age.

$$\text{Age Dependency Ratio} = \frac{(\text{0 to 17 age group} + \text{65 and over age group})}{\text{18 to 64 age group}} \times 100$$

Old-age dependency ratio - The number of seniors (65+) compared to the number of persons of working age (18-64 yrs).

$$\text{Old -age Dependency Ratio} = \frac{\text{65 and over age group}}{\text{18 to 64 age group}} \times 100$$

Source: Statistics Canada. D. Kerr and B. Ram. Focus on Canada - Population Dynamics in Canada. Ottawa, 1994 (1991 Census of Canada, Cat.No. 96-305E, p53).

Age and Old-age Dependency Ratios
Canada, 1961-1991

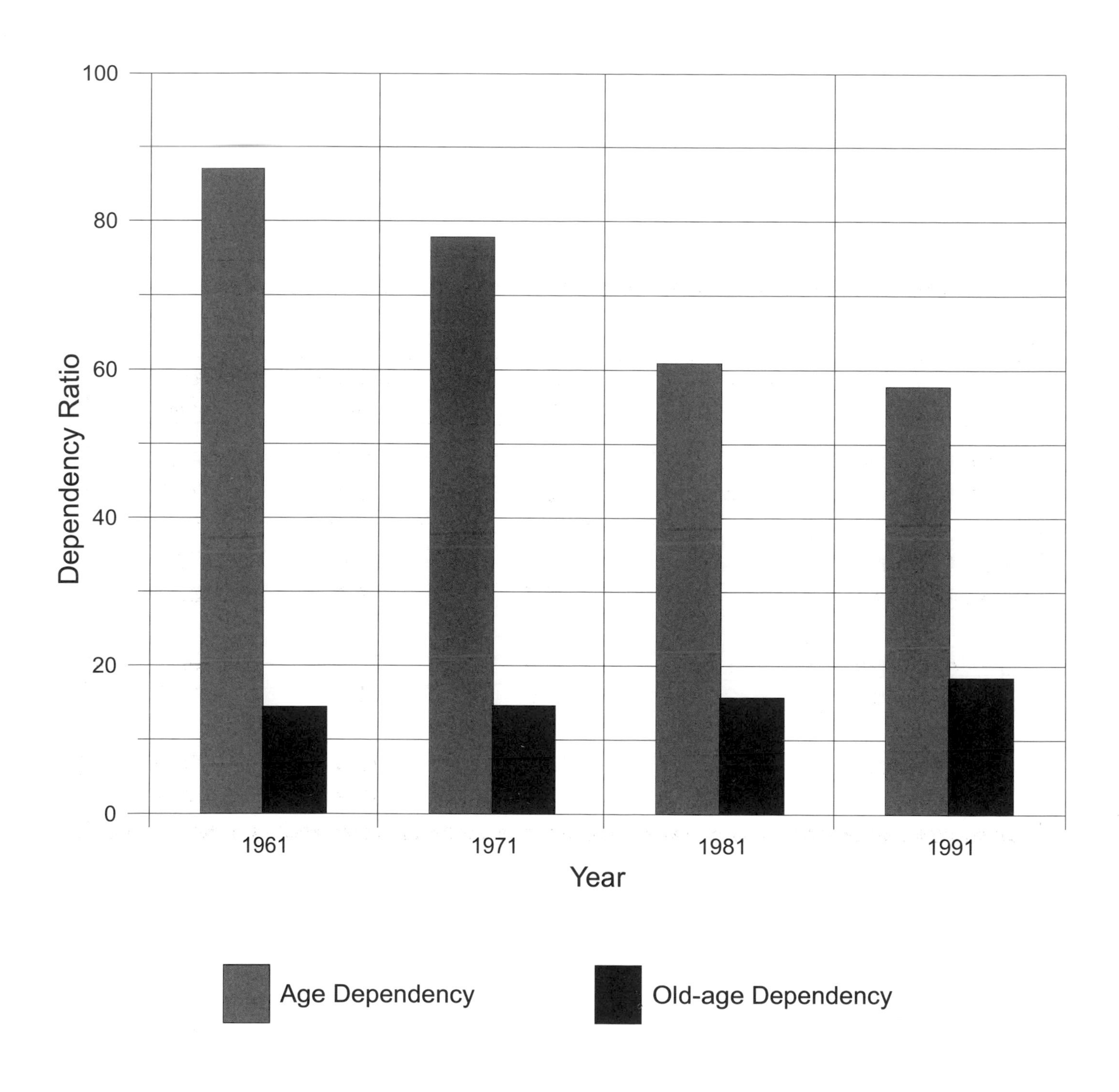

Source: *Statistics Canada. D. Kerr and B. Ram. Focus on Canada - Population Dynamics in Canada. Ottawa, 1994.*

A.8: Marital status of Canadians 65+, by age and gender, 1991

Age Group	Divorced (%)	Single (%)	Widowed (%)	Married (%)
65+ Females	3.0	7.7	46.7	42.6
65+ Males	2.8	6.9	12.9	77.3
65-74 Females	4.0	6.5	33.5	56.0
65-74 Males	3.4	6.7	7.7	82.2
75-84 Females	1.9	8.8	59.2	30.1
75-84 Males	2.0	7.0	18.3	72.7
85+ Females	0.8	10.4	78.8	10.0
85+ Males	1.2	8.7	39.2	50.9

Source: Statistics Canada. J.A. Norland, Focus on Canada - Profile of Canada's Seniors. Ottawa, 1994 (Cat.No. 96-312E, p22).

Marital Status, Population Aged 65+
By Age and Gender, 1991

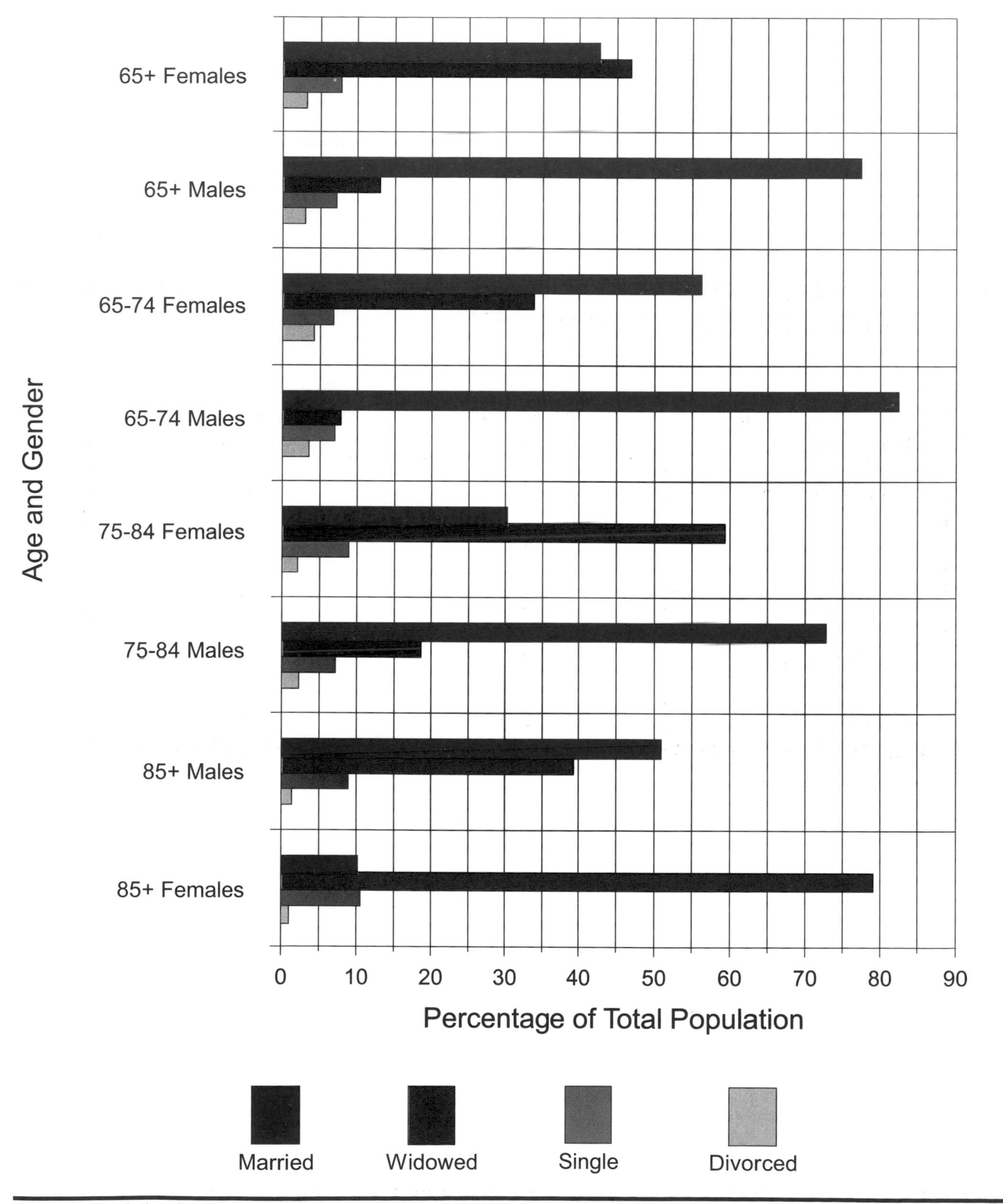

Source: *Statistics Canada. J.A. Norland. Focus on Canada - Profile of Canada's Seniors. Ottawa, 1994.*

A.9: *Percentage distribution of widowed Canadians 65+, by length of time that they had been widowed, 1991*

Length of Time Widowed	Males 65+ (%)	Females 65+ (%)
2 Years or less	23.0	11.0
3-5 Years	18.0	14.0
6-10 Years	24.0	22.0
11-20 Years	22.0	29.0
Other	13.0	24.0

Source: Health Canada. Ageing and Independence: Provincial Highlights. Ottawa, 1993 (1991 Survey), Table 4.

Widowed Canadians Aged 65+, 1991
By Length of Time Widowed

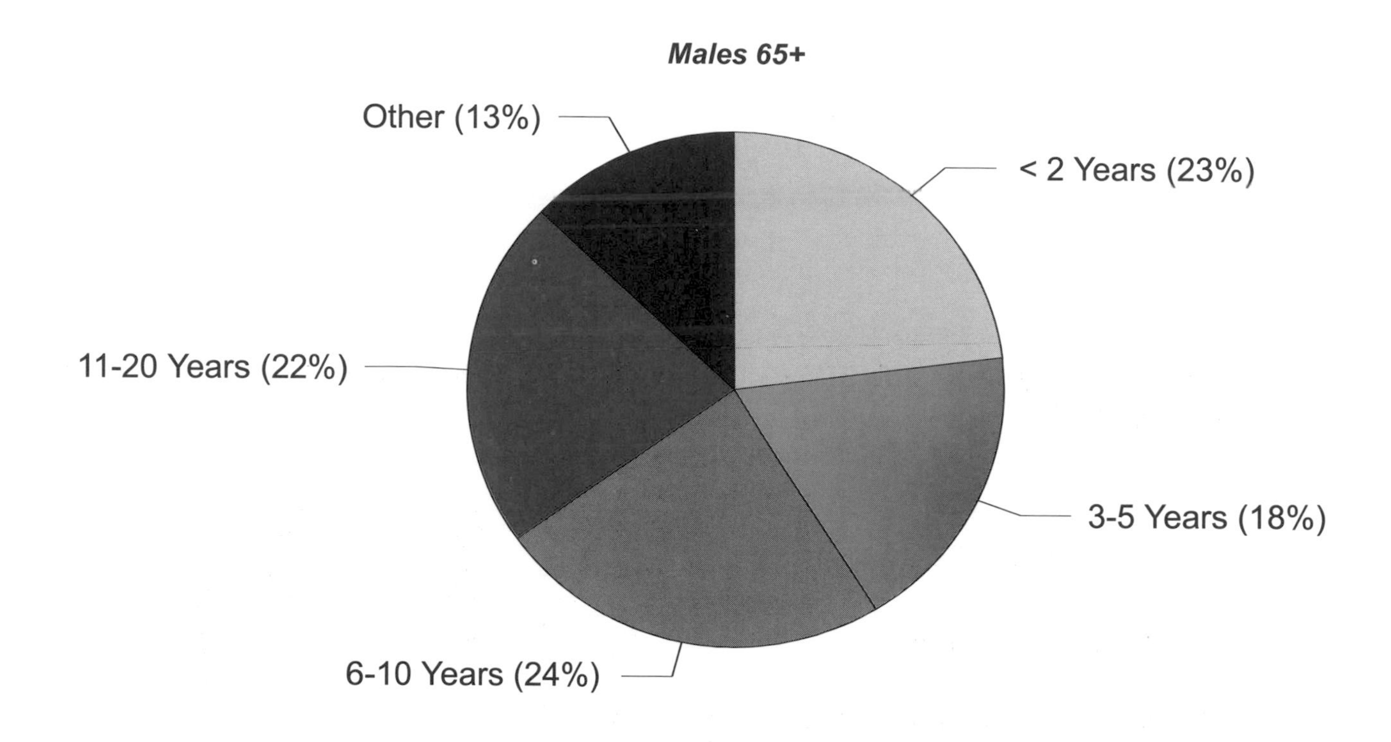

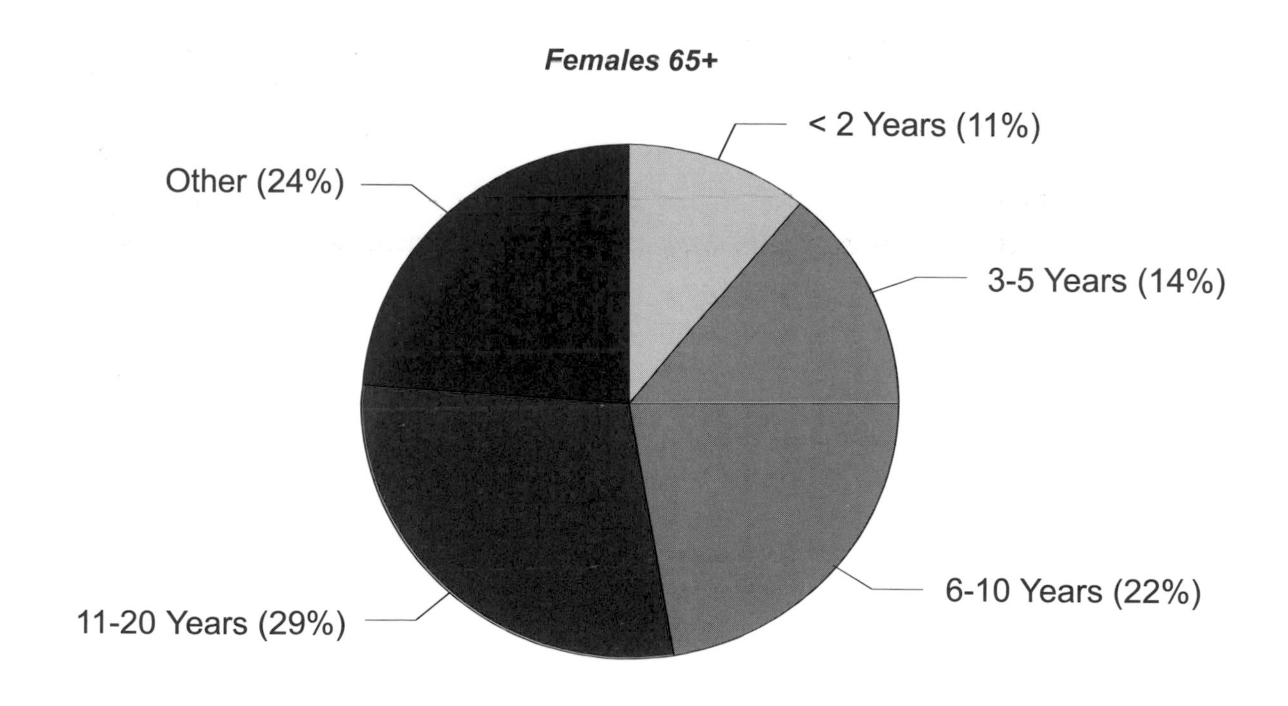

Source: Health Canada. Ageing and Independence: Provincial Highlights. Ottawa, 1993.

A.10: Size and type of community in which Canadians 45+ live, by age group, 1991

Community Size	45-64 (%)	65+ (%)	80+ (%)
Urban: 500,000+	46	43	43
Urban: 100,000-500,000	14	14	14
Urban: 30,000-99,999	9	9	8
Urban: 15,000-29,999	4	4	4
Small Urban	9	11	13
Rural	18	19	18

Source: Health Canada. Ageing and Independence: Overview of a National Survey. Ottawa, 1993 (1991 Survey; p17).

Size and Type of Community
Where Canadians Aged 45+ Live, 1991

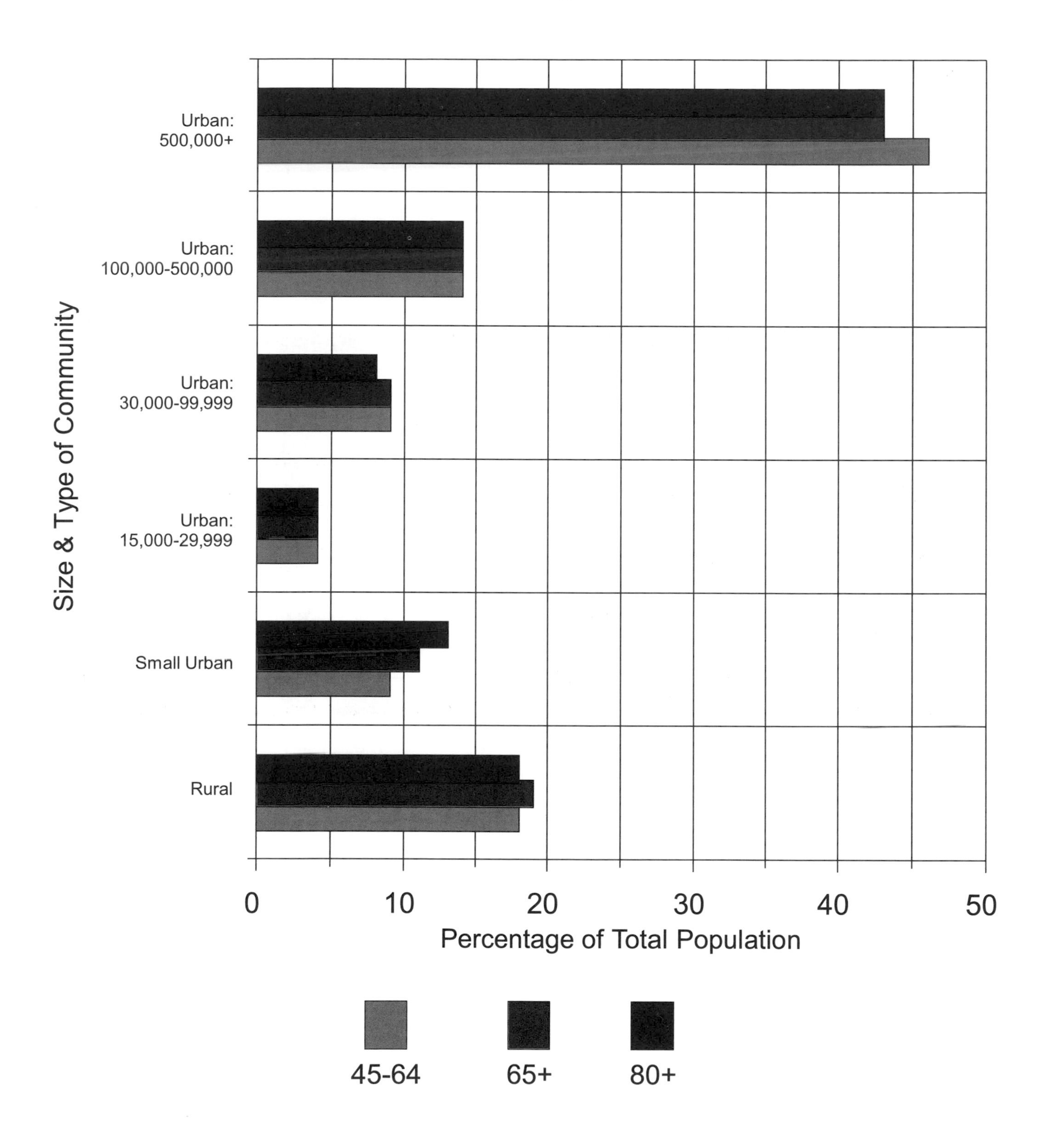

Source: *Health Canada. Ageing and Independence: Overview of a National Survey. Ottawa, 1993.*

A.11: Mobility of Canadians 45+, by age and gender, 1991

Mobility	45-64 (%)	65+ (%)	80+ (%)
Moved in Past 5 Years (Males)	25	19	13
Moved in Past 5 Years (Females)	28	21	18
Did Not Move in Past 5 Years (Males)	75	81	87
Did Not Move in Past 5 Years (Females)	72	79	82

Source: Health Canada. Ageing and Independence: Overview of a National Study. Ottawa, 1993 (1991 Survey, p19).

Mobility of Canadians Aged 45+
By Age and Gender, 1991

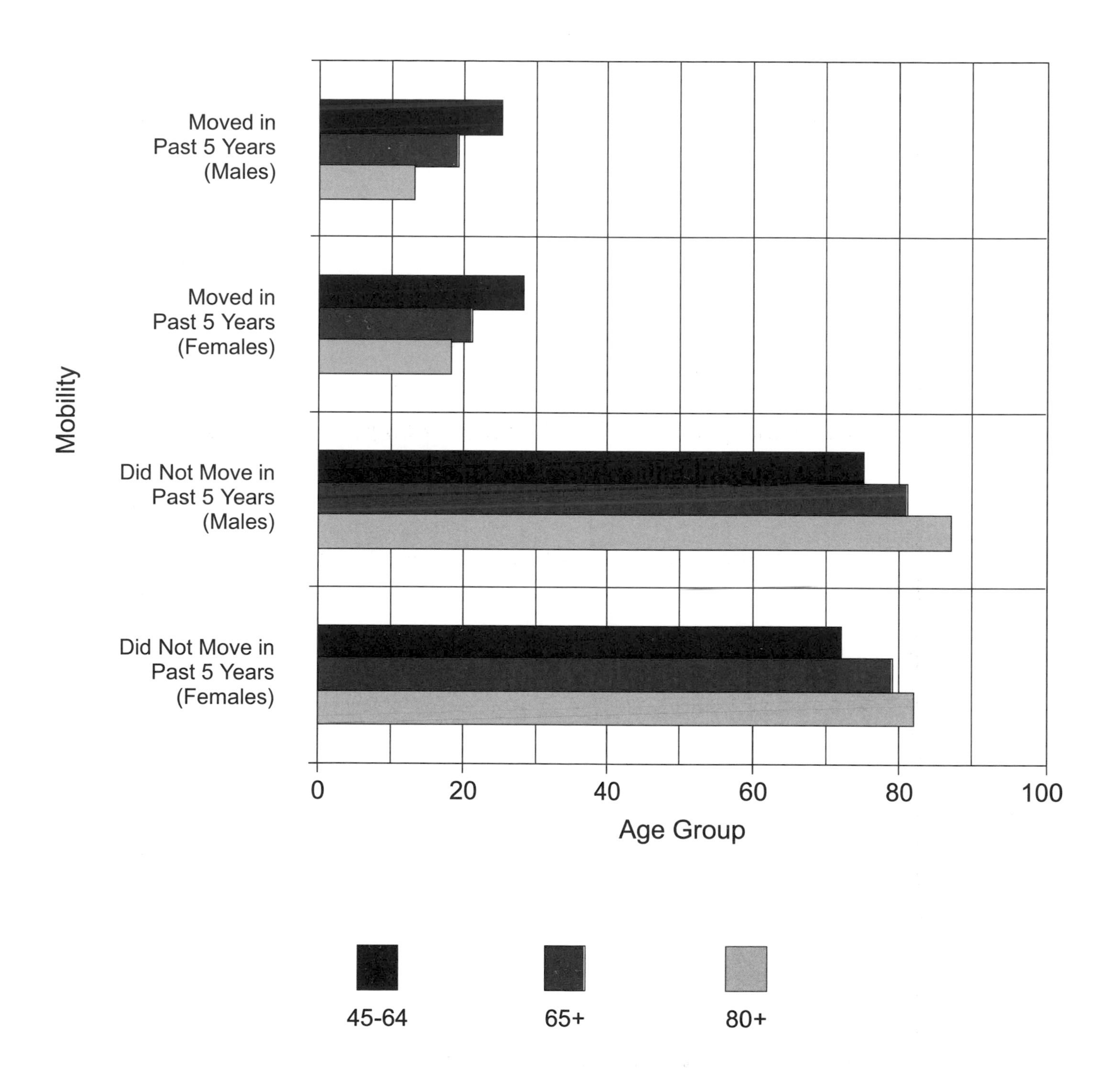

Source: *Health Canada. Ageing and Independence: Overview of a National Study. Ottawa, 1993.*

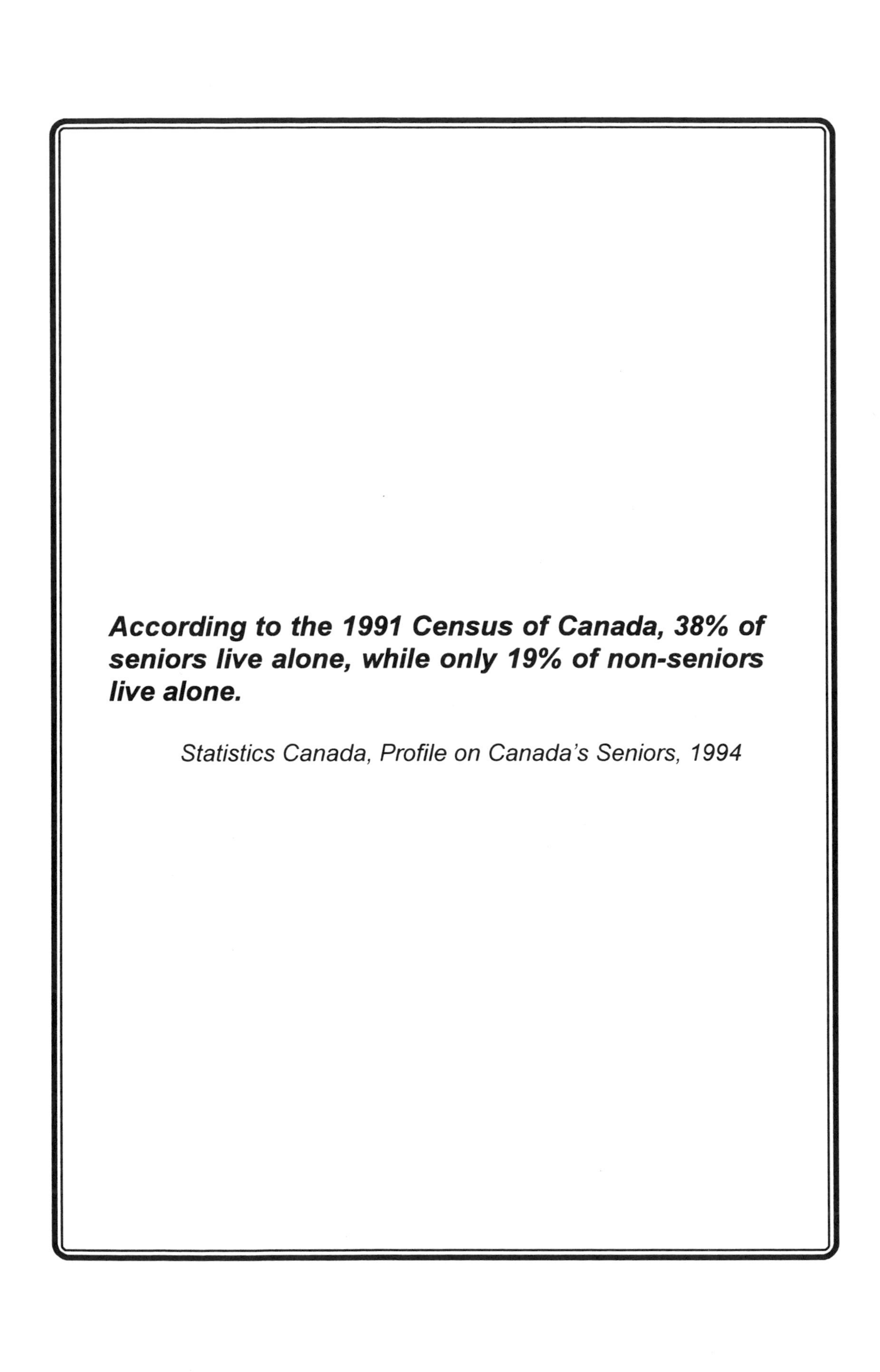

According to the 1991 Census of Canada, 38% of seniors live alone, while only 19% of non-seniors live alone.

Statistics Canada, Profile on Canada's Seniors, 1994

SECTION B

Social Support & Contributions

B.1: Number of friends of Canadian adults, by age and gender, 1990

Number of Friends	Males 15+ (%)	Females15+ (%)	Males 65+ (%)	Females 65+ (%)
No Friends	7	6	18	14
1-2 Friends	14	18	13	16
3-5 Friends	30	37	17	26
6-9 Friends	17	16	14	15
10+ Friends	31	22	35	26

Note: Column totals do not sum to 100 due to the exclusion of results from people who did not provide information regarding their number of friends.

Source: Statistics Canada. Family and Friends. Ottawa, 1994 (1990 General Social Survey; Cat.No. 11-612, p107).

Number of Friends, By Age & Gender
Canada, 1990

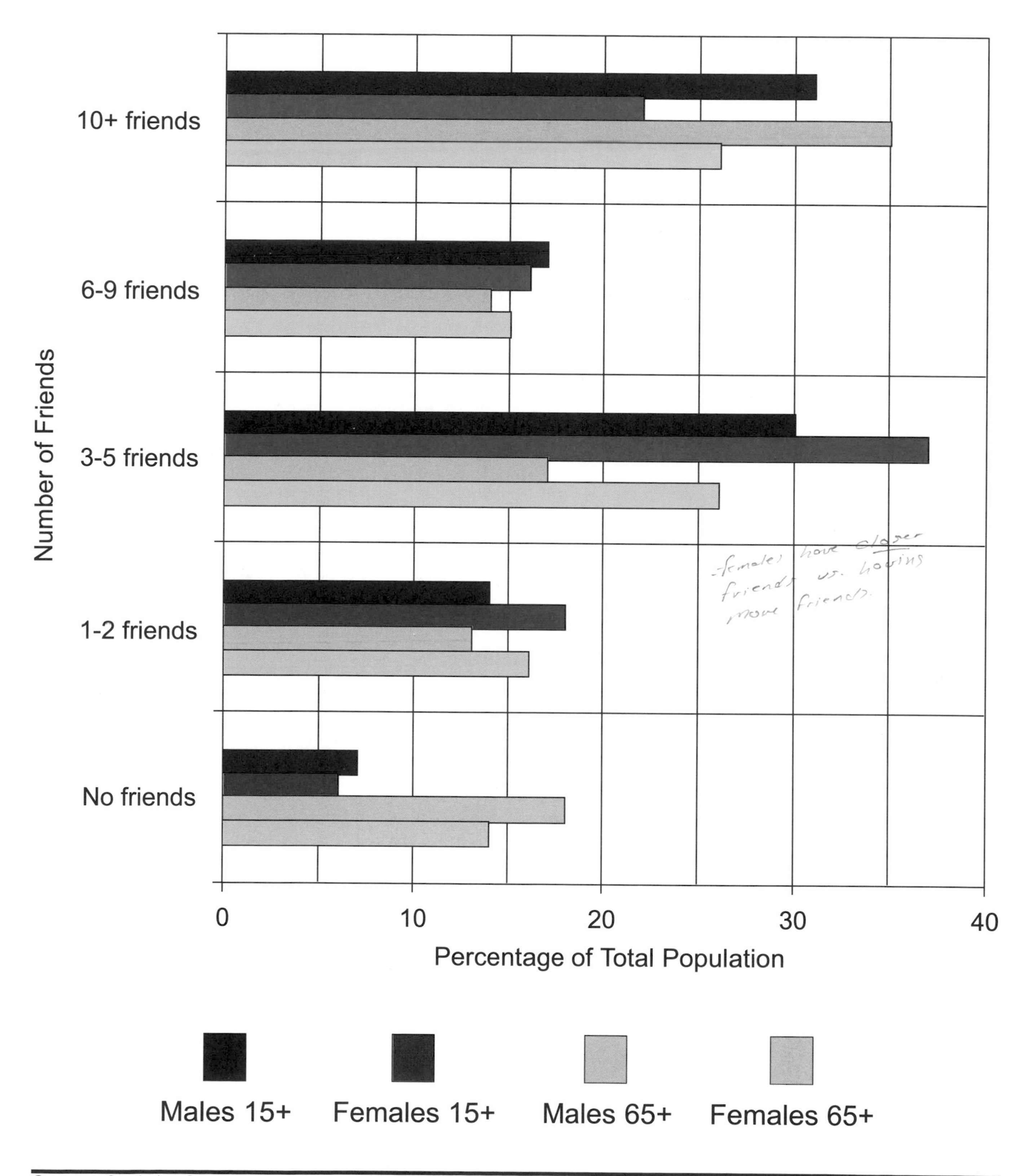

Source: Statistics Canada. Family and Friends. Ottawa, 1994.

B.2: *Frequency of personal contact of Canadian adults with closest friend, 1990*

Frequency of Contact *	Age 15+ (%)	Age 65+ (%)
Daily	19	11
At least once a week	39	42
At least once a month	21	21
Less than once a month	17	20
Not within past 12 months	3	4

* Results include only Canadian adults not living with friend who have at least one friend.

Note: Columns do not sum to 100% due to the exclusion of results of people who did not provide information regarding frequency of contact.

Source: Statistics Canada. Family and Friends. Ottawa, 1994 (1990 General Social Survey; Cat.No. 11-612, p93).

Frequency of Personal Contact
With Closest Friend, Canada 1990

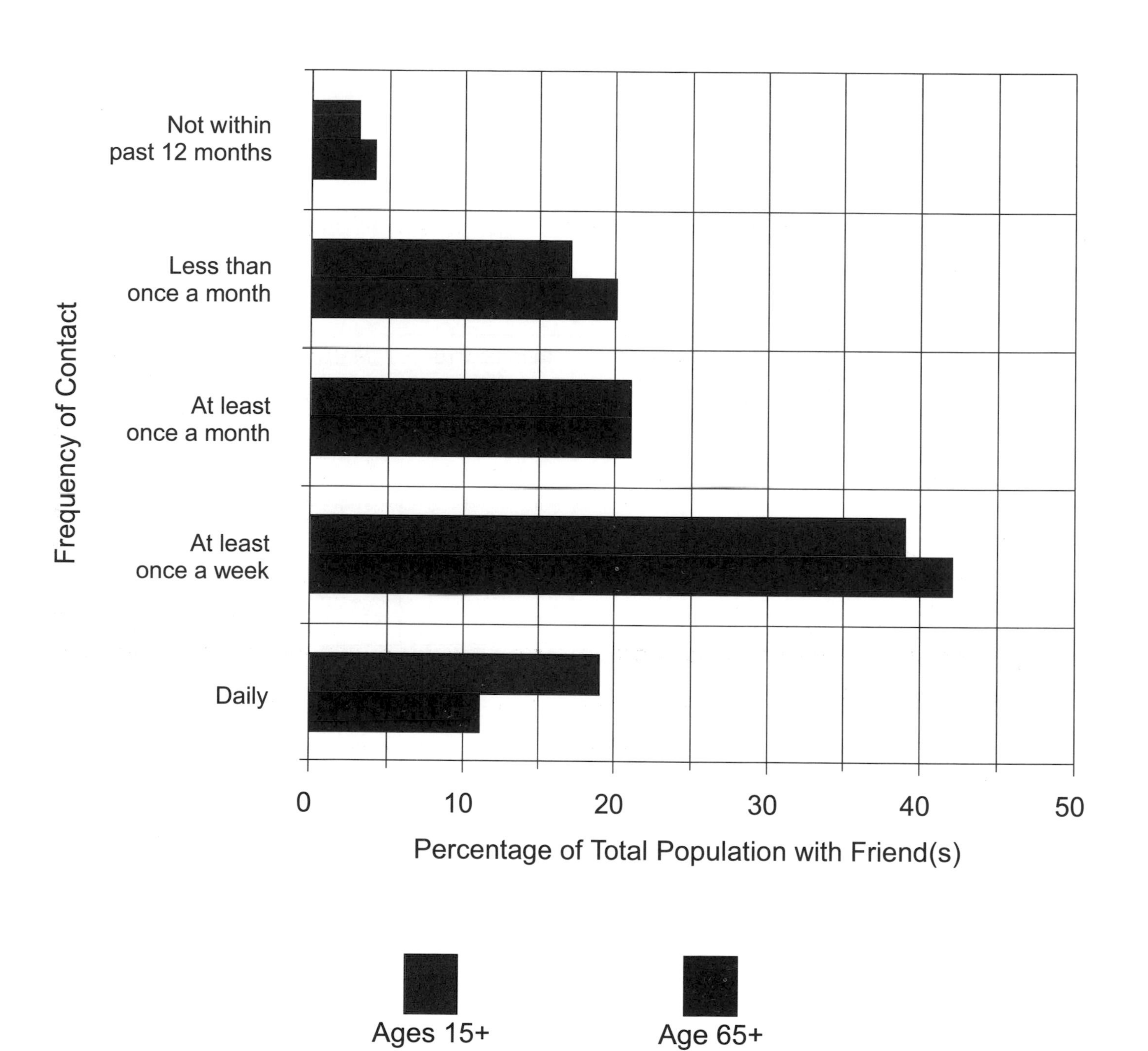

Source: Statistics Canada. Family and Friends. Ottawa, 1994.

B.3: Frequency of personal contact of Canadian adults with sibling(s), 1990

Frequency of Contact *	Males 15+ (%)	Females 15+ (%)	Males 65+ (%)	Females 65+ (%)
Daily	8	7	5	6
At least once a week	26	27	17	18
At least once a month	25	24	19	17
Less than once a month	31	32	36	43
Not within past 12 months	10	9	22	15

* Results include only Canadian adults not living with sibling and who have at least one living sibling.

Note: Columns do not sum to 100% due to the exclusion of results of people who did not provide information regarding frequency of contact.

Source: Statistics Canada. Family and Friends. Ottawa, 1994 (1990 General Social Survey; Cat.No. 11-612, p103).

Frequency of Personal Contact
With Sibling(s), Canada 1990

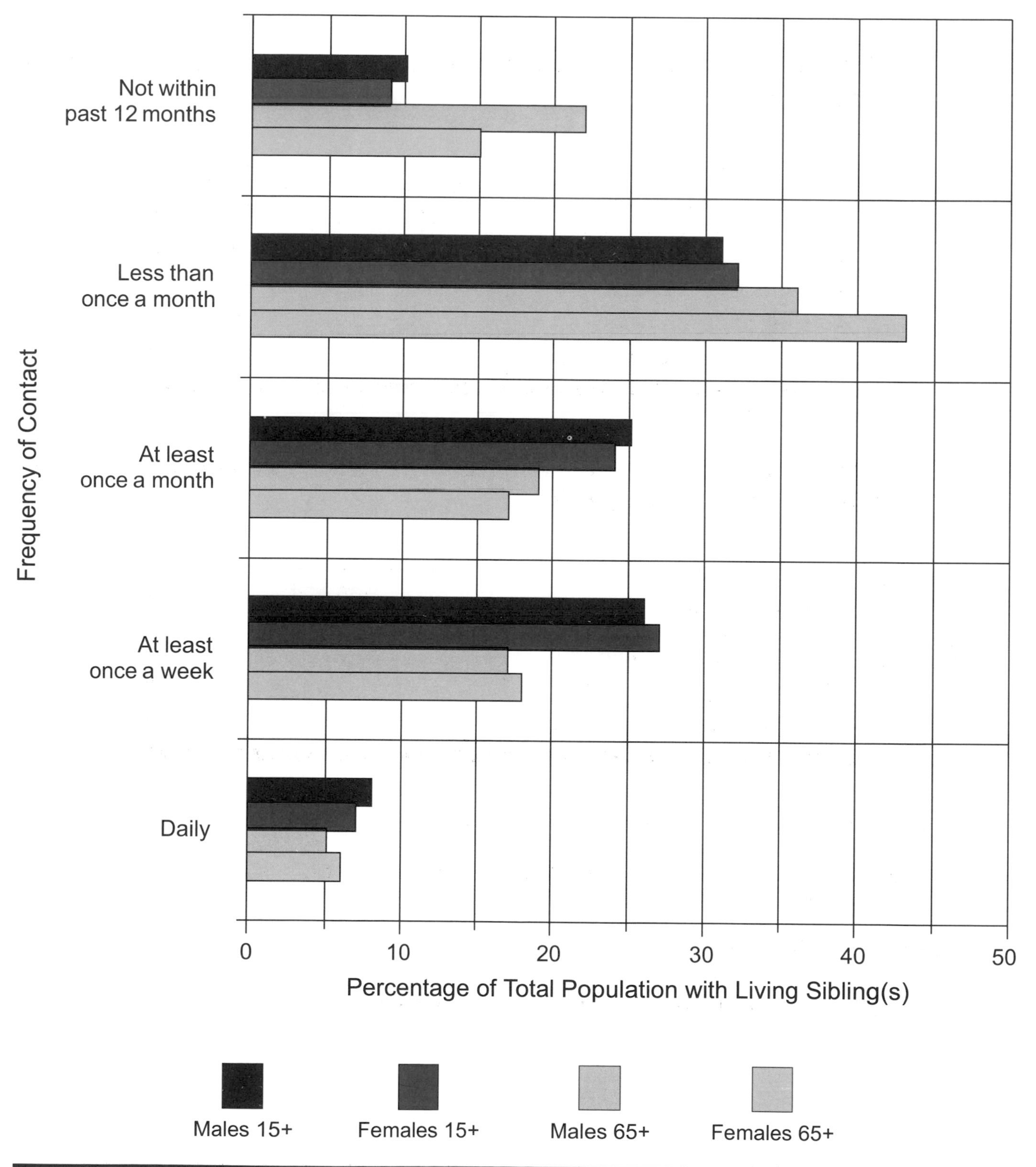

Source: Statistics Canada. Family and Friends. Ottawa, 1994.

B.4.a: *Frequency of personal contact of Canadians 65+ with reference child, 1990*

Frequency of Contact *	Males 65+ (%)	Females 65+ (%)
Daily	12	14
At least once a week	44	44
At least once a month	21	22
Less than once a month	22	18

B.4.b: *Satisfaction of Canadians 65+ with frequency of personal contact with reference child, 1990*

Personal Contact *	Age 65+ (%)
Less often than would like	27
About the right amount	71
More often than would like	1

* Results include only Canadian adults not living with reference child.

Note: Columns in both tables do not sum to 100% due to the exclusion of results of people who did not provide information regarding frequency of contact.

Statistics Canada Definition:

Reference child - child with whom parent has the most contact.

Source: Statistics Canada. Family and Friends. Ottawa, 1994 (1990 General Social Survey; Cat.No. 11-612, p119 & 120).

Frequency of Personal Contact
of Canadians 65+ with Reference Child, 1990

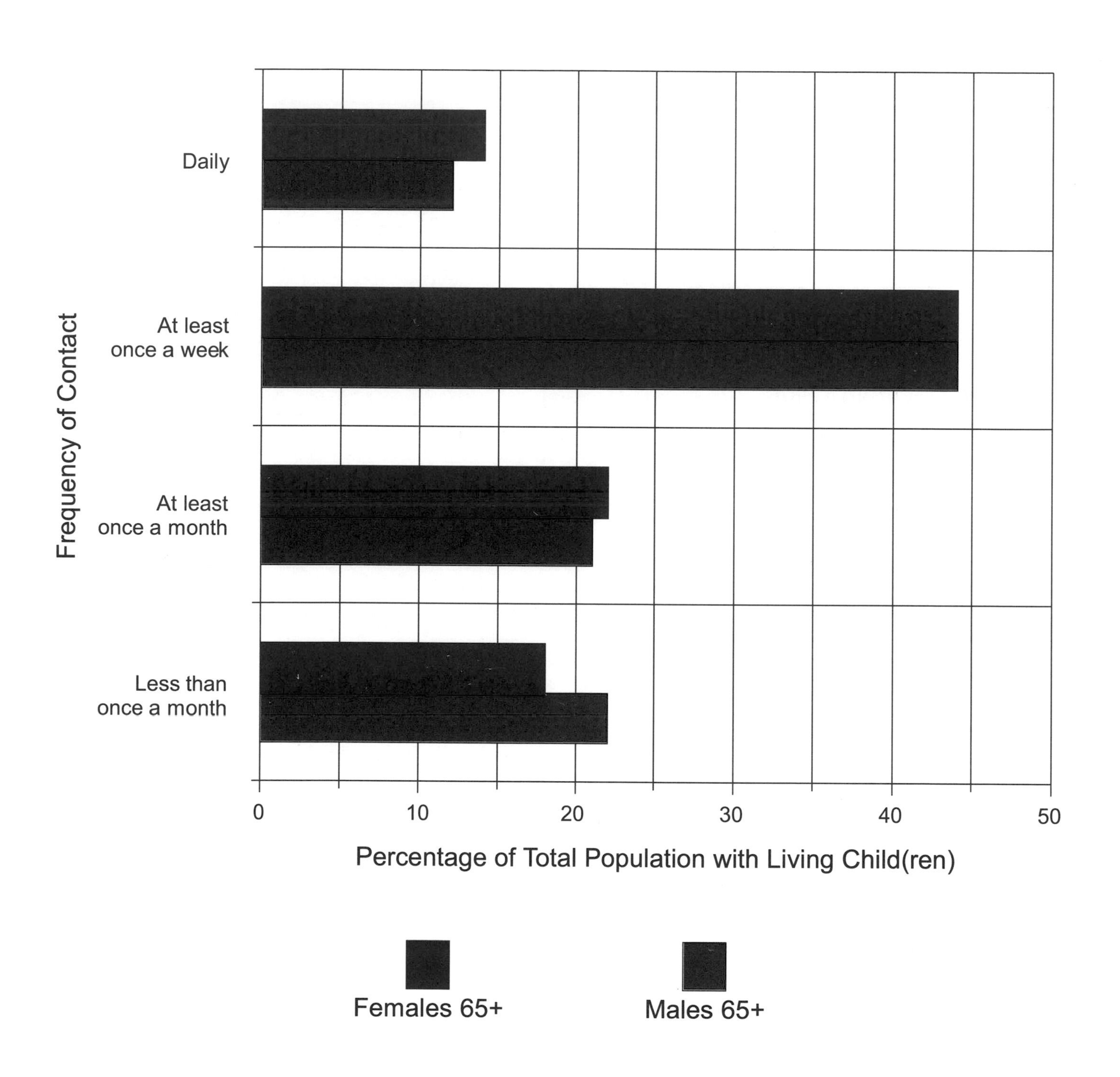

Source: Statistics Canada. Family and Friends. Ottawa, 1994.

B.5: Distance from reference child* of Canadians 65+, 1990

Distance	Males 65+ (%)	Females 65+ (%)
Within 10 km	47	49
11-50 km	21	23
51-100	8	8
Over 100 km	23	18

* Results include only Canadian adults not living with reference child.

Note: Columns do not sum to 100% due to the exclusion of results of people who did not provide information regarding distance from reference child.

Statistics Canada Definition:

Reference child - child with whom parent has the most contact.

Source: Statistics Canada. Family and Friends. Ottawa, 1994 (1990 General Social Survey; Cat.No. 11-612, p114).

Distance from Reference Child
Canadians Aged 65+, 1990

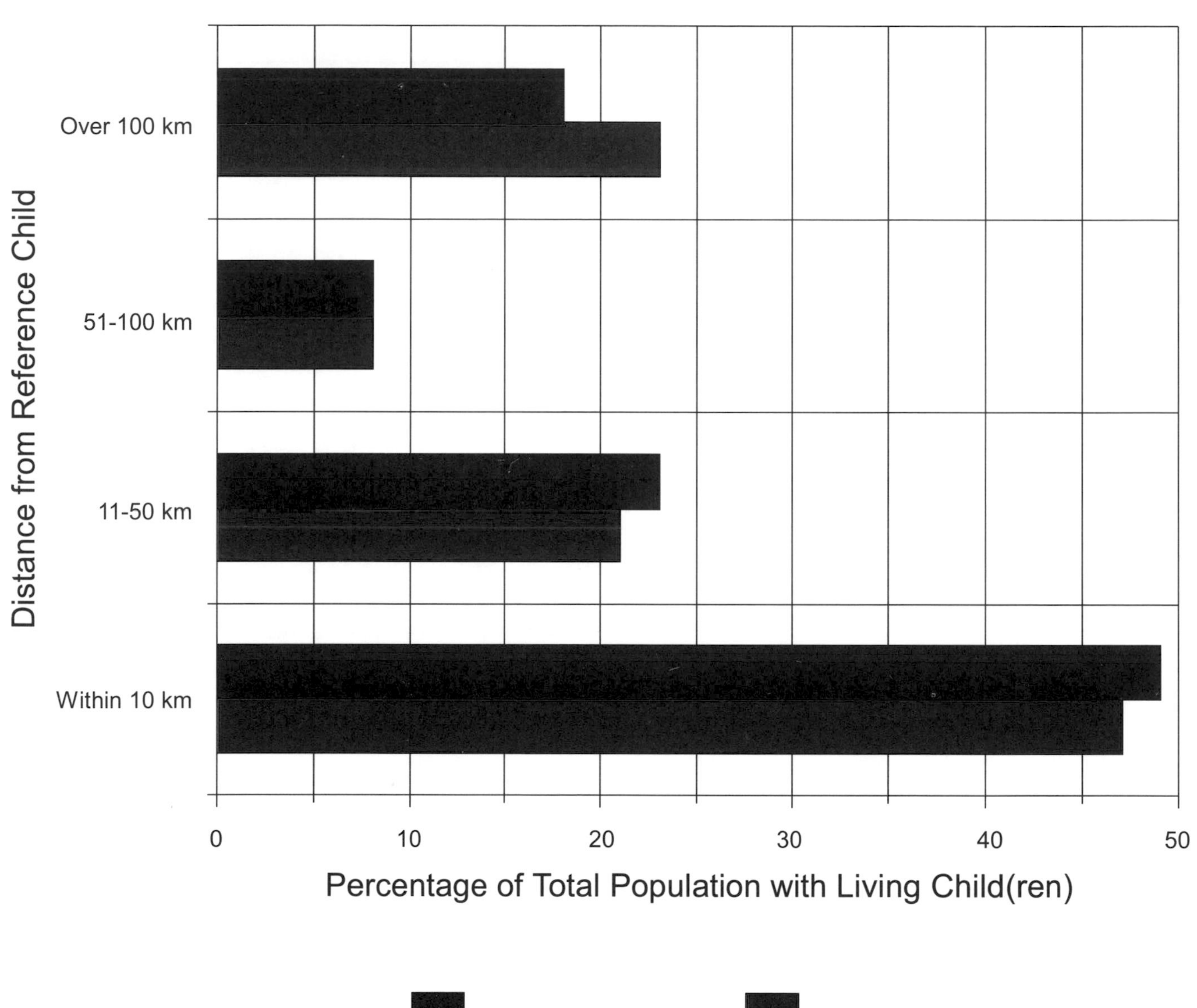

Source: *Statistics Canada. Family and Friends. Ottawa, 1994.*

B.6: *Whom Canadians 65+ turn to first for help when feeling down or depressed, 1990*

Person turned to	Males 65+ (%)	Females 65+ (%)
Spouse/Partner	36	16
Relative	23	43
Friend	10	15
Professional	11	11
No One	8	7
Other/Not Stated	13	8

Note: Not all columns sum to 100% due to rounding in source table.

Statistics Canada Definitions:

Relative - includes son, daughter, sibling, other relatives and in-laws.

Friend - includes neighbour or co-worker.

Professional - includes counsellor, doctor, church, God or clergy.

Source: Statistics Canada. Family and Friends. Ottawa, 1994 (1990 General Social Survey; Cat.No. 11-612, p59).

Whom Canadians 65+ Turn To First
When Down or Depressed, 1990

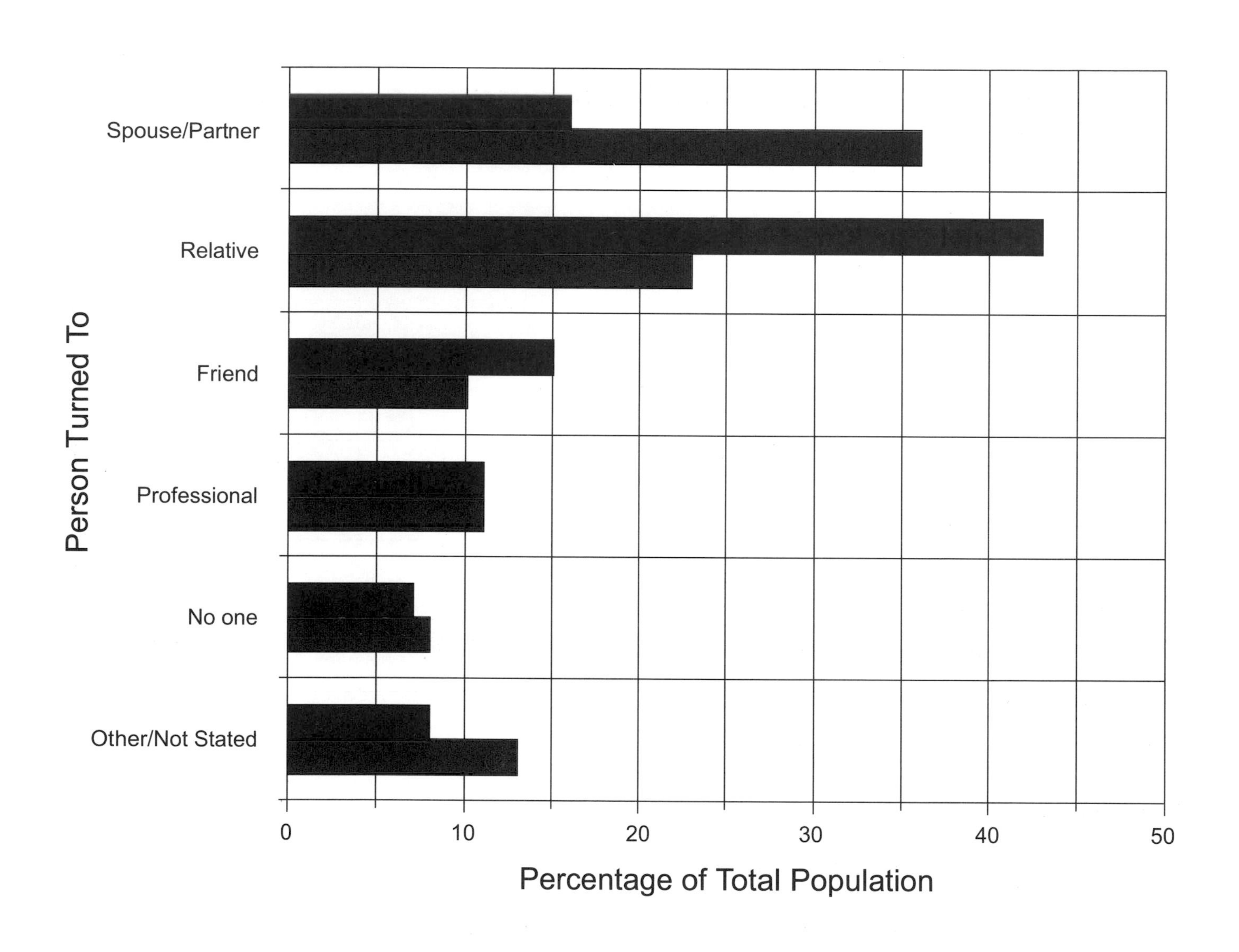

Source: Statistics Canada. Family and Friends. Ottawa, 1994.

B.7: *Proportion of Canadian adults providing unpaid support to people outside of their household, by age and type of assistance provided, 1990*

Type of Assistance *	Males 15+ (%)	Females15+ (%)	Males 65+ (%)	Females 65+ (%)
Housework	13	22	4	12
Household Maintenance	48	16	20	5
Transportation	52	47	37	22
Child Care	24	39	14	22
Financial Support	27	23	26	22

* Support provided in the 12 months prior to survey.

Note: Multiple answers were accepted.

Statistics Canada Definitions:

Housework - includes cooking, sewing, cleaning.

Household Maintenance - includes repairs, painting, carpentry, lawn mowing, and snow shovelling.

Transportation - includes driving someone to an appointment or shopping.

Source: Statistics Canada. Family and Friends. Ottawa, 1994 (1990 General Social Survey; Cat.No. 11-612, p80).

Type of Unpaid Support Provided to Others
By Age and Gender, Canada, 1990

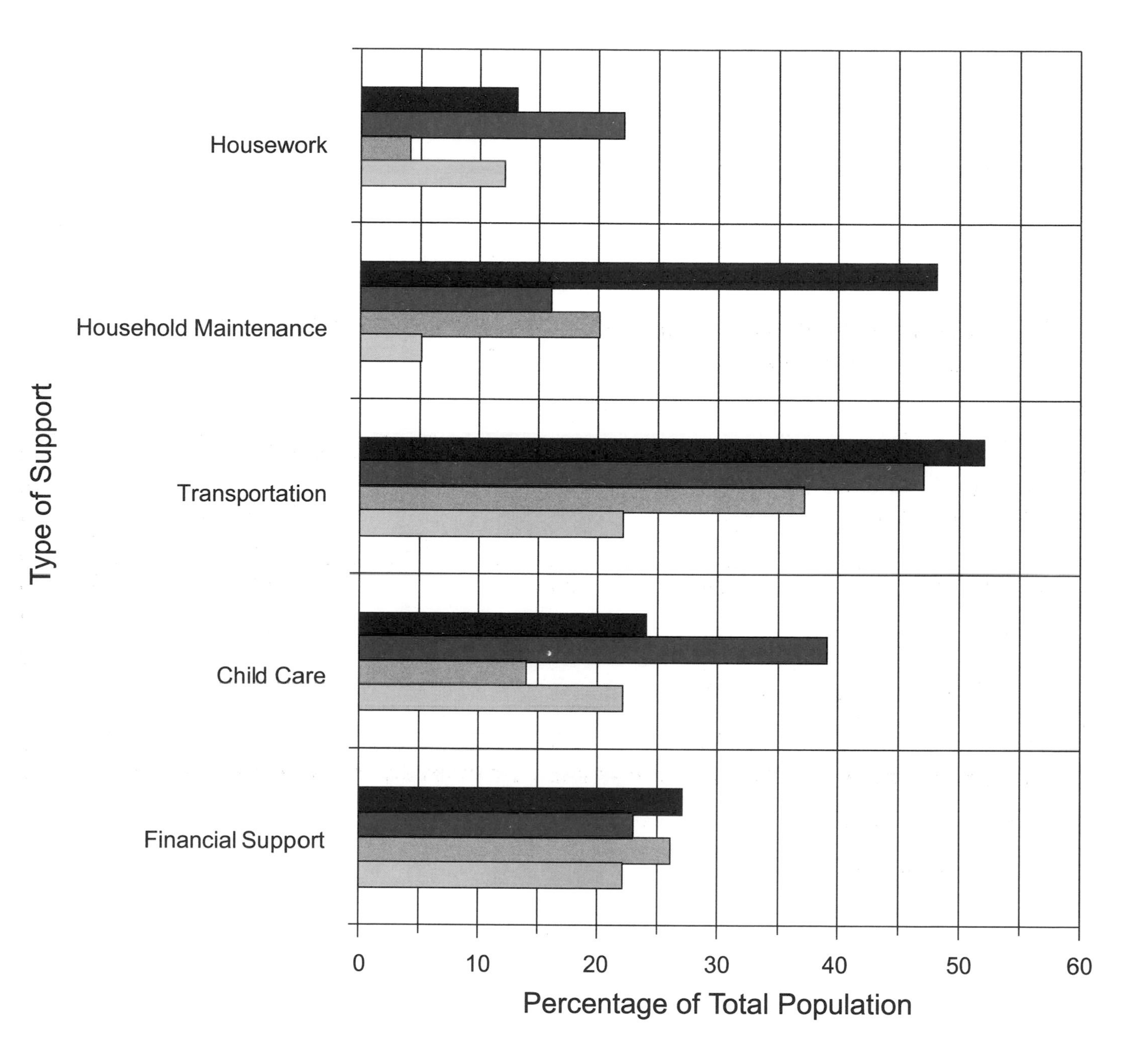

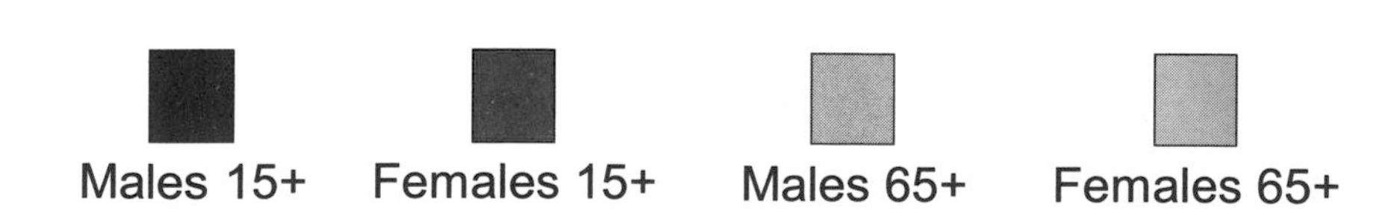

Source: *Statistics Canada. Family and Friends. Ottawa, 1994.*

B.8: *Proportion of Canadians 45+ providing assistance, by recipient of assistance, 1991*

Age/Gender of those providing assistance *	Recipient of Assistance **				
	Spouse/ Partner (%)	Daughter (%)	Son (%)	Friend/ Neighbour (%)	Grandchild (%)
45-64 Males	69	38	37	42	14
45-64 Females	40	44	35	46	35
65+ Males	66	27	26	41	24
65+ Females	32	33	24	46	27

* Assistance provided in the 12 months prior to survey.

** Multiple answers were accepted.

Source: Health Canada. Ageing and Independence: Overview of a National Study. Ottawa, 1993 (1991 Survey; p75).

Canadians 45+ Providing Assistance
By Recipient of Assistance, 1991

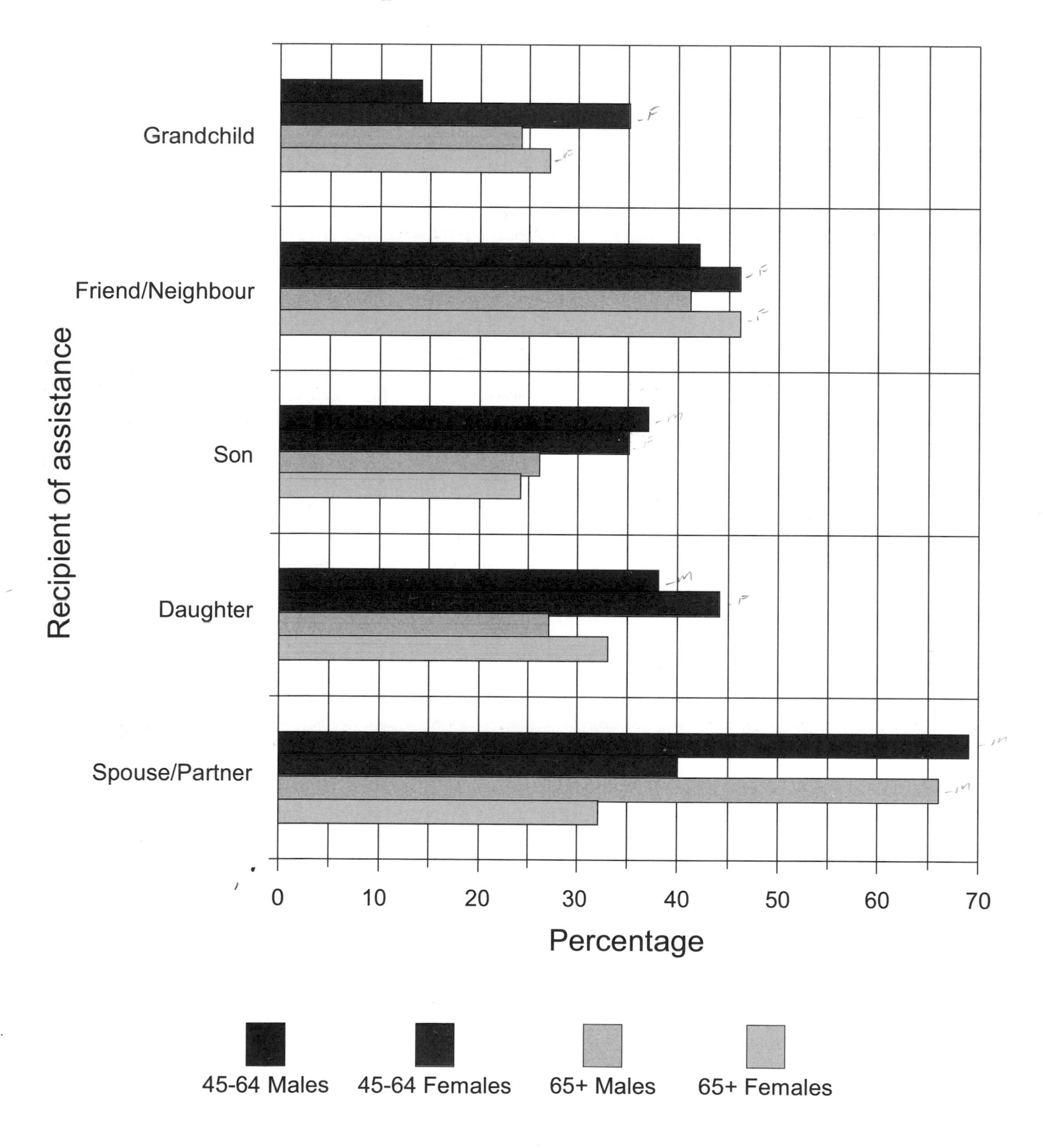

Source: *Health Canada. Ageing and Independence: Overview of a National Study. Ottawa, 1993.*

B.9: *Proportion of Canadians 45+ receiving unpaid assistance from others, by type of assistance received, 1991*

Age/Gender of those receiving assistance *	Type of Assistance Received **			
	Housework (%)	Meals (%)	Transportation (%)	Emotional Support (%)
45-64 Males	38	38	23	33
45-64 Females	32	26	32	42
65+ Males	37	34	20	26
65+ Females	35	20	43	33
80+ Males	49	39	34	29
80+ Females	51	29	57	35

* Assistance received in the 12 months prior to survey.

** Multiple answers were accepted.

Source: Health Canada. Ageing and Independence: Overview of a National Study. Ottawa, 1993 (1991 Survey; p79).

Recipients of Unpaid Assistance
By Type of Assistance, Canadians 45+

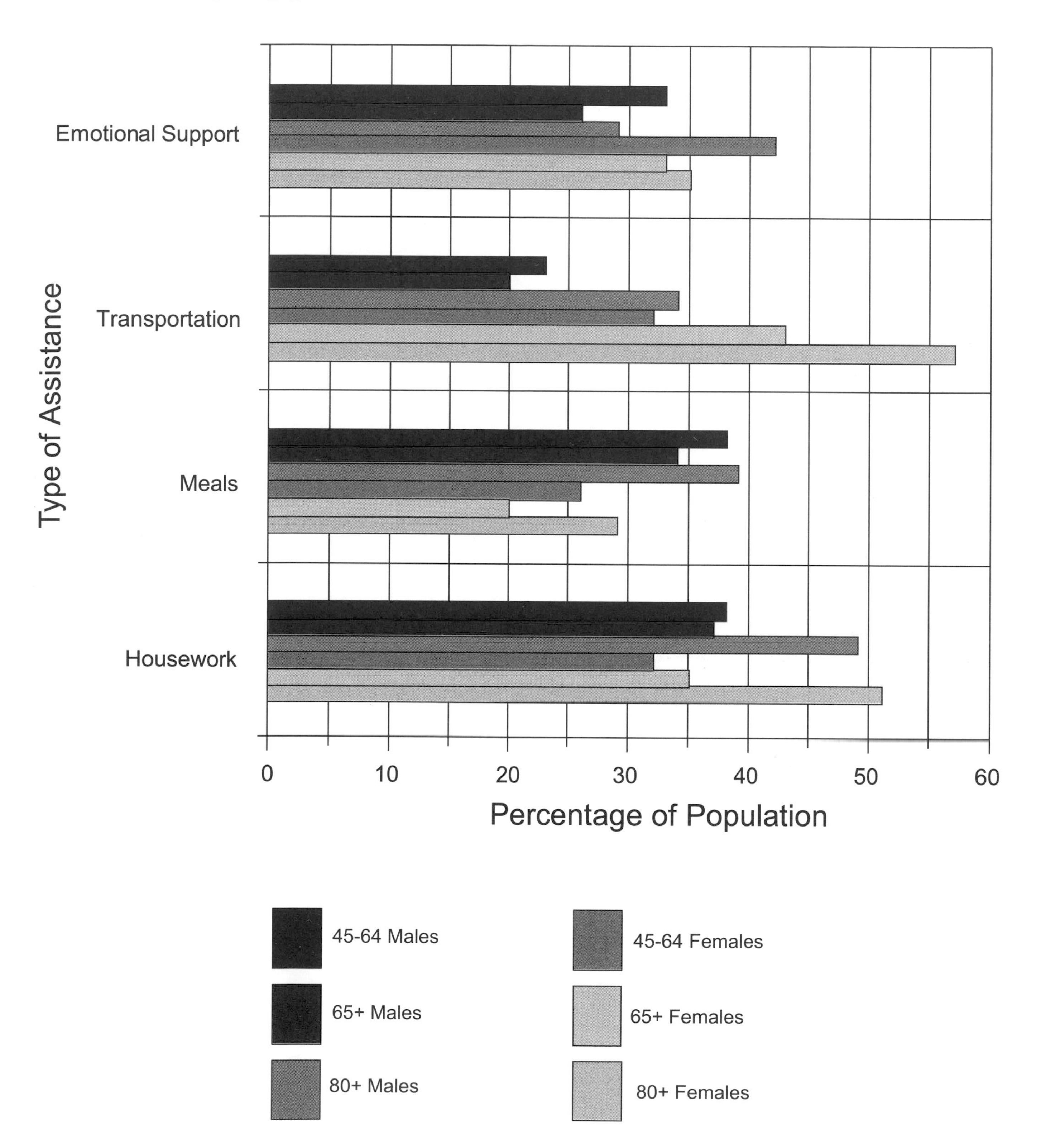

Source: Health Canada. Ageing and Independence: Overview of a National Study. Ottawa, 1993.

B.10: Proportion of Canadians 65+ receiving unpaid assistance from others, by provider of assistance, 1991

Age/Gender of those receiving assistance *	Spouse/ Partner (%)	Daughter (%)	Son (%)	Friend/ Neighbour (%)	Grandchild (%)	Volunteer Groups (%)
65+ Males	**65**	**24**	**26**	**26**	**9**	**7**
65+ Females	**30**	**40**	**28**	**31**	**14**	**10**

* Assistance received in the 12 months prior to survey.

Note: Multiple answers were accepted.

Source: Health Canada. Ageing and Independence: Overview of a National Study. Ottawa, 1993 (1991 Survey; p81).

Proportion of Canadians 65+ Receiving Unpaid Assistance from Others

By Provider of Assistance, 1991

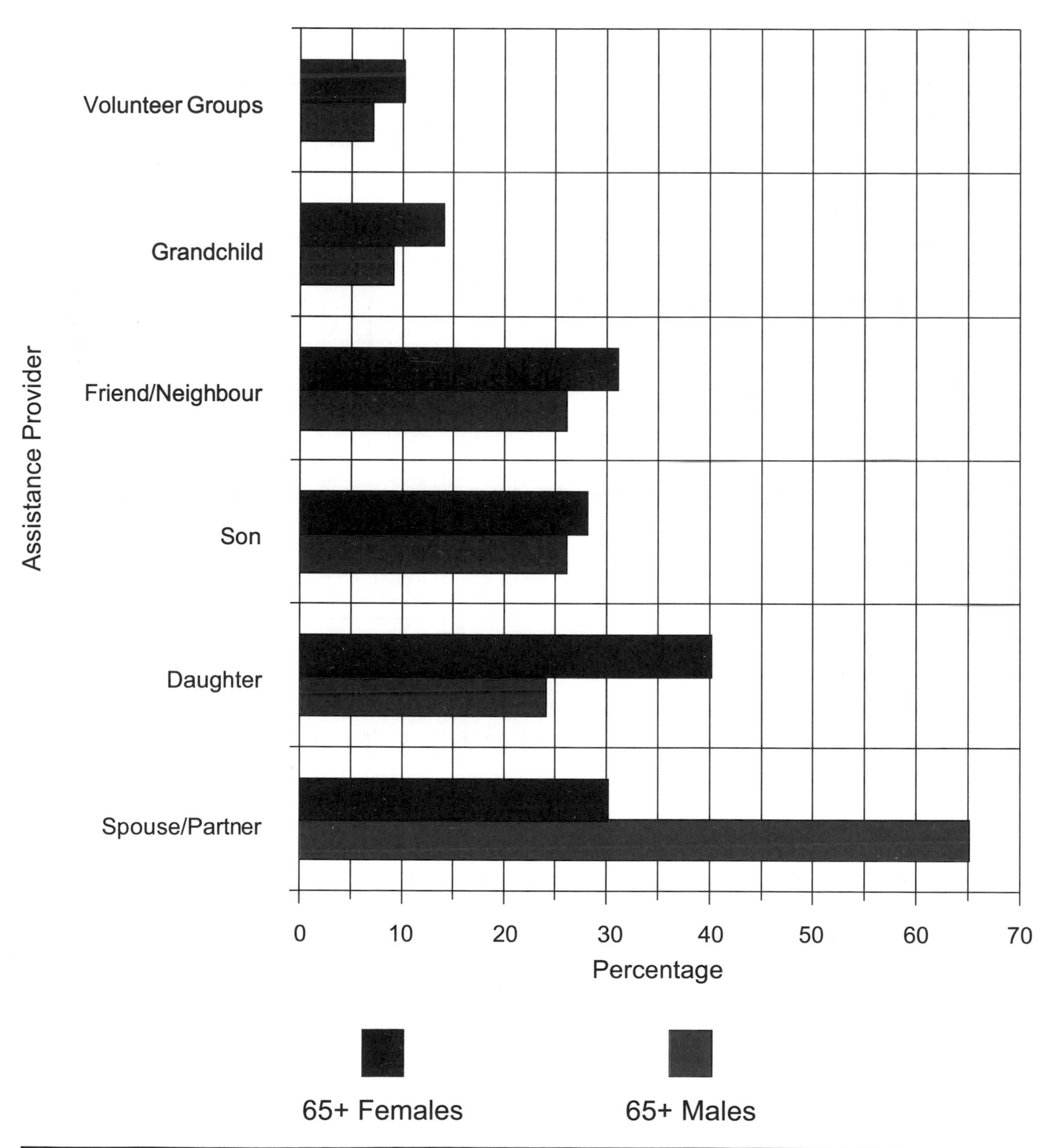

Source: Health Canada. Ageing and Independence: Overview of a National Study. Ottawa, 1993.

B.11: Proportion of Canadians receiving paid support from outside of their household, by type of support received, 1990

Type of Assistance *	Males 15+ (%)	Females15+ (%)	Males 65+ (%)	Females 65+ (%)
House Cleaning/Laundry	8	9	14	18
Household Maintenance	12	13	21	21
Transportation	5	7	6	12

* Support received in the 12 months prior to survey.

Note: Multiple answers were accepted.

Statistics Canada Definitions:

House Cleaning/Laundry - includes cooking, sewing, and cleaning.

Household Maintenance - includes repairs, painting, carpentry, lawn mowing, and snow shovelling.

Transportation - includes shopping and driving someone to an appointment.

Source: Statistics Canada. Family and Friends. Ottawa, 1994 (1990 General Social Survey; Cat.No. 11-612, p86).

Proportion of Canadians Receiving Paid Support

By Type, Age and Gender, 1990

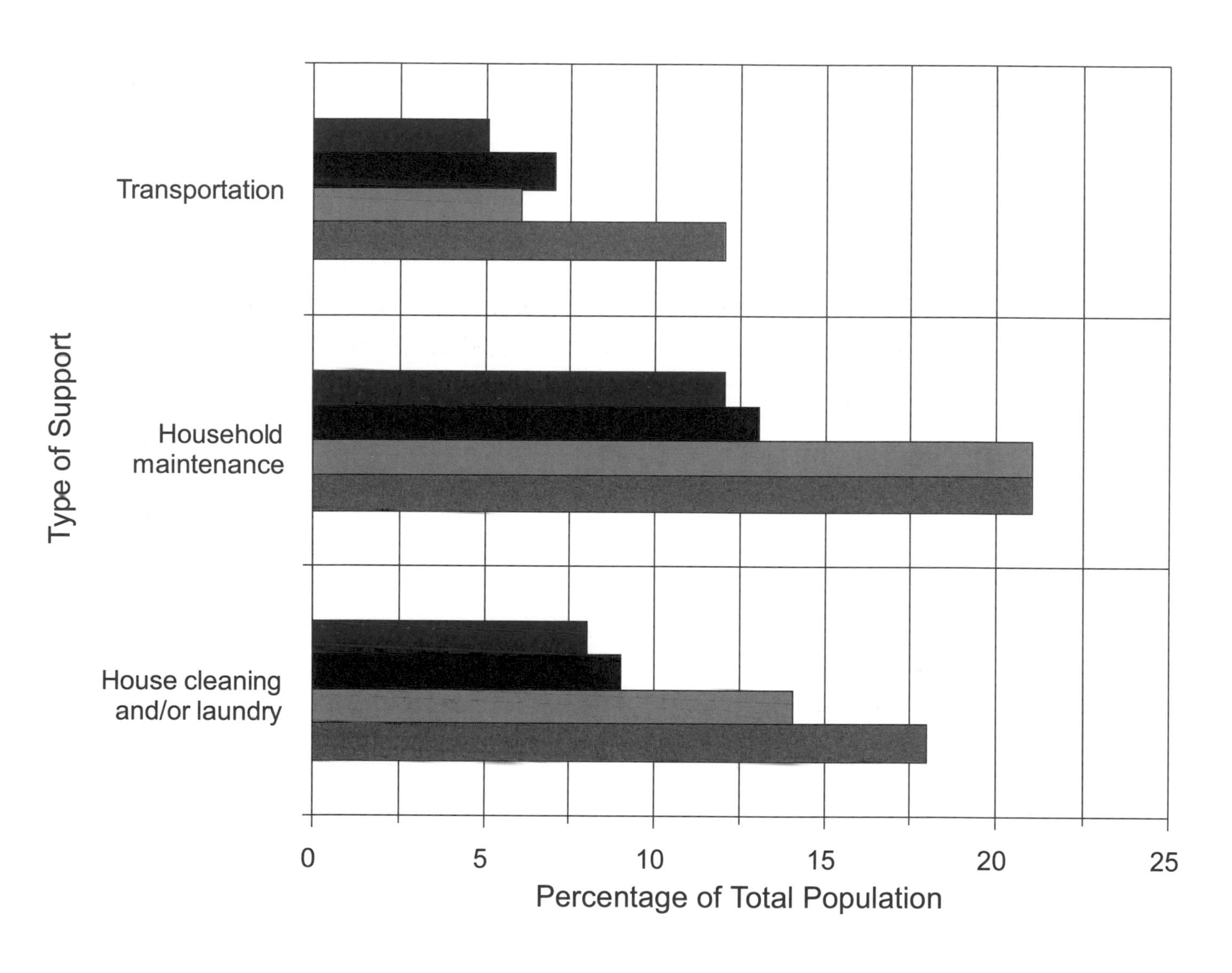

Source: *Statistics Canada. Family and Friends. Ottawa, 1994.*

Canada's church and synagogue attendance declined about 20% between 1957 and 1988.

Canada's Social Trends, Autumn, 1991

In 1990, 42% of those 65 years of age and over attended a religious service at least once a week, compared with 32% in the 45-64 age group and 18% in the 24-44 age group.

Canada's Social Trends, Autumn, 1991

SECTION C

Cultural Characteristics

C.1: Percentage of Canadians 65+ born outside Canada, 1961-1986

Year	Born outside Canada (%)
1961	38.8
1971	36.5
1981	27.6
1986	24.6

Source: Statistics Canada. Demography Division, B. Desjardins. Population Ageing and the Elderly. Ottawa, 1993 (1986 Census of Canada; Cat.No. 91-533E, p41).

Canadians Aged 65+ Born Outside Canada
1961-1986

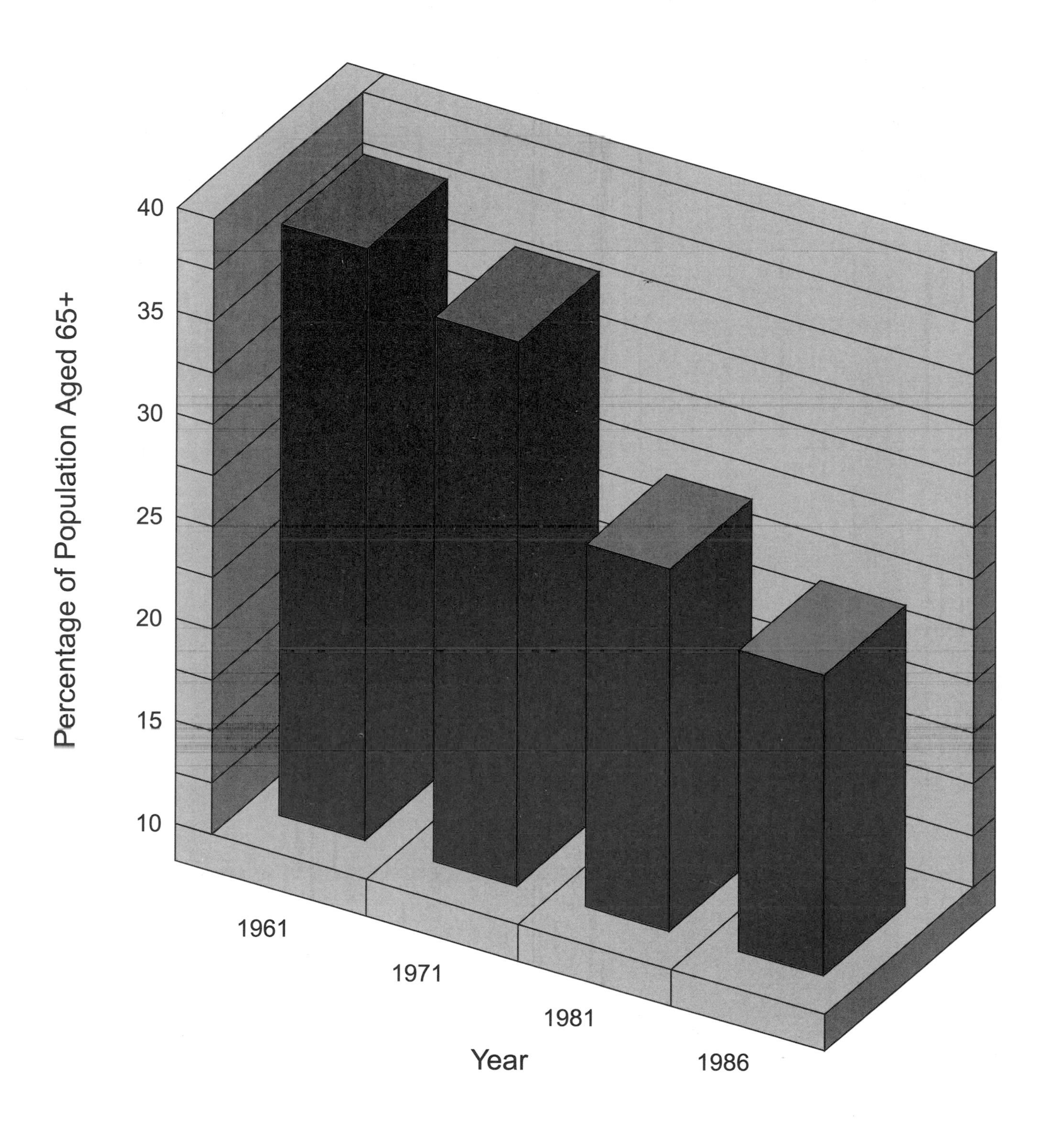

Source: Statistics Canada. Demography Division, B. Desjardins. Population Ageing and the Elderly. Ottawa, 1993.

C.2: Canada's Immigrant Population aged 65+, by place of birth, 1991

Place of Birth	% 65+	Place of Birth	% 65+
United States	6.96	Ethiopia	0.01
El Salvador	0.08	Kenya	0.09
Guatemala	0.02	Tanzania	0.15
Mexico	0.05	Egypt	0.54
Barbados	0.16	Morocco	0.19
Haiti	0.40	Republic of S. Africa	0.27
Jamaica	0.86	Iran	0.19
Trinidad & Tobago	0.31	Israel	0.08
Czech & Slovak Fed. Repub	1.48	Lebanon	0.33
Chile	0.12	Syria	0.11
Guyana	0.64	Turkey	0.39
Austria	1.08	Hong Kong	0.49
Belgium	0.66	Japan	0.24
Argentina	0.06	Kampuchea	0.24
France	0.84	Korea	0.29
Germany	4.42	Laos	0.04
Hungary	2.37	Malaysia	0.10
Italy	8.63	People's Rep of China	4.57
Netherlands	3.65	Philippines	1.32
Poland	7.79	Taiwan	0.06
Portugal	1.59	Vietnam	0.55
Republic of Ireland	0.72	India	2.03
Greece	1.36	Pakistan	0.20
Romania	1.22	Sri Lanka	0.17
Scandinavia	2.34	Australia	0.17
Spain	0.17	Fiji	0.09
Switzerland	0.27	U.S.S.R.	7.96
United Kingdom	27.12	Yugoslavia	2.06

Note: Not all birthplaces are included in this table.

Statistics Canada Definitions:

Immigrant population - refers to persons who are, or have been, landed immigrants in Canada; a landed immigrant is a person who is not a Canadian citizen by birth, but who has been granted the right to live in Canada permanently.

Non-immigrant population - refers to persons who are Canadian citizens by birth.

Source: Statistics Canada. Immigration and Citizenship: The Nation. Ottawa, 1993 (1991 Census of Canada; Cat.No. 93-316, p38-71).

C.3: Canadians 65+ by ethnic origin, 1991

Ethnicity	% 65+	Ethnicity	% 65+
English	26.04	Italian	3.55
Irish	5.42	Maltese	0.05
Scottish	7.91	Portuguese	0.55
Welsh	0.25	Spanish	0.14
French	26.65	Jewish	1.97
Acadian	0.04	Egyptian	0.06
Austrian	0.28	Lebanese	0.19
Belgian	0.25	Arab	0.03
Dutch	1.85	Armenian	0.14
German	5.94	Iranian	0.06
Swiss	0.34	East Indian	0.65
Finish	0.34	Punjabi	0.04
Danish	0.34	Pakistani	0.06
Icelandic	0.14	Sri Lankan	0.03
Norwegian	0.69	Chinese	1.89
Swedish	0.48	Philipino	0.40
Scandinavian	0.11	Cambodian	0.01
Estonian	0.22	Laotian	0.01
Latvian	0.20	Vietnamese	0.12
Lithuanian	0.21	Japanese	0.28
Czech	0.13	Korean	0.09
Czechoslovakian	0.17	Other Africa	0.02
Slovak	0.11	Chilean	0.01
Hungarian	0.80	Salvadorean	0.01
Polish	2.11	Other latin	0.02
Romanian	0.20	Guyanese	0.03
Russian	0.37	Haitian	0.05
Ukrainian	3.85	Jamaican	0.03
Croatian	0.15	West Indian	0.03
Macedonian	0.07	Black	0.36
Serbian	0.07	Inuit	0.03
Yugoslav	0.23	Metis	0.13
Greek	0.46	North American	0.59
American	0.08	Canadian	2.16

Note: These data are based on single responses. Not all ethnic origins are included in this table.

Statistics Canada Definitions:

Ethnic origin - the ethnic or cultural group(s) to which the respondent's ancestors belong. Ethnic or cultural origin refers to the ethnic 'roots' or ancestral background of the population and should not be confused with citizenship or nationality.

Source: Statistics Canada. Ethnic Origin: The Nation. Ottawa, 1992 (1991 Census of Canada; Cat.No. 91-315, p128-135).

C.4: Percentage of Canadians 65+, by mother tongue, 1991

Mother Tongue	% 65+	Mother Tongue	% 65+
English	57.11	French	22.57
Cree	0.15	Inuktitut	0.02
Italian	2.19	Portuguese	0.40
Spanish	0.19	German	3.12
Yiddish	0.41	Dutch	0.85
Croatian	0.11	Czech	0.14
Polish	1.20	Russian	0.28
Ukrainian	2.23	Slavic Languages	0.12
Finnish	0.22	Hungarian	0.58
Greek	0.31	Armenian	0.09
Arabic	0.15	Gujarati	0.09
Hindi	0.05	Persian(Farsi)	0.04
Punjabi	0.24	Tamil	0.03
Japanese	0.14	Korean	0.07
Chinese	1.33	Vietnamese	0.08
Tagalog (Philipino)	0.21	Other	2.10

Note: Not all mother tongues are included in this table.

Source: Statistics Canada. Mother Tongue: The Nation. Ottawa, 1992 (1991 Census of Canada; Cat.No. 93-313, p66-71).

Mother Tongue of Canadians 65+, 1991

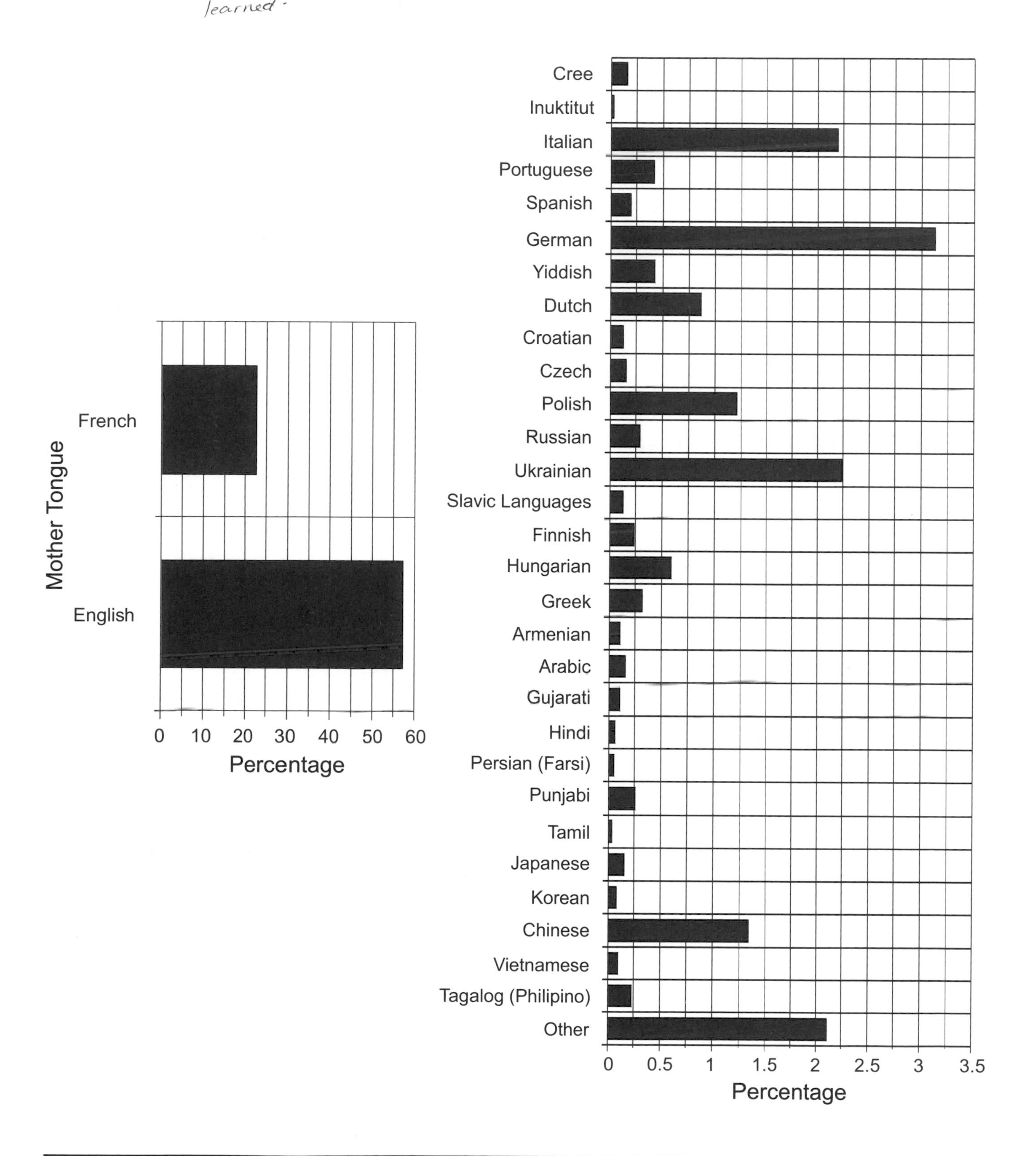

Source: Statistics Canada. Mother Tounge: The Nation. Ottawa, 1992.

C.5: *Percentage of Canadians 60+, by religious affiliation, 1981 and 1991*

Religious Affiliation	Age 60-69		Age 70+	
	1981 (%)	1991 (%)	1981 (%)	1991 (%)
Catholic	41.70	44.80	37.90	39.00
Protestant	50.20	43.30	54.40	50.10
Eastern Non-Christian	0.60	1.60	0.40	1.10
Jewish	2.00	1.50	2.30	2.20
Eastern Orthodox	1.60	1.80	1.90	1.80
Para-religious groups	0.05	0.04	0.06	0.01
No religious affiliation	3.90	6.90	3.00	5.60
Other	0.01	0.03	0.02	0.02

Statistics Canada Definitions:

Catholic - includes Roman Catholic, Ukrainian Catholic, and other Catholic.

Protestant - includes United Church, Anglican, Presbyterian, Lutheran, Baptist, Pentecostal, Mennonite, Jehovah's Witnesses, Salvation Army, Latter Day Saints (Mormons), Reformed bodies, Methodist bodies, Adventist, Christian and Missionary Alliance, Brethren in Christ, Churches of Christ, Hutterite, Church of the Nazarene, Unitarian, and other Protestant.

Eastern Non-Christian - includes Islam, Buddhist, Hindu, Sikh,and Baha'i.

No religious affiliation - includes no religion, agnostic, atheist, and other.

Source: Statistics Canada. Religions in Canada: The Nation. Ottawa, 1993 (1991 Census of Canada; Cat.No. 93-319, p102-107).

Religious Affiliations
Canadians 60+, 1981 and 1991

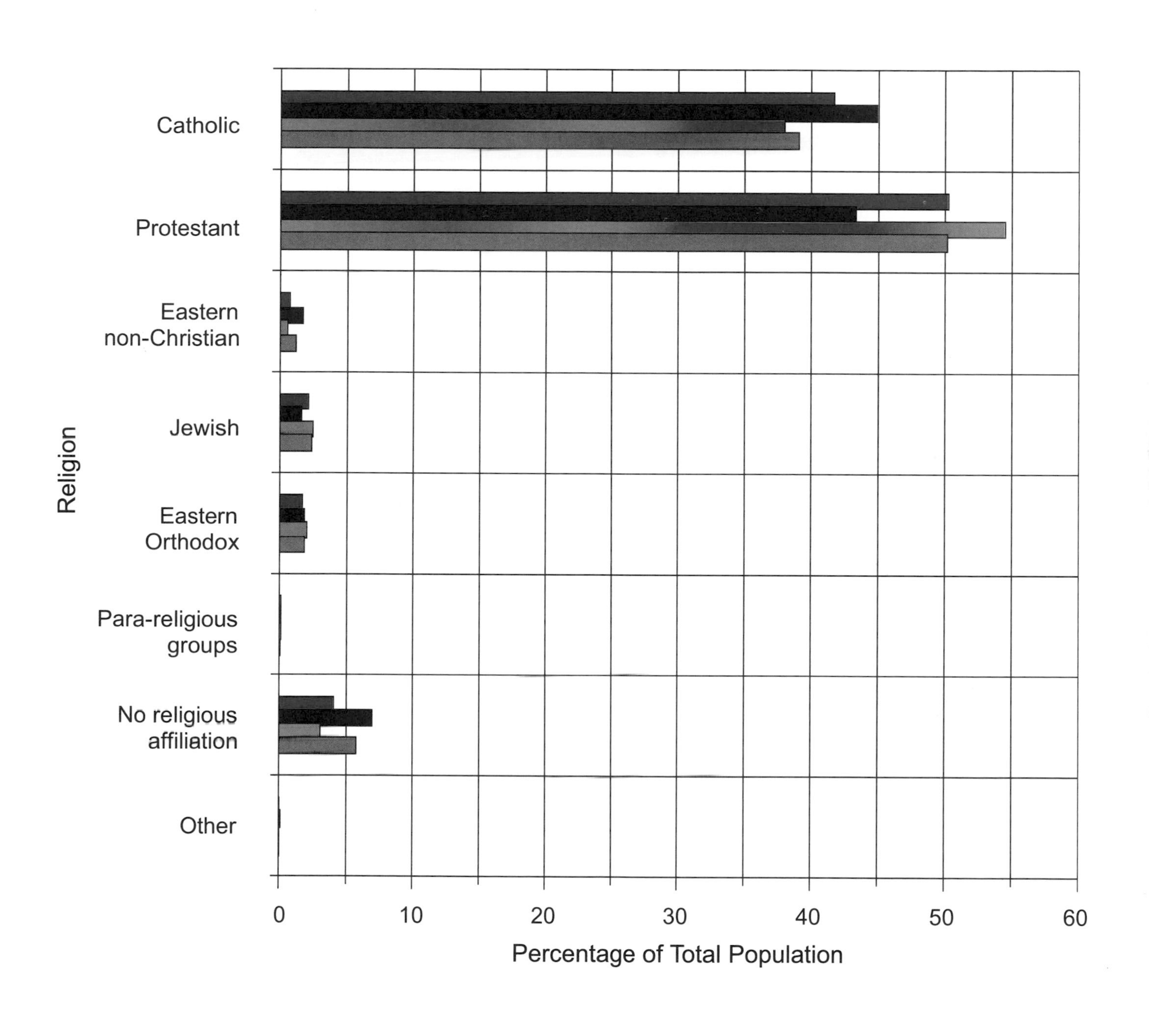

Source: Statistics Canada. Religions in Canada: The Nation. Ottawa, 1993.

After food and shelter costs, personal taxes and transportation costs are the highest expenses for seniors.

Statistics Canada, Profile of Canada's Seniors, 1994

SECTION D

Housing

D.1: Living arrangements of Canadians 65+, by gender, 1991

Living Arrangement	Males 65+ (%)	Females 65+ (%)
In a collective household	**6.1**	**10.3**
In a private household		
As a couple	**71.3**	**38.7**
Alone	**14.3**	**34.2**
Not as a couple/with a relative*	**4.6**	**14.8**
With an unrelated person	**2.7**	**2.0**

Statistics Canada Definition:

Collective households - include hospitals, special care centres, prisons, correctional institutions, religious institutions, tourist homes, boarding houses, military & worker camps, Hutterite colonies, etc.

* The category "not as a couple" includes some people who live with non-relatives only but who fall within the Statistics Canada definition of living in a family household.

Source: Statistics Canada. Demography Division, B. Desjardins. Population Ageing and the Elderly. Ottawa, 1993 (1991 Cencus of Canada; Cat.No. 91-533E, p64).

Living Arrangements of Canadians 65+,
By Gender, 1991

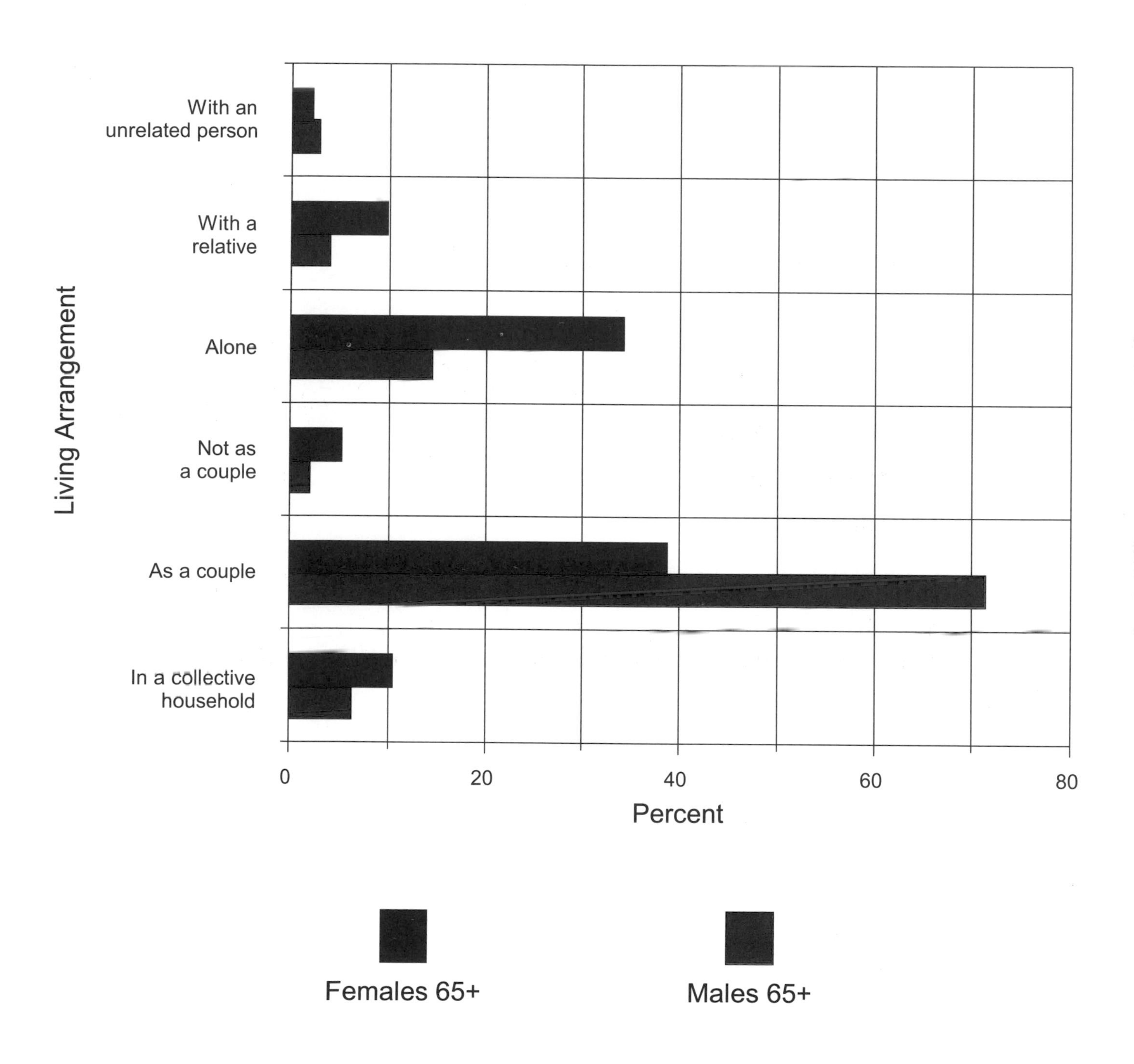

Source: Statistics Canada. Demography Division, B. Desjardins. Population Ageing and the Elderly. Ottawa, 1993.

D.2: *Housing tenure of Canadians 45+, 1991*

Housing tenure	Age 45-64 (%)	Age 65-79 (%)	Age 80+ (%)
Own, no mortgage	49	60	48
Own, with mortgage	28	6	0
Rent	18	27	38
Not stated	4	4	6
Other *	1	3	8

* Not defined in source data.

Source: Health Canada. Ageing and Independence: Overview of a National Survey. Ottawa, 1993 (1991 Survey; p148).

Housing Tenure of Canadians 45+, 1991

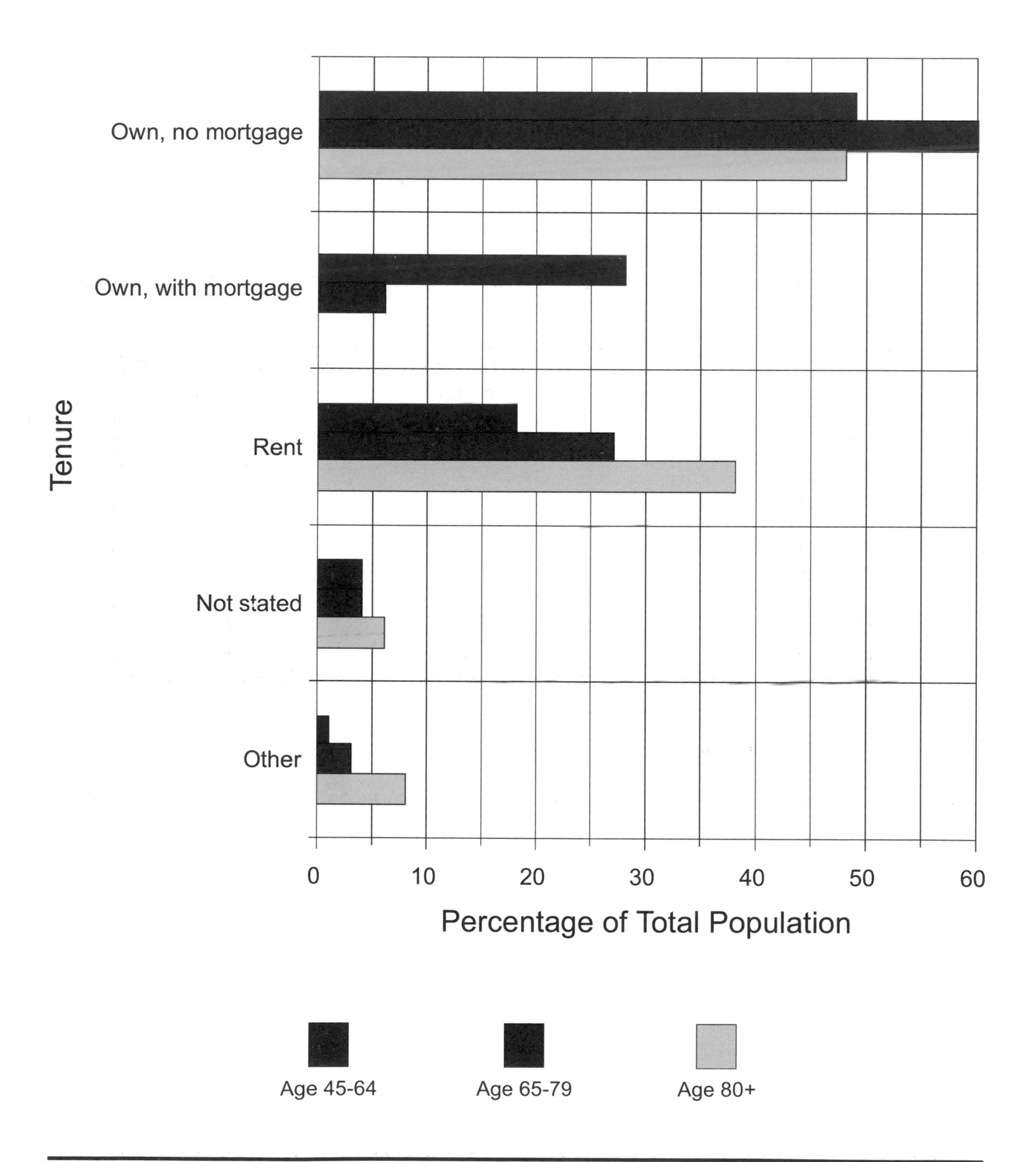

Source: *Health Canada. Ageing and Independence: Overview of a National Survey. Ottawa, 1993.*

D.3: Percentage of Canadians 65+ residing in collective dwellings, 1991

Age/Gender	Special Care Homes (%)	Hospitals & Related Institutions (%)
Males 65-74	1.4	0.5
Females 65-74	1.7	0.3
Males 75-84	6.1	0.9
Females 75-84	9.6	0.8
Males 85+	23.3	2.2
Females 85+	36.3	2.4

Statistics Canada Definition:

Hospitals and related institutions - does not include religious institutions or rooming houses.

Source: Statistics Canada. J.A. Norland. Focus on Canada - Profile of Canada's Seniors. Ottawa, 1994 (Cat. No. 96-312E, p91).

Canadians in Collective Dwellings
By Age and Gender, 1991

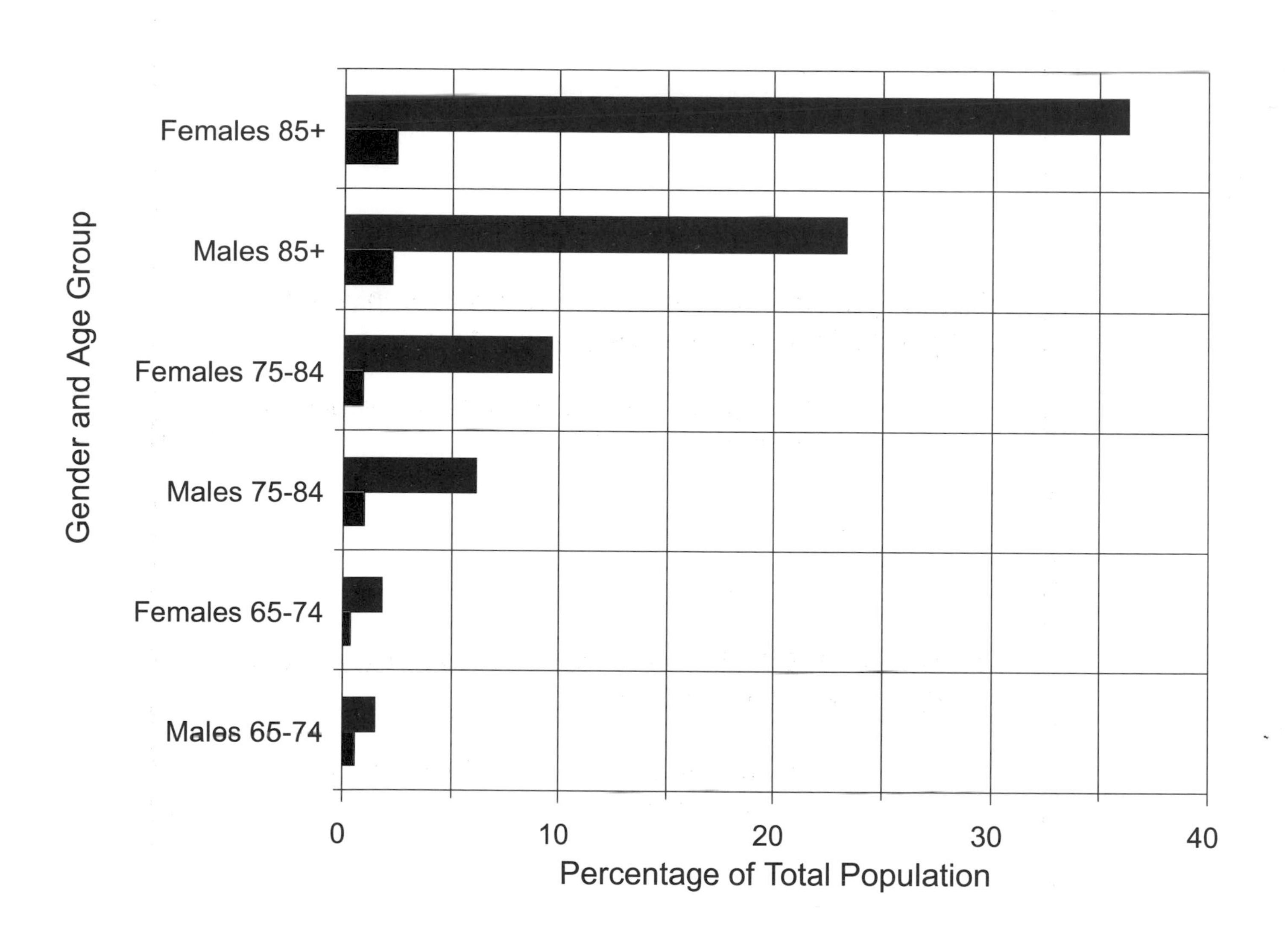

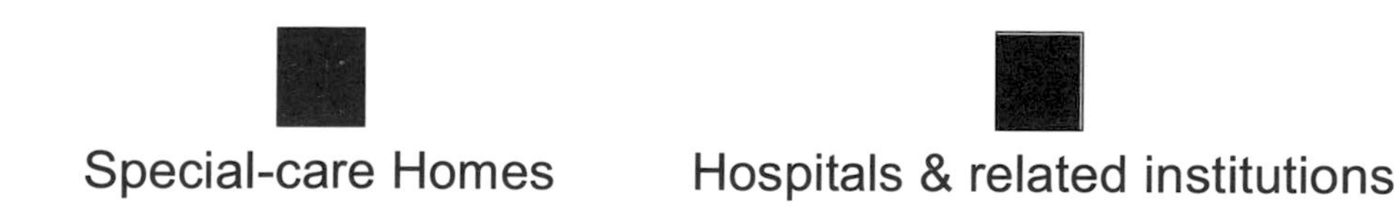

Source: *Statistics Canada. J.A. Norland. Focus on Canada - Profile of Canada's Seniors. Ottawa, 1994.*

Three-quarters (75%) of seniors believe that action on pollution control is very important.

Canada's Health Promotion Survey, Health and Welfare Canada, 1990

Over half (57%) of seniors aged 65 and over recycle bottles, cans and papers.

Canada's Health Promotion Survey, Health and Welfare Canada, 1990

SECTION E

Education

E.1: Highest level of formal education of Canadians, by age, 1991

Age	None (%)	Grades 1-8 (%)	Grades 9-13 (%)	Post Secondary (%)
15-64	0.5	9.2	39.7	50.5
65-69	1.9	33.3	36.0	28.8
70-74	2.1	35.5	36.6	25.8
75-79	2.8	39.2	34.6	23.4
80-84	4.1	43.0	30.9	22.0
85+	5.7	46.7	27.8	19.7
65+	2.6	36.9	34.8	25.6

Source: Statistics Canada. J.A. Norland. Focus on Canada - Profile of Canada's Seniors. Ottawa, 1994 (Cat. No. 96-312E; p40).

Highest Level of Formal Education
of Canadians, by Age, 1991

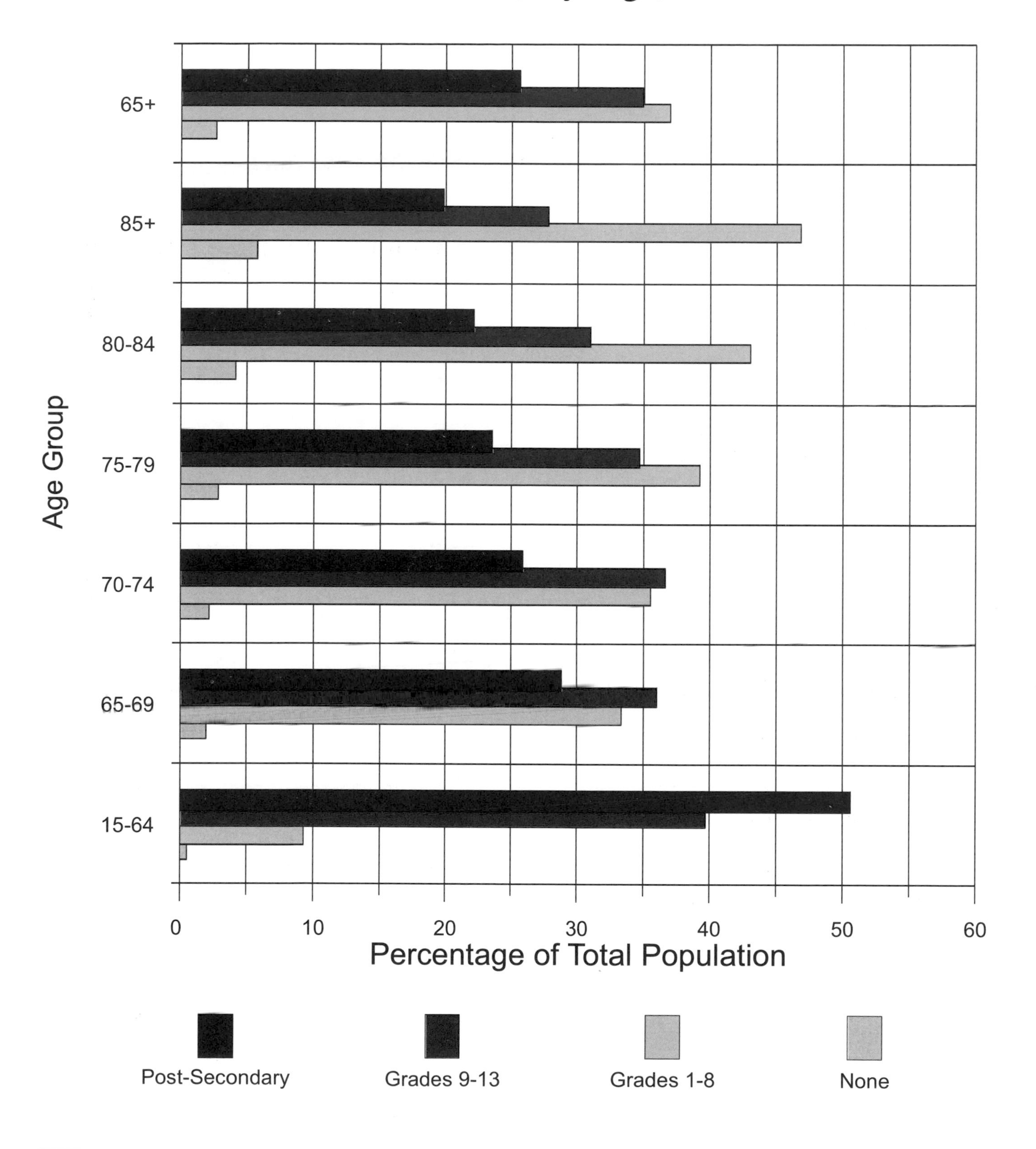

Source: *Statistics Canada. J.A. Norland. Focus on Canada - Profile of Canada's Seniors. Ottawa, 1994.*

E.2: Highest degree attained by Canadians, by age, 1991

Age	No Degree (%)	Below B.A. Level (%)	B.A. Level & Above (%)
15-64	36.3	51.3	12.4
65-69	63.3	30.8	5.9
70-74	66.1	28.8	5.1
75-79	69.5	26.0	4.5
80-84	72.4	23.6	4.0
85+	75.5	21.0	3.5
65+	67.0	27.9	5.1

Statistics Canada Definition:

Below B.A. Level - primarily comprised of diplomas and certificates of non-university post-secondary institutions.

B.A. Level and Above - includes university degrees and some certificates and diplomas (primarily from universities).

Source: Statistics Canada. J.A. Norland. Focus on Canada - Profile of Canada's Seniors. Ottawa, 1994 (1991 Census of Canada; Cat. No. 96-312E; p40).

Highest Degree Attained
By Canadians, 1991

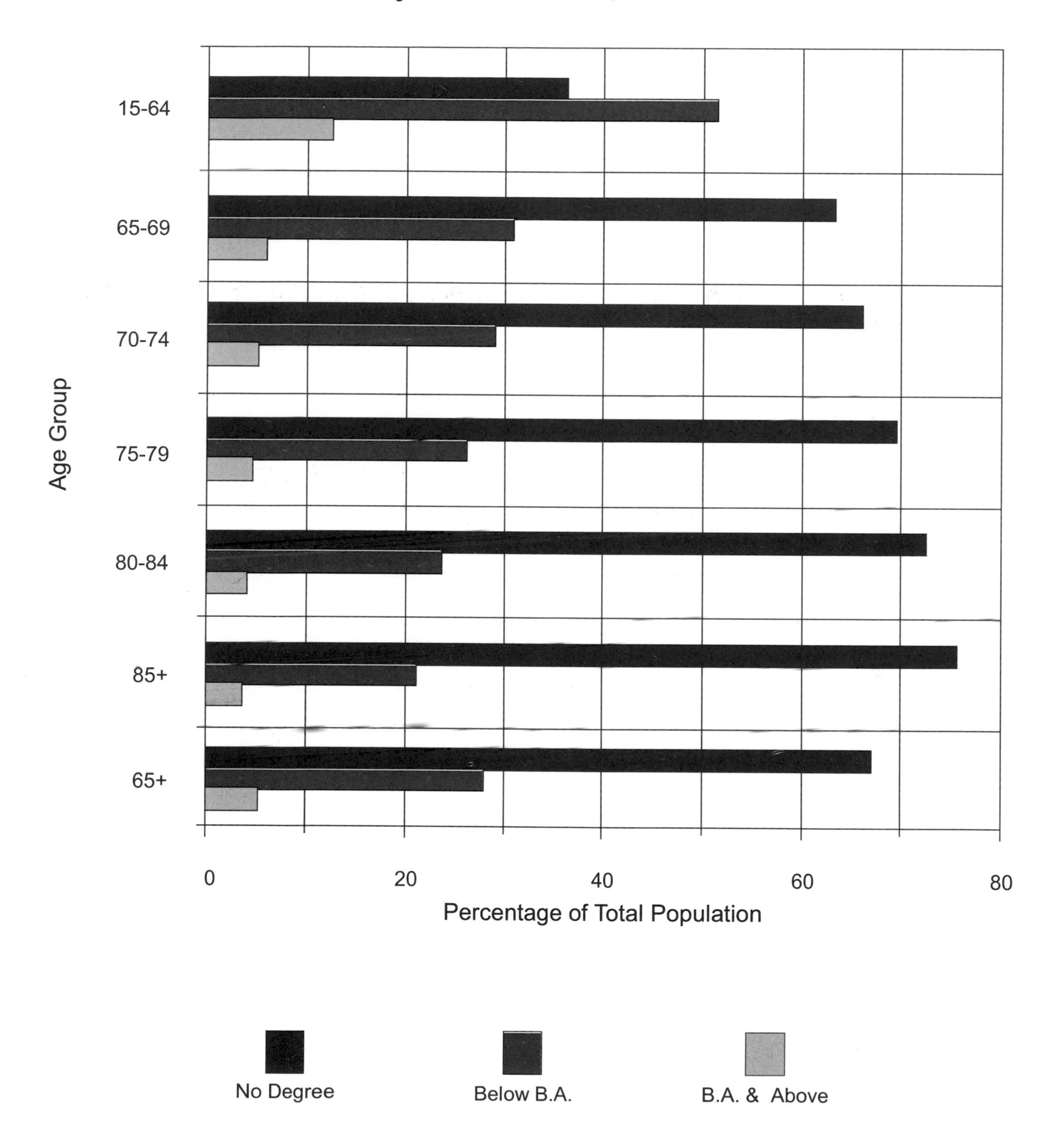

Source: Statistics Canada. J.A. Norland. Focus on Canada - Profile of Canada's Seniors. Ottawa, 1994.

E.3: *Full- and part-time university enrolment of Canadians 40+, 1983 and 1988*

Age	Year			
	Full-time Studies		Part-time Studies	
	1983	1988	1983	1988
40-49	5,463	9,540	38,747	54,012
50-59	1,098	1,389	10,638	10,749
60+	279	441	4,285	4,920

Source: Statistics Canada. Housing, Family and Social Statistics Division. A Portrait of Seniors in Canada. Ottawa, 1990 (1988 data; Cat. No. 89-519, p49).

Full- & Part-time University Enrolment
Canadians Aged 40+, 1983 and 1988

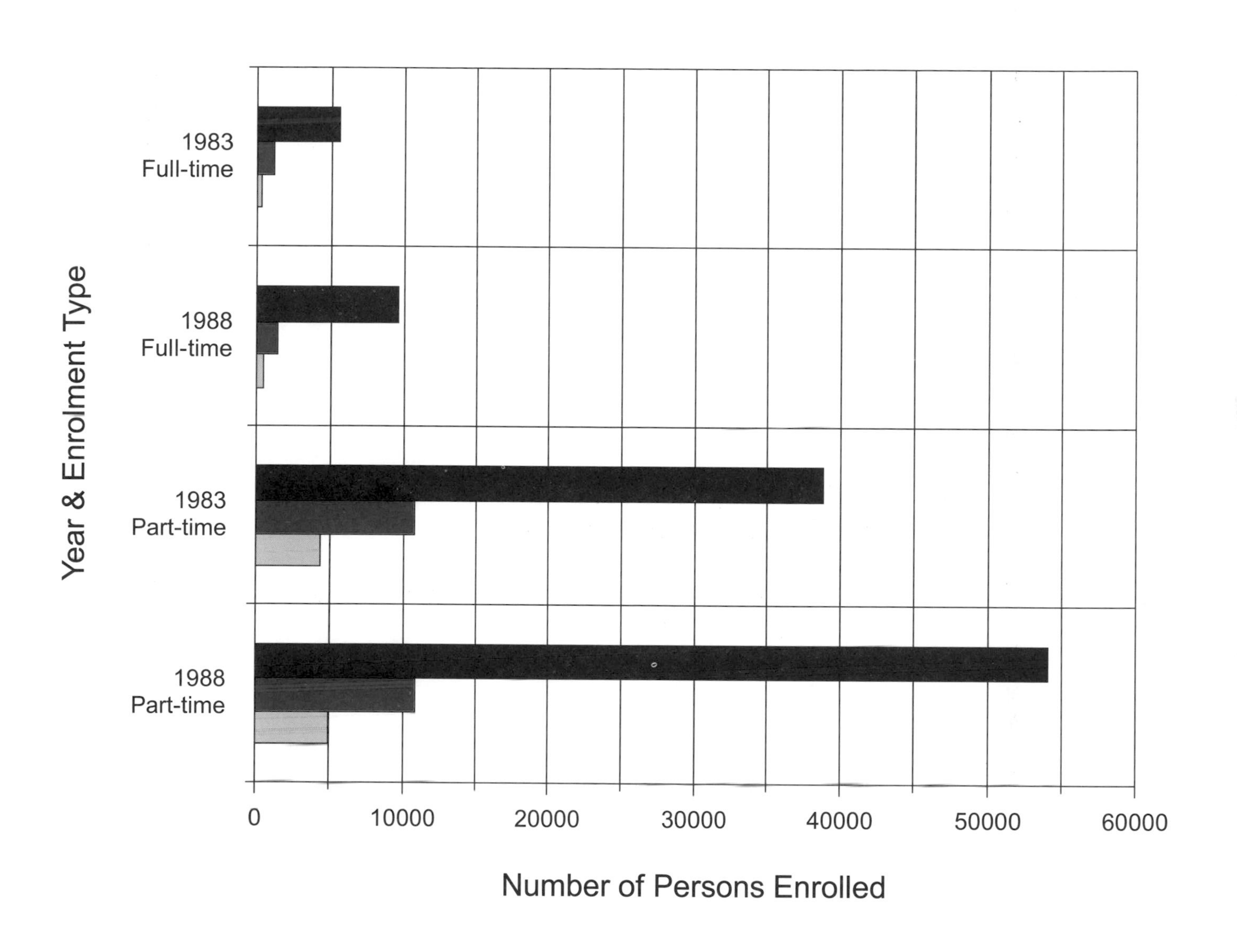

Source: Statistics Canada. Housing, Family and Social Statistics Division. A Portrait of Seniors in Canada. Ottawa, 1990.

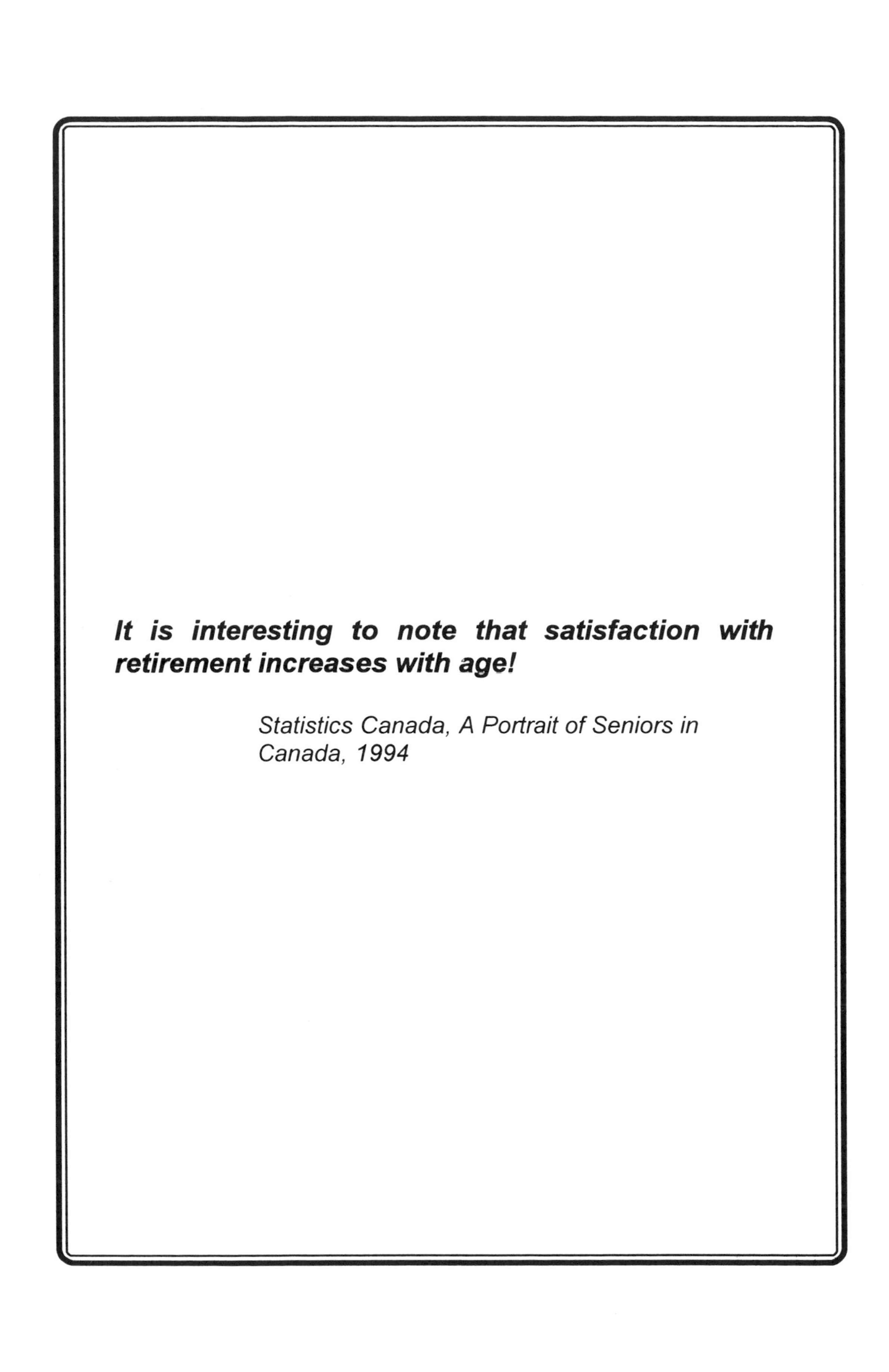

It is interesting to note that satisfaction with retirement increases with age!

Statistics Canada, A Portrait of Seniors in Canada, 1994

SECTION F

Leisure

F.1: *Percentage of Canadian adults engaging in "active" and "sedentary" leisure-time physical activity, 1991*

Age Group	"Active" Leisure		"Sedentary" Leisure	
	Males (%)	Females (%)	Males (%)	Females (%)
15-24	65	44	6	14
25-44	43	28	20	23
45-64	25	17	24	27
65+	13	10	28	42

Statistics Canada Definitions:

"Level of leisure time physical activity is based on an index of energy expenditure values. These were developed from a series of questions about the usual total time per week spent on activities described as light, moderate or vigorous. Energy expenditure values were assigned."

Respondents were then classified as:

- Sedentary - less than 500 kcal/week energy expenditure.
- Active - minimum 2000 kcal/week energy expenditure.

Source: Statistics Canada. Health Status of Canadians. Ottawa, 1994 (1991 General Social Survey; Cat.No. 11-612E, p156).

Physical Leisure Activity
Canadians, 1991

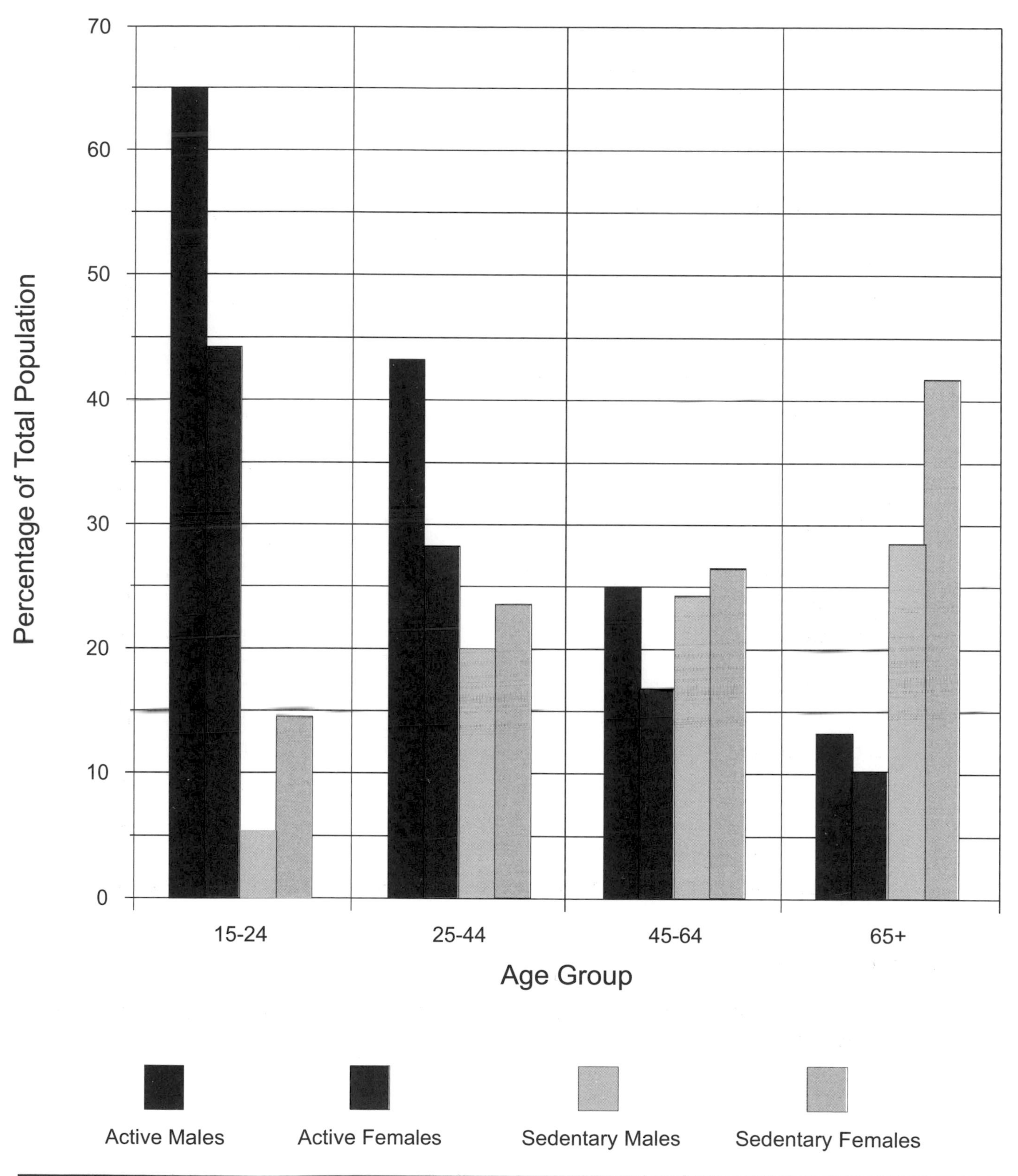

Source: *Statistics Canada. Health Status of Canadians. Ottawa, 1994.*

F.2: Participation by Canadian adults in regular physical activity, by age and gender, 1985 and 1990

Age and Gender	Year	
	1985 (%)	1990 (%)
18-24 Males	64	70
18-24 Females	60	54
25-44 Males	55	44
25-44 Females	51	42
45-64 Males	46	41
45-64 Females	51	48
65+ Males	59	55
65+ Females	47	43
Total - Males	55	49
Total - Females	52	46
Total - Both genders	53	47

Health and Welfare Canada Definition:

Regular physical activity - vigorous physical activity of at least 15 minutes in duration three or more times weekly.

Source: Health Canada. Canada's Health Promotion Survey 1990: Technical Report. Ottawa, 1993 (1990 Health Promotion Survey; p142).

Participation, by Canadian Adults, in Regular Physical Activity
By Age and Gender, 1985 and 1990

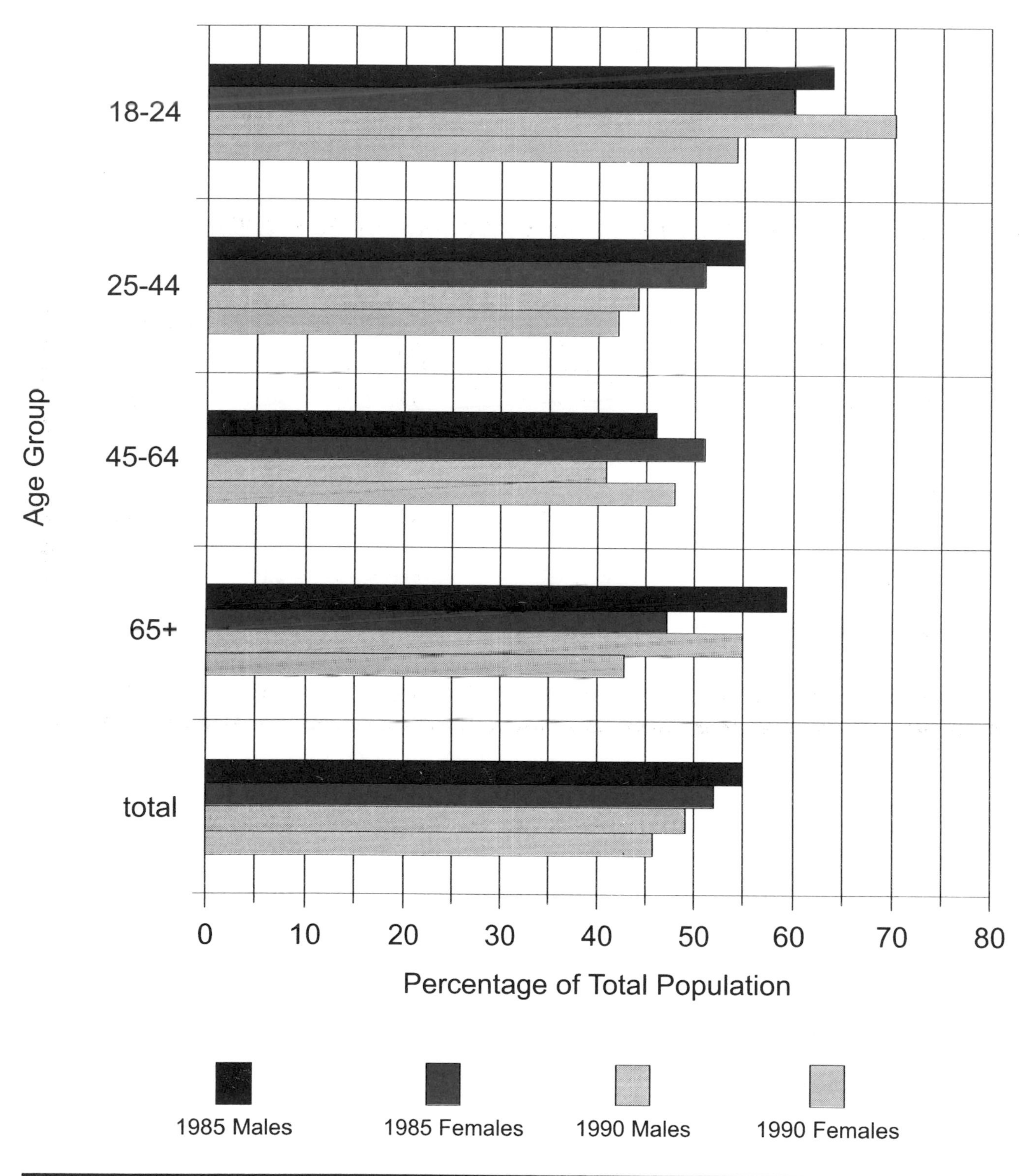

Source: Health Canada. Canada's Health Promotion Survey 1990: Technical Report. Ottawa, 1993.

F.3: *Activities engaged in at home by Canadians 65+, 1991*

Type of Activity	Males 65+ (%)	Females 65+ (%)	Males 80+ (%)	Females 80+ (%)
Watch television	49	51	49	51
Listen to radio	38	49	35	40
Talk on phone	16	44	15	41
Arts & crafts	23	34	20	27
Read	61	66	56	57
Have family/friends over	43	49	36	38

Note: Multiple answers were accepted.

Source: Health Canada. Ageing and Independence: Overview of a National Study. Ottawa, 1993 (1991 Survey; p41).

Activities Engaged in at Home By Canadians 65+,

By Age and Gender, 1991

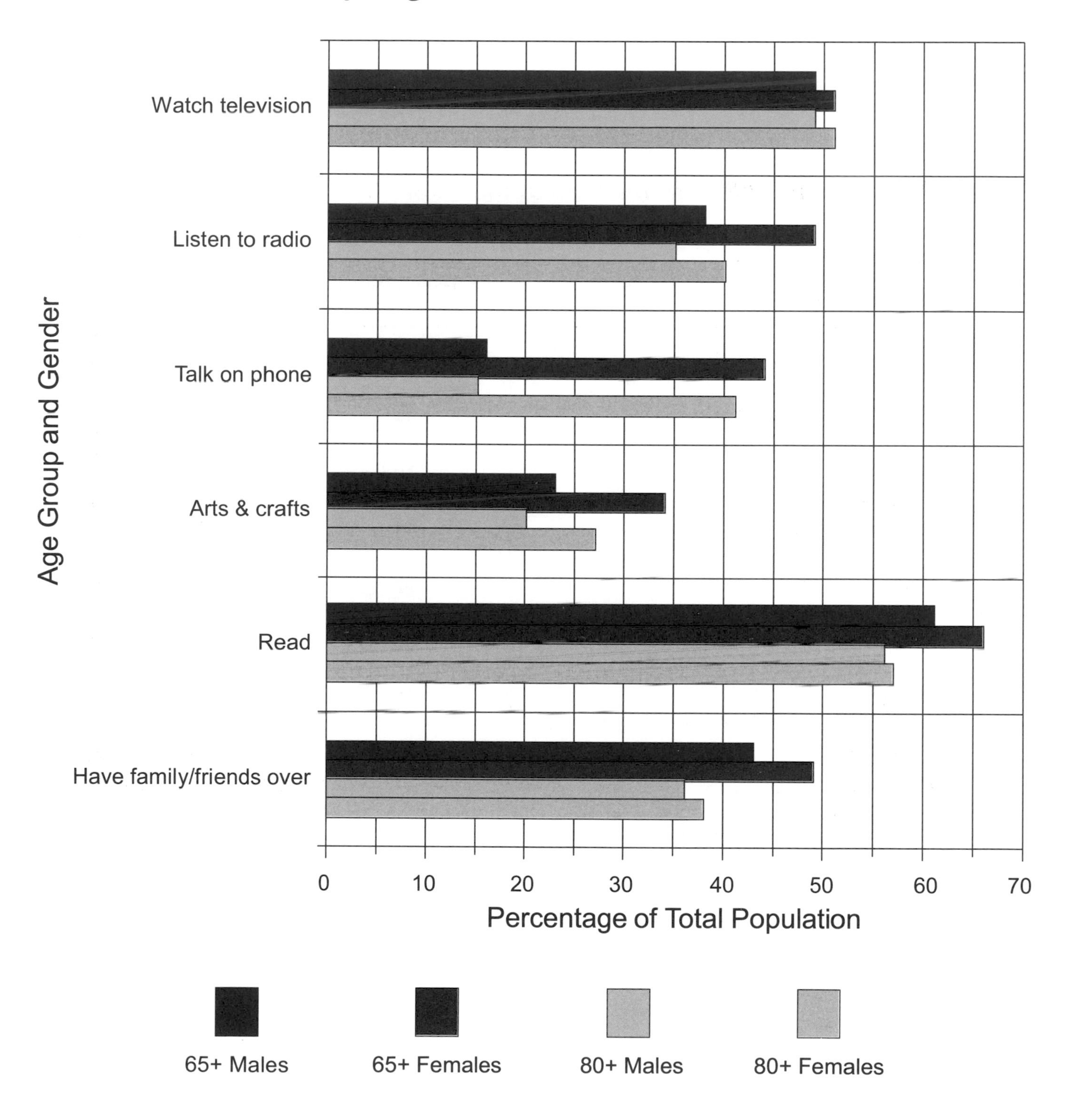

Source: *Health Canada. Ageing and Independence: Overview of a National Study. Ottawa, 1993.*

F.4: Activities engaged in outside of the home by Canadians 65+, 1991

Type of Activity	Males 65+ (%)	Females 65+ (%)
Visit relatives/friends	31	36
Shop (excl. groceries)	23	32
Eat out	19	21
Go for a drive	31	24
Walk	52	46
Clubs/Church/Community Centre	36	42
Library	10	12
Cards/Games	25	27

Note: Multiple answers were accepted.

Source: Health Canada. Ageing and Independence: Overview of a National Study. Ottawa, 1993 (1991 Survey; p45).

Activities Engaged in Outside the Home By Canadians 65+,

By Gender, 1991

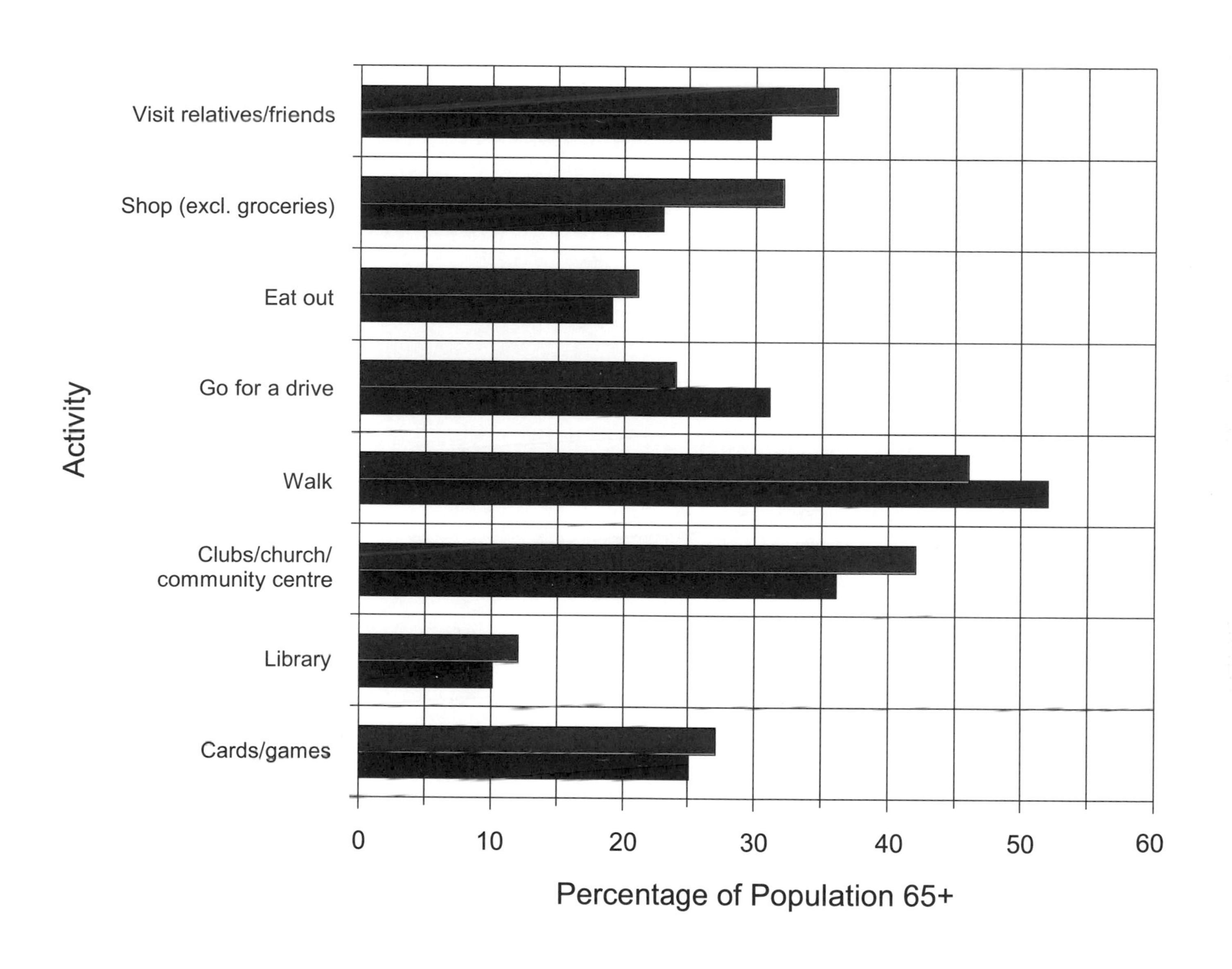

Source: *Health Canada. Ageing and Independence: Overview of a National Study. Ottawa, 1993 (1991 Survey).*

F.5: *Percentage of population aged 65 and over reporting involvment in selected organizations, by gender, 1988*

Type of Organization	Males 65+ (%)	Females 65+ (%)
Work/business-related	4	4
Social/cultural/ethnic	11	6
Religious/church	18	21
Charitable/volunteer/service	19	22
Neighbourhood/community/school	18	23
Political	49	50

Note: Multiple answers were accepted.

Source: Statistics Canada. Housing, Family and Social Statistics Division. A Portrait of Seniors in Canada. Ottawa, 1990 (1988 data; p54).

Involvement in Selected Organizations
By Canadians Aged 65+, 1988

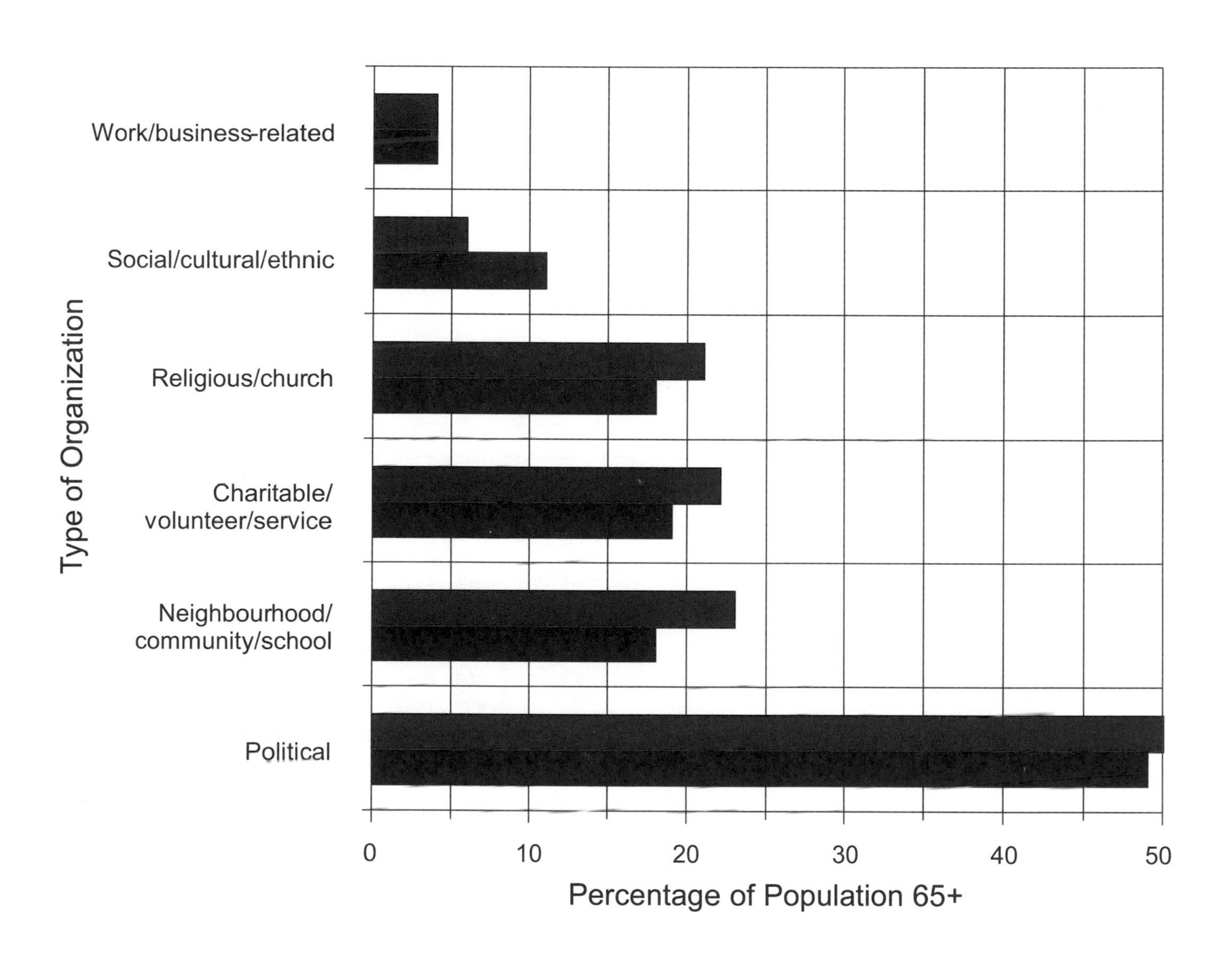

Source: *Statistics Canada. Housing, Family and Social Statistics Division. A Portrait of Seniors in Canada. Ottawa, 1990.*

F.6: Percentage of Canadians 45+ who are licenced to drive, 1991

Age Group	Males (%)	Females (%)
45-64	92	74
65+	80	37

Source: Health Canada. Ageing and Independence: Overview of a National Study. Ottawa, 1993 (1991 Survey; p29).

Canadians 45+ Licenced to Drive
By Age Group, 1991

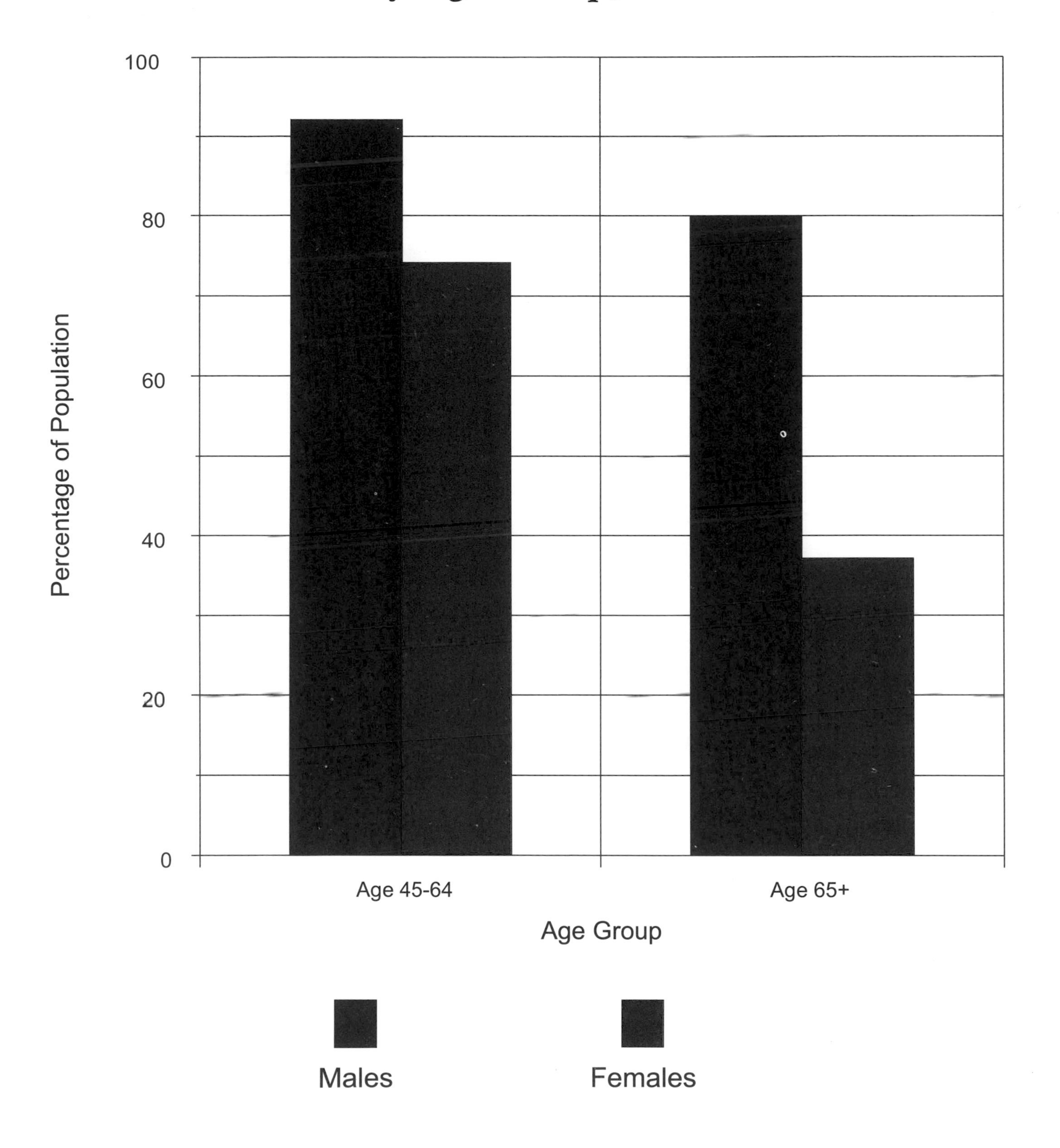

Source: Health Canada. Ageing and Independence: Overview of a National Study. Ottawa, 1993.

F.7: Percentage of Canadians 45+ who travel, 1991

Age Group/Gender	Travelling* (%)
45-64 Males	11
45-64 Females	11
65+ Males	17
65+ Females	12
80+ Males	15
80+ Females	10

*Travelled for at least 4 weeks in the 12 months prior to survey (excluding business trips).

Source: Health Canada. Ageing and Independence: Overview of a National Study. Ottawa, 1993 (1991 Survey; p48).

Proportion of Canadians 45+ Who Travel
By Age Group and Gender, 1991

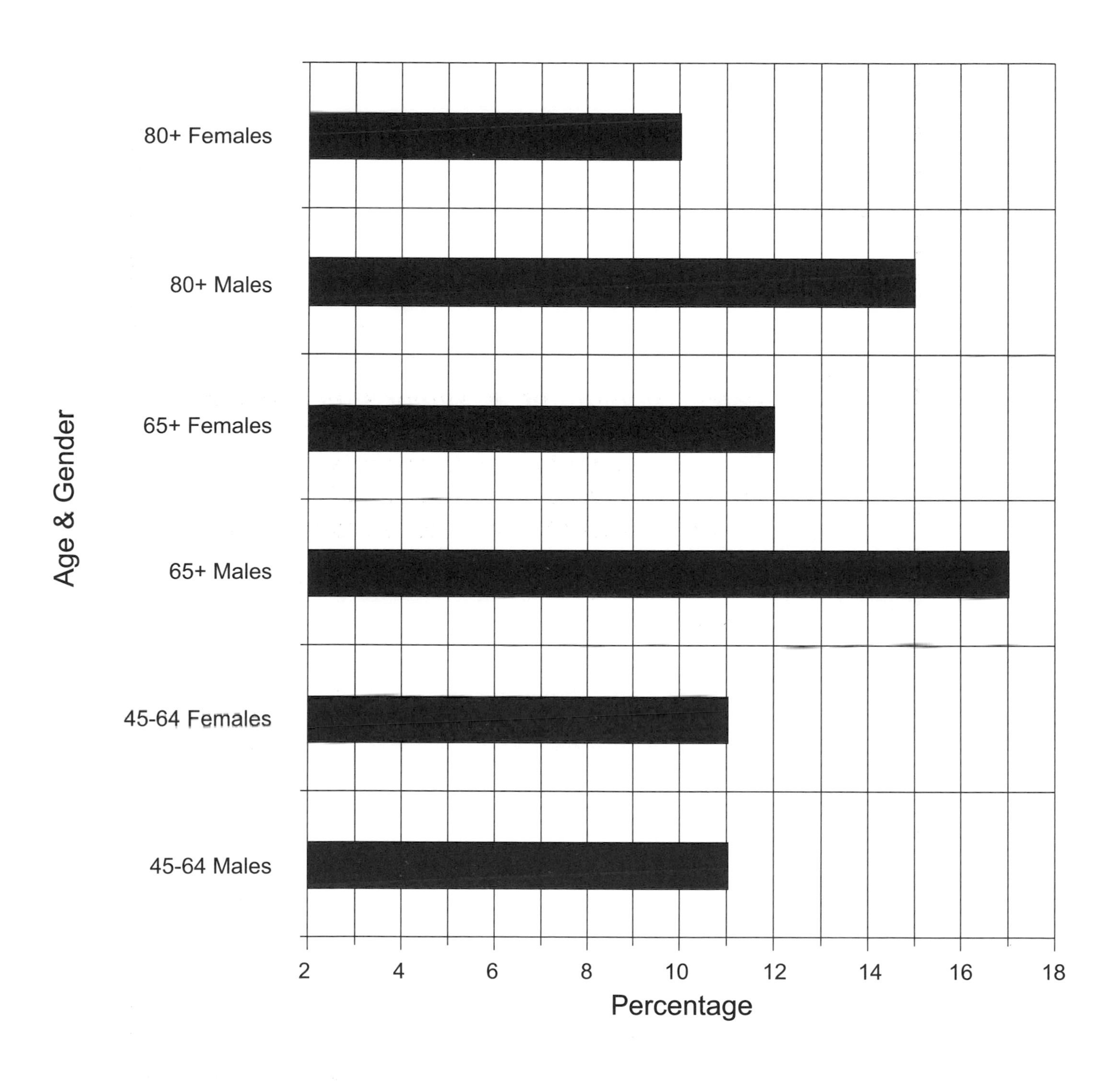

Source: Health Canada. Ageing and Independence: Overview of a National Study. Ottawa, 1993.

The greatest portion of a senior's household income goes towards shelter costs. For every dollar, 21 cents is spent on shelter costs, 17 cents on personal taxes, 14 cents on food, 11 cents on gifts/contributions and 10 cents on transportation.

Statistics Canada, Profile of Canada's Seniors, 1994

SECTION G

Labour Force

G.1: Labour force participation rates* of Canadians 45+, 1991

Age Group	Males (%)	Females (%)
45-49	93.1	76.3
50-54	89.5	66.4
55-59	78.3	49.9
60-64	54.1	28.1
65-69	21.9	9.6
70-74	12.6	4.8
75-84	7.4	2.7
85+	7.3	2.9

*Note: Includes both full- and part-time labour force participation.

Source: Statistics Canada. J.A. Norland. Focus on Canada - Profile of Canada's Seniors. Ottawa, 1994 (1991 Census of Canada; Cat. No. 96-312E; p103).

Labour Force Participation Rates
of Canadians 45+, by Gender, 1991

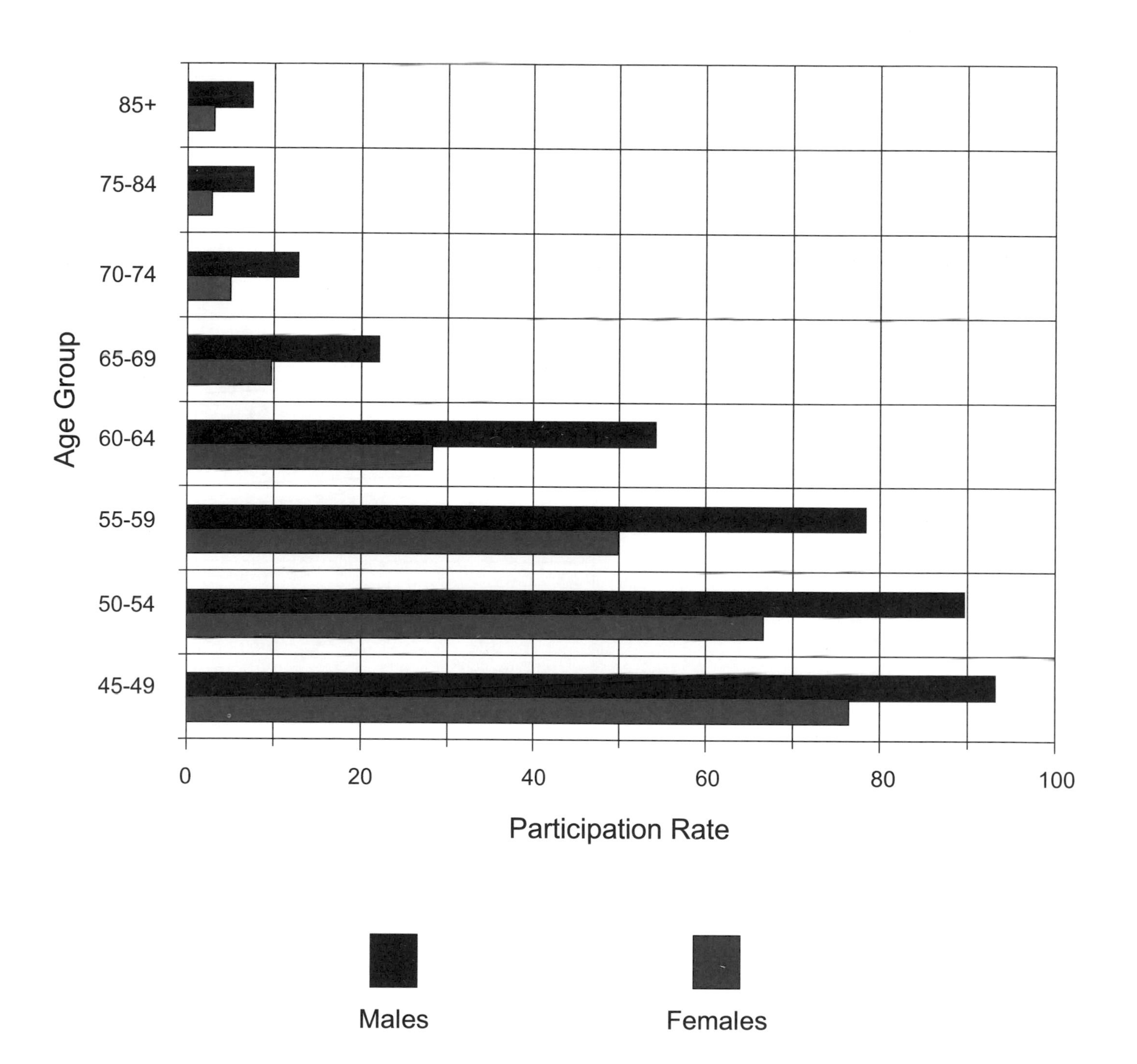

Source: Statistics Canada. J.A. Norland. Focus on Canada - Profile of Canada's Seniors. Ottawa, 1994.

G.2: *Full- and part-time employment status of the Canadian employed labour force aged 45+, 1991*

Age Group	Full-time (%)	Part-time (%)
45-64 Males	95	5
45-64 Females	73	27
65+ Males	62	38
65+ Females	36	64

Source: Health Canada. Ageing and Independence: Overview of a National Study. Ottawa, 1993 (1991 Survey; p94).

Full- and Part-time Employment Status
Employed Labour Force Aged 45+, Canada, 1991

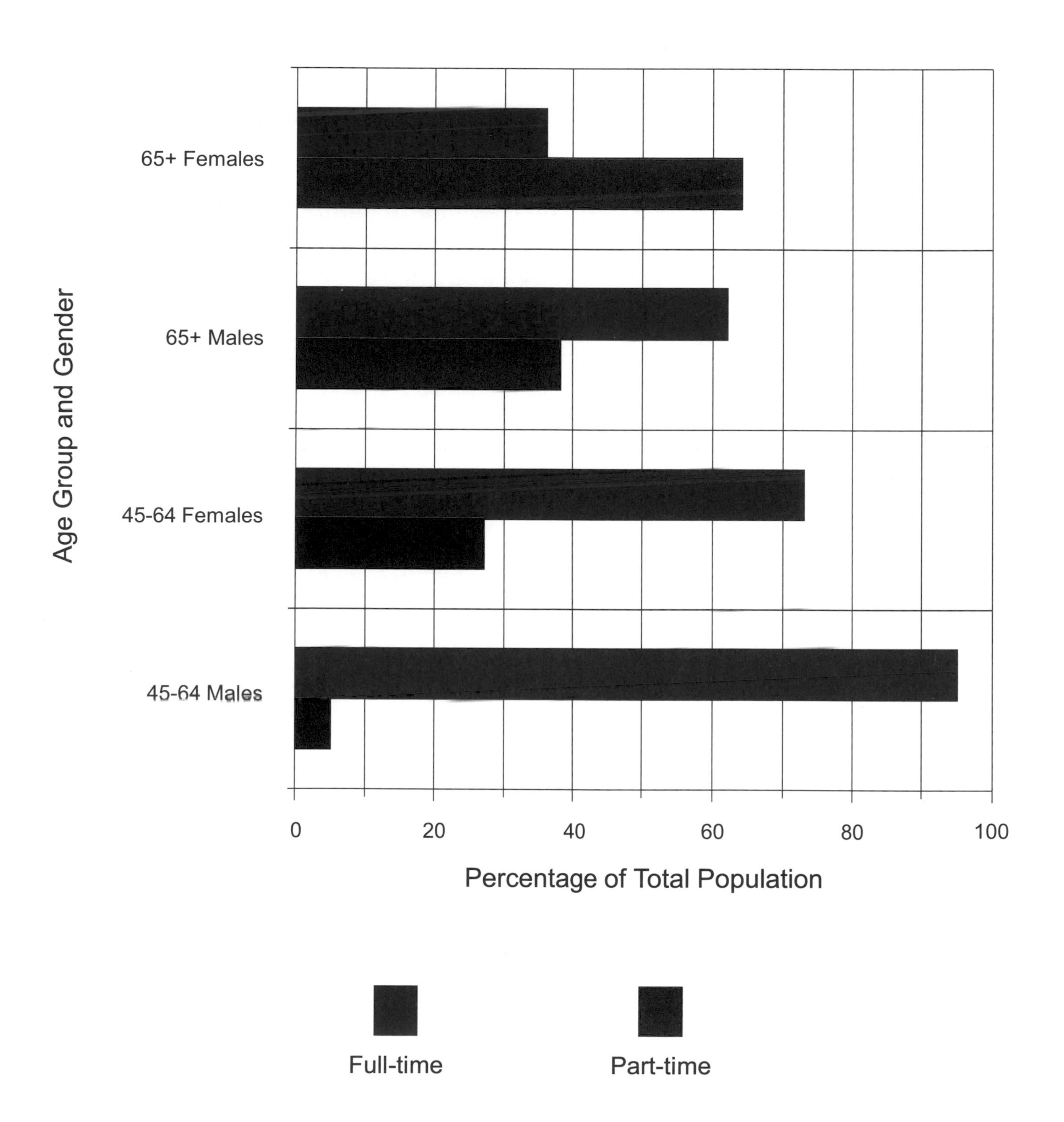

Source: *Health Canada. Ageing and Independence: Overview of a National Study. Ottawa, 1993.*

G.3: Mean number of weeks worked per year by employed Canadians 45+, 1990

Age Group	Number of Weeks
45-49	46.7
50-54	46.4
55-59	45.1
60-64	42.8
65-69	39.2
70-74	39.0
75+	41.7

Source: Statistics Canada. J.A. Norland. Focus on Canada - Profile of Canada's Seniors. Ottawa, 1994 (1991 Cencus of Canada; Cat. No. 96-312E; p105).

Mean Number of Weeks Worked
By Employed Canadians 45+, 1990

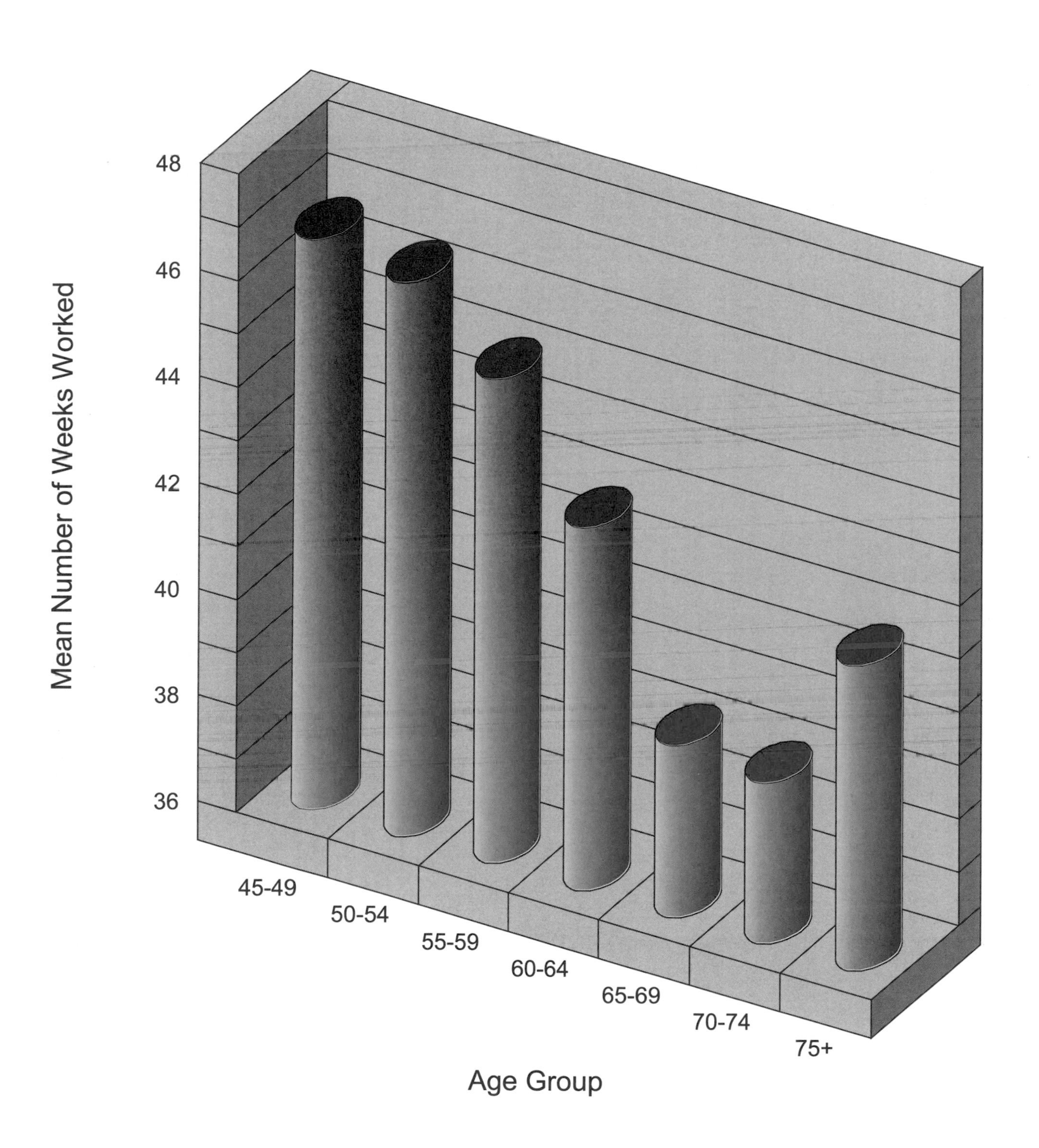

Source: Statistics Canada. J.A. Norland. Focus on Canada - Profile of Canada's Seniors. Ottawa, 1994.

G.4: *Percentage distribution of the Canadian labour force aged 50+, by major occupational group, 1986*

MALES : Occupation Types	50-54	55-59	60-64	65-69	70-74	75-79	80-84	85+	65+
Occupations in natural sciences, social sciences, engineering, medicine & health, teaching & artistic & literary professions	10.8	9.4	10.1	10.5	11.7	8.8	9.6	10.9	10.6
Managerial & administrative related	17.1	15.8	14.1	14.9	13.1	14.1	13.3	16.4	14.3
Clerical & related	5.1	5.8	6.5	7.2	6.8	5.7	6.4	1.8	6.9
Sales occupations	8.3	8.5	8.2	11.7	10.2	11.8	9.6	12.7	11.3
Service occupations	8.7	9.1	10.8	10.7	10.6	10.7	10.6	9.1	10.7
Primary and processing industries	11.9	13.4	14.7	20.1	28.9	32.2	36.2	27.3	24.3
Machining, fabricating, assembling repairing, construction, trades,	31.6	30.8	28.3	18.4	12.0	11.4	11.2	14.5	15.7
Religion, material handling and other occupations	6.5	7.3	7.3	6.5	6.8	5.3	3.2	7.3	6.3

Source: Statistics Canada. Demography Division, B. Desjardins. Population ageing and the elderly; Current Demographic Analysis, Ottawa, 1993 (Cat. No. 91-533E, p 76).

G.4: Percentage distribution of the Canadian labour force aged 50+, by major occupational group, 1986 (Cont'd)

FEMALES: Occupation Types	50-54	55-59	60-64	65-69	70-74	75-79	80-84	85+	65+
Occupations in natural sciences, social sciences, engineering, medicine & health, teaching & artistic & literary professions	18.4	16.5	15.7	14.3	16.0	21.4	22.5	14.3	15.7
Managerial & administrative related	8.5	7.9	7.0	6.6	5.6	7.6	7.1	14.3	6.7
Clerical & related	30.4	29.9	31.2	31.1	25.5	27.1	20.5	18.4	28.8
Sales occupations	9.9	11.1	11.6	15.1	16.4	11.0	12.2	6.1	14.7
Service occupations	17.0	19.0	19.0	17.9	20.6	18.6	17.3	20.4	18.6
Primary and processing industries	6.2	6.1	7.5	8.6	8.0	7.1	12.2	8.2	8.5
Machining, fabricating, assembling repairing, construction, trades,	7.0	7.1	5.2	4.2	3.4	2.9	7.1	12.2	4.2
Religion, material handling and other occupations	2.7	2.5	2.8	2.2	4.4	4.3	1.0	6.1	2.9

Source: Statistics Canada. Demography Division, B. Desjardins. Population ageing and the elderly; Current Demographic Analysis, Ottawa, 1993 (Cat. No. 91-533E, p 76).

G.5: *Job tenure (current positions) of Canadians 45+ employed full- & part-time, by age group, 1991*

Job Tenure (Years in Current Job)	Age 45-64 (%)*	Age 65+ (%)
Under 1	8	4
1-5	19	11
6-10	14	9
11-20	25	16
20+	28	48
Not Stated	5	12

* This column does not sum to 100% due to rounding in source table.

Source: Health Canada. Ageing and Independence: Overview of a National Study. Ottawa, 1993 (1991 Survey; p99).

Job Tenure of Canadians 45+ & 65+ Employed Full- and Part-Time, 1991

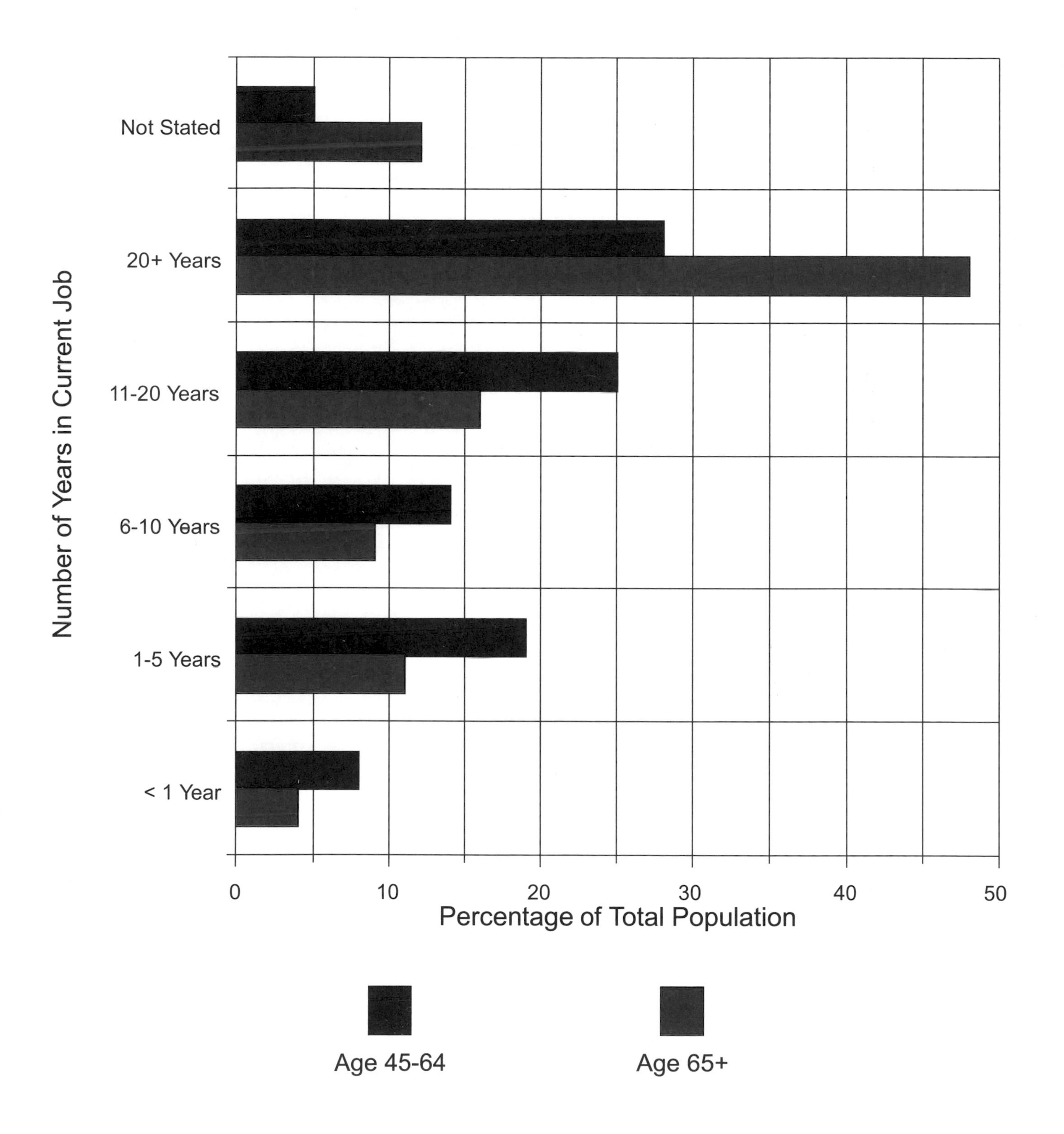

Source: *Health Canada. Ageing and Independence: Overview of a National Study. Ottawa, 1993.*

The mean income of men 65 years of age or over is nearly $10,000 higher ($24,500) than for women in the same age group ($15,300), according to the 1991 Census of Canada.

Statistics Canada, Profile of Canada's Seniors, 1994

The mean income of men in the 65-69 age group was $27,500 in 1990, compared to $14,800 for women in the same age group. The gap between men's and women's income was much smaller in the 85+ age group in 1990, with men reporting a mean income of $18,700 and women reporting $15,300.

Statistics Canada, Profile of Canada's Seniors, 1994

Government income is the major source of income for retired Canadian seniors, accounting for 40% of their total income.

Statistics Canada, Profile of Canada's Seniors, 1994

Section H

Income Sources / Distribution

H.1: Average annual pension plan benefits, Canada, 1983-1991

Income Source	Average Annual Benefits (per Year)		
	1983	1987	1991
OAS/GIS	$3,985	$4,769	$5,515
C/QPP	$2,310	$3,250	$4,027
RPP	$5,973	$7,735	$9,771

OAS/GIS - Old Age Security/Guaranteed Income Supplement

C/QPP - Canada/Quebec Pension Plans

RPP - Registered Pension Plans (frequently referred to as private pension plans)

Source: Statistics Canada. Pension Plans in Canada. Ottawa, 1992 (1991 Census of Canada; Cat. No. 74-401; p14).

Average Annual Pension Benefits
Canada, 1983-1991

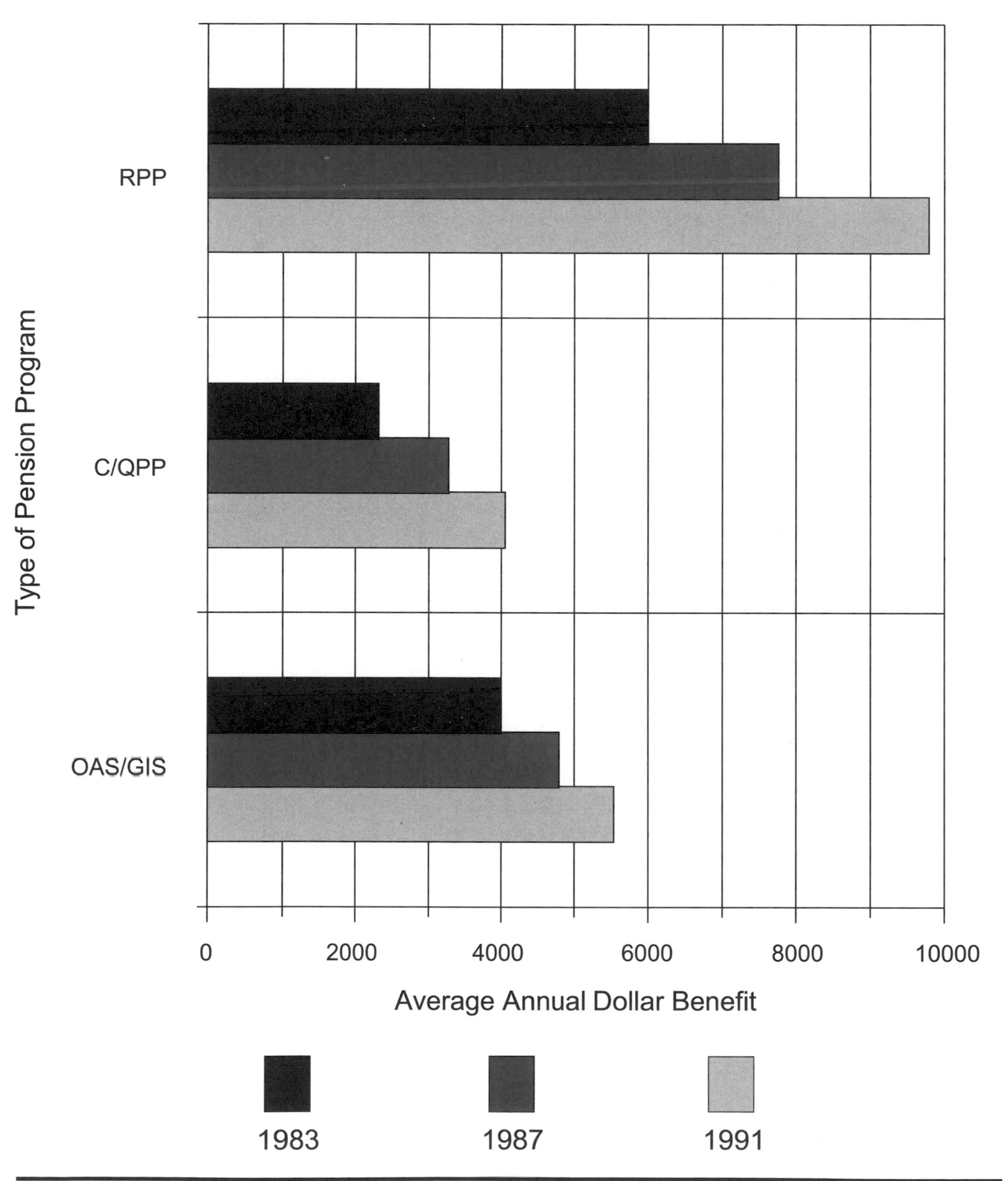

Source: Statistics Canada. Pension Plans in Canada. Ottawa, 1992.

H.2: *Sources of income of Canadians 65+, 1991*

Income source	% Receiving Income Source
Old Age Security	97.2
Canada/Quebec Pension Plans	80.1
Investments	78.6
Private Pension Plans	44.6
Paid work	8.0
Business & Professional employment	2.7
Unemployment Insurance	1.5
Other	15.1

Statistics Canada Definition:

Private Pension Plan - an employee retirement benefit program which is provided by employers or by unions in both the public and private sectors of the economy.

Source: Statistics Canada. Pension Plans in Canada. Ottawa, 1992 (1991 Census of Canada; Cat. No. 74-401; p56).

Proportion of Canadians 65+ Receiving Various Sources of Income, 1991

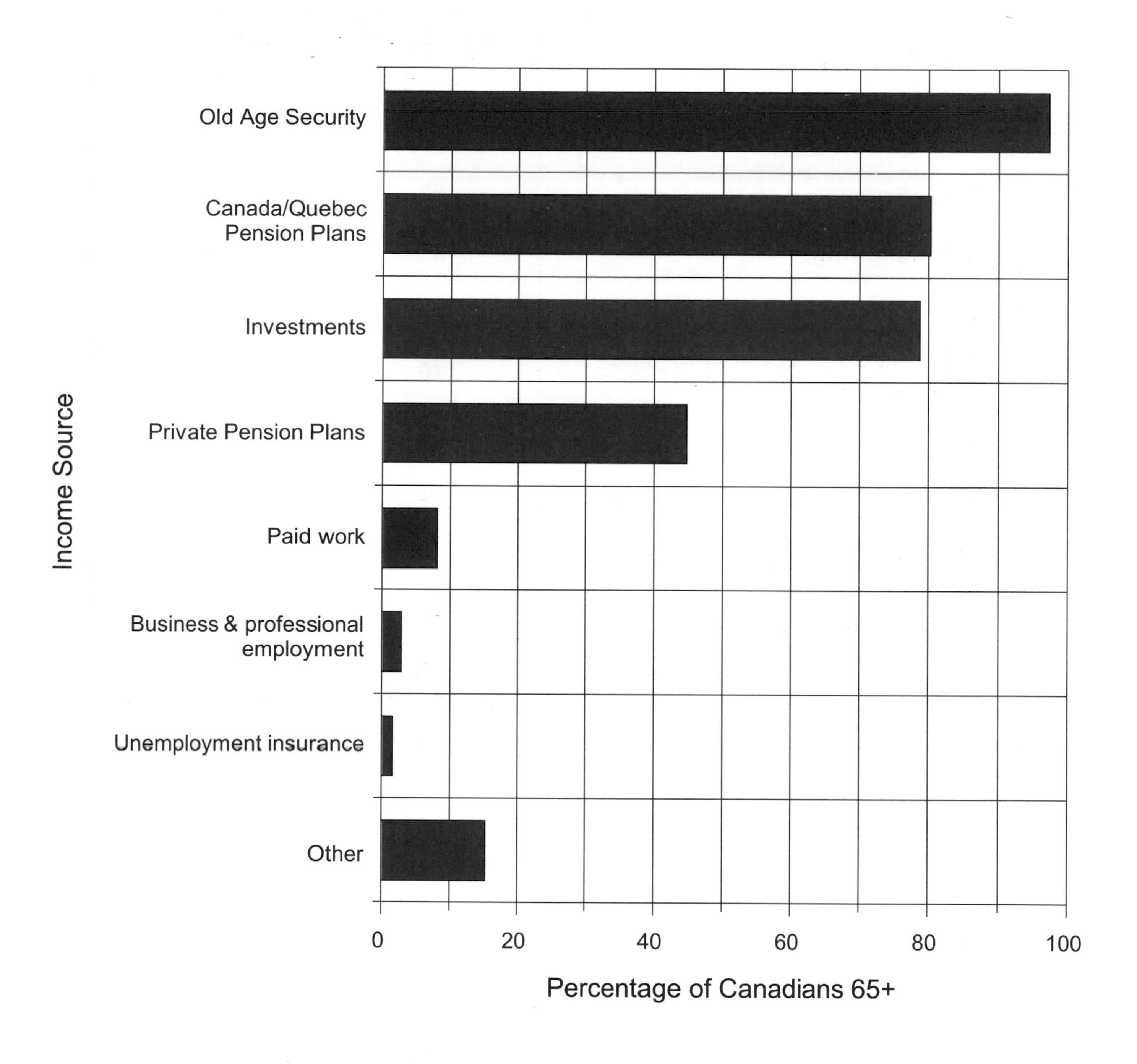

Source: *Statistics Canada. Pension Plans in Canada. Ottawa, 1992.*

H.3: Private pension plan coverage rates by industry, 1989

Industry Type	% of Population with coverage *	
	Males	Females
Agriculture	12	5
Other Primary	52	43
Manufacturing	61	39
Construction	37	20
Transportation/Communication/ Other utilities	70	60
Trade	35	24
Finance/ Insurance/ Real Estate	63	56
Community Service	75	59
Business/ Personal/ Other Services	27	15
Government Services	82	72

* Population surveyed = Paid workers (i.e. all employed workers except unpaid family workers and self-employed) aged 20+.

Statistics Canada Definitions:

Private Pension Plan - an employee retirement benefit program which is provided by employers or by unions in both the public and private sectors of the economy.

Other Primary - forestry, fishing and mining.

Community Services - health and social services and education services.

Business, Personal and Other Services - business services, accommodation, food and beverage services and other services.

Source: Statistics Canada. Employer- sponsored pension plans - who is covered?, Perspectives on Labour and Income. Ottawa, 1992 (1989 data; Cat. No. 75-001; p30).

Private Pension Coverage by Industry
Canada, 1989

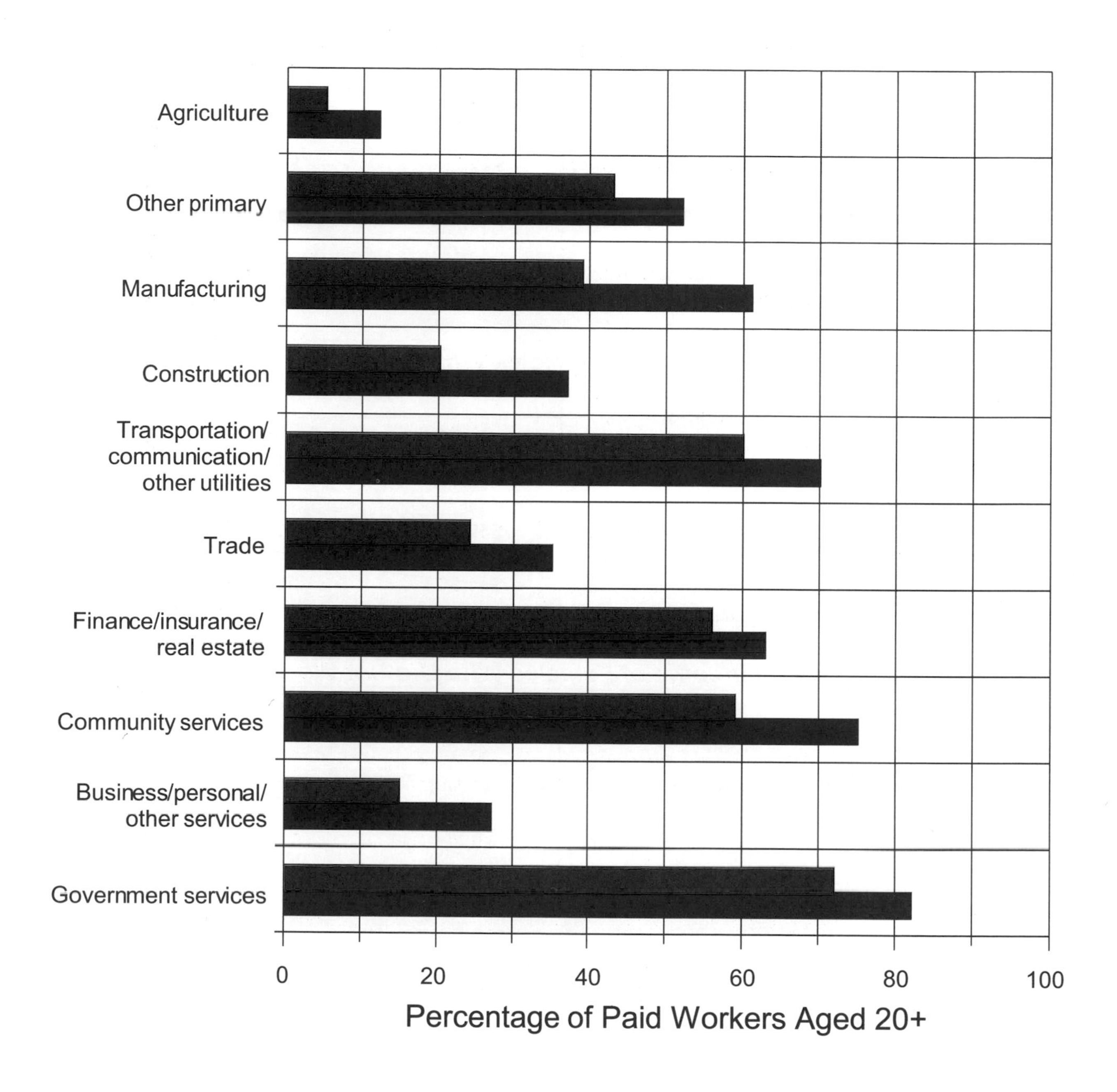

Source: Statistics Canada. Employer-sponsored pension plans-who is covered?, Perspectives on Labour and Income. Ottawa, 1992.

H.4: Mean income of Canadians aged 25+, by gender, age group, labour force activity and education, 1990

Mean Income of Males Who Did Not Work in 1990

Education	Age	
	25-64	65+
Less than Secondary	$12,200	$15,600
Secondary	$15,500	$21,300
Post-secondary	$18,900	$28,000

Mean Income of Males Who Worked in 1990

Education	Age	
	25-64	65+
Less than Secondary	$27,600	$27,600
Secondary	$32,200	$38,900
Post-secondary	$41,800	$53,300

Mean Income of Females Who Did Not Work in 1990

Education	Age	
	25-64	65+
Less than Secondary	$7,900	$11,500
Secondary	$9,200	$14,400
Post-secondary	$11,500	$20,200

Mean Income of Females Who Worked in 1990

Education	Age	
	25-64	65+
Less than Secondary	$15,000	$17,900
Secondary	$18,600	$24,400
Post-secondary	$25,500	$29,300

Source: Statistics Canada, J.A. Norland. Focus on Canada - Profile of Canada's Seniors. Ottawa, 1994 (1991 Census of Canada; Cat. No. 96-312E; p107).

Mean 1990 Income of Non-working Males
By Education and Age

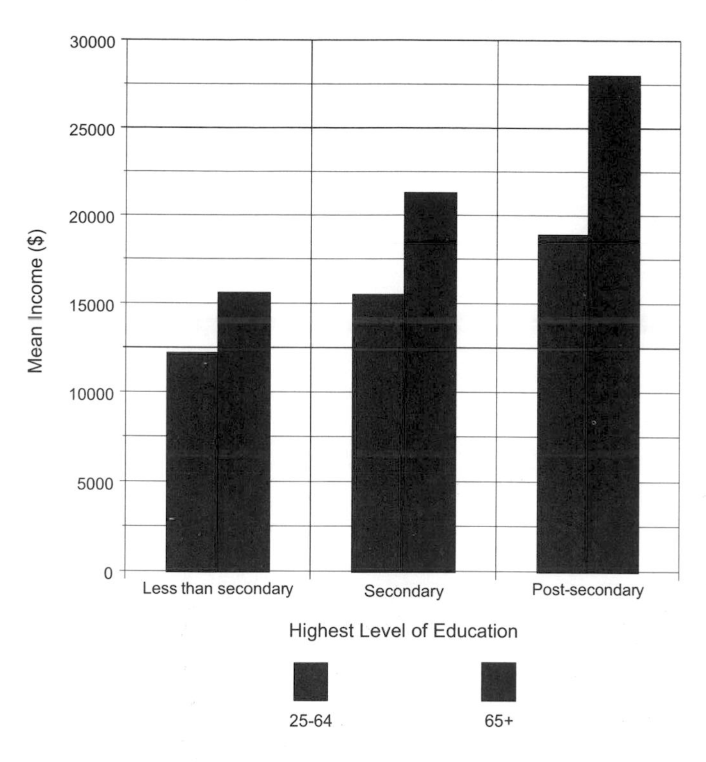

Mean 1990 Income of Working Males
By Education and Age

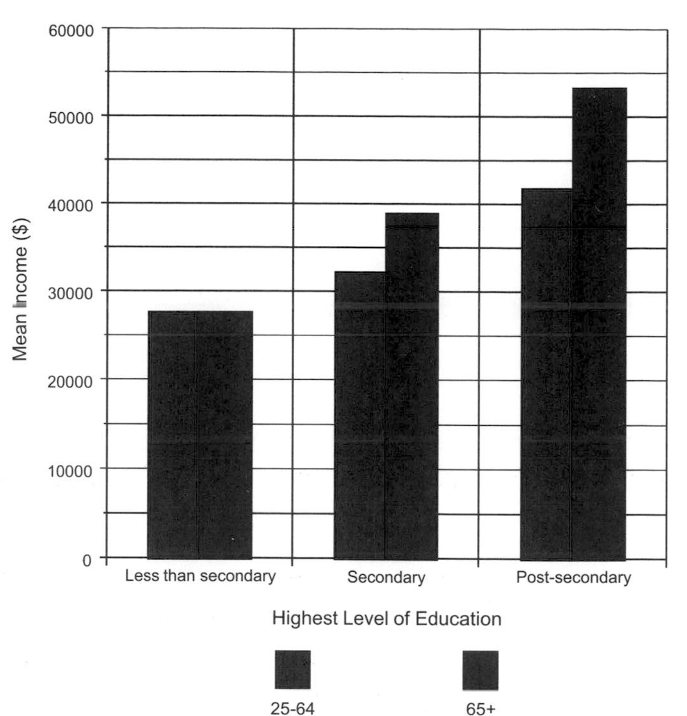

Mean 1990 Income of Non-working Females
By Education and Age

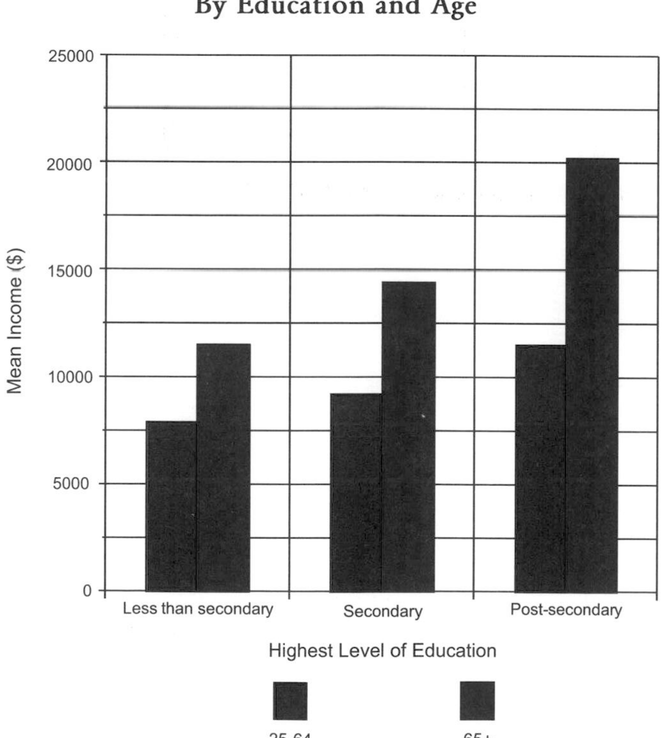

Mean 1990 Income of Working Females
By Education and Age

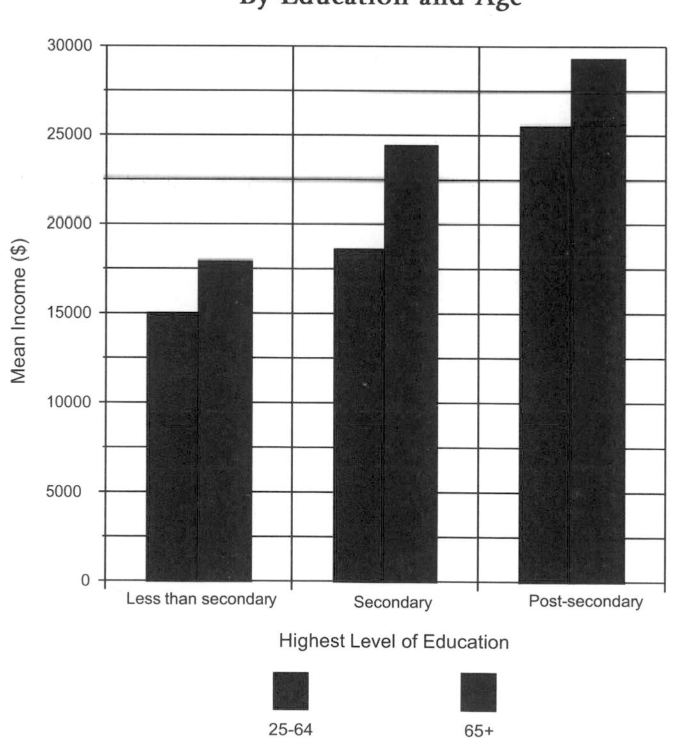

Source: Statistics Canada. J.A. Norland. Focus on Canada - Profile of Canada's Seniors. Ottawa, 1994.

H.5: Household income of Canadian adults, 1990

Household Income	Age 15-64 (%)	Age 65+ (%)
<$15,000	6	28
$15,000 - 29,999	16	24
$30,000 - 59,999	37	12
$60,000+	21	4
Not Stated	20	32

Source: Statistics Canada. Family and Friends. Ottawa, 1994 (1990 General Social Survey; Cat.No. 11-612, p51).

Total Household Income
Canadian Adults, 1990

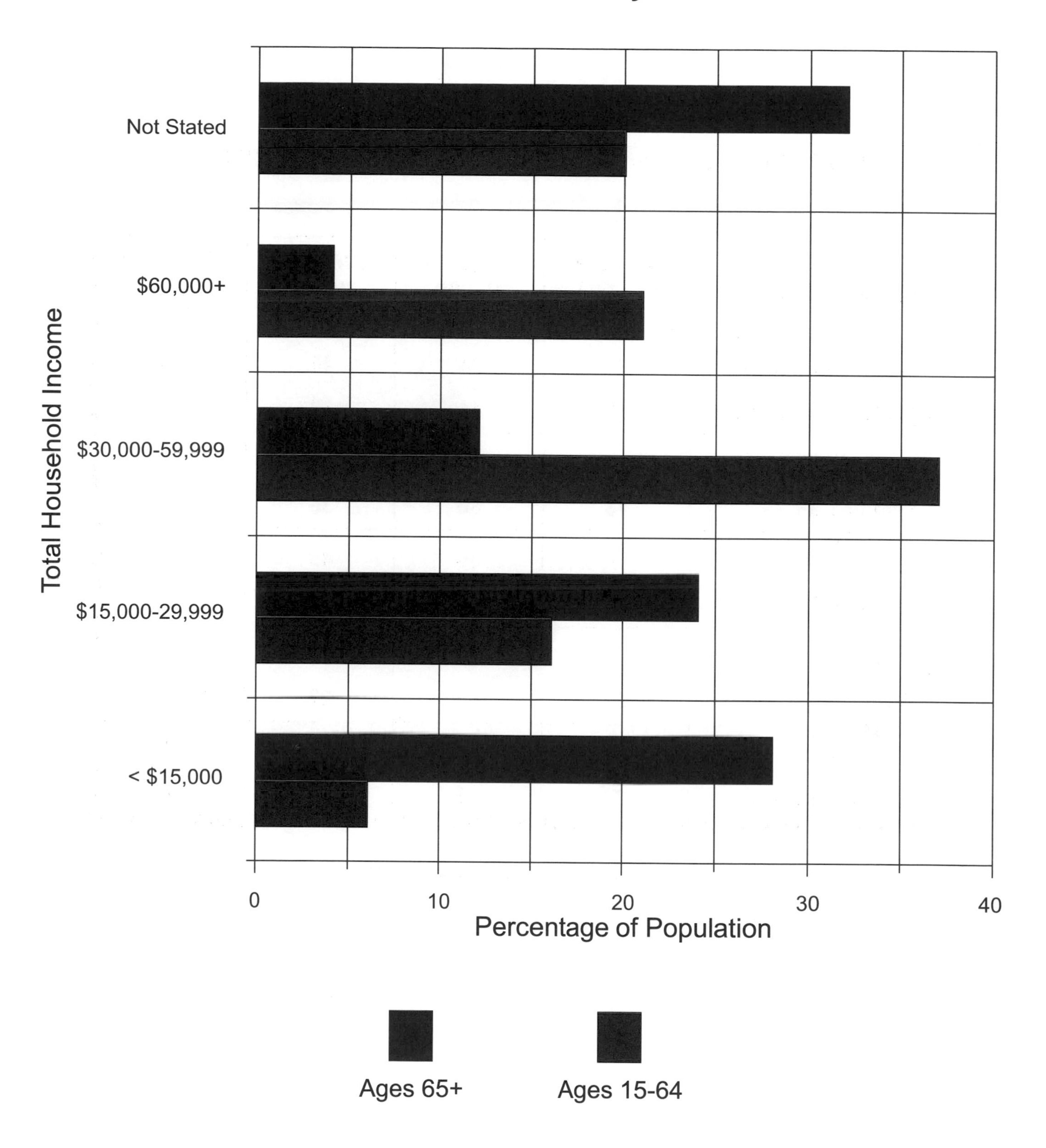

Source: *Statistics Canada. Family and Friends. Ottawa, 1994.*

H.6: Household income of Canadians 65+, by gender, 1993

Age and Gender	Less than $10,000 (%)	$10,000-19,999 (%)	$20,000-39,999 (%)	$40,000 or greater (%)
Males 65 or over	7	34	40	19
Females 65 or over	19	41	30	10
Males 65-69	-	29	41	25
Females 65-69	15	36	35	14
Males 70-74	-	35	42	17
Females 70-74	19	40	31	9
Males 75-79	-	43	37	13
Females 75-79	22	45	27	6
Males 80 or over	15	36	37	12
Females 80 or over	27	45	21	7

(-) The sampling variability associated with this estimate is too high to be published.

* Note: Includes those who reported no income.

Source: Statistics Canada. Ageing and Independence: Provincial Highlights. Ottawa, 1993 (1991 Survey; Table 31-Canada).

Household Income of Canadians 65+
By Gender, 1993

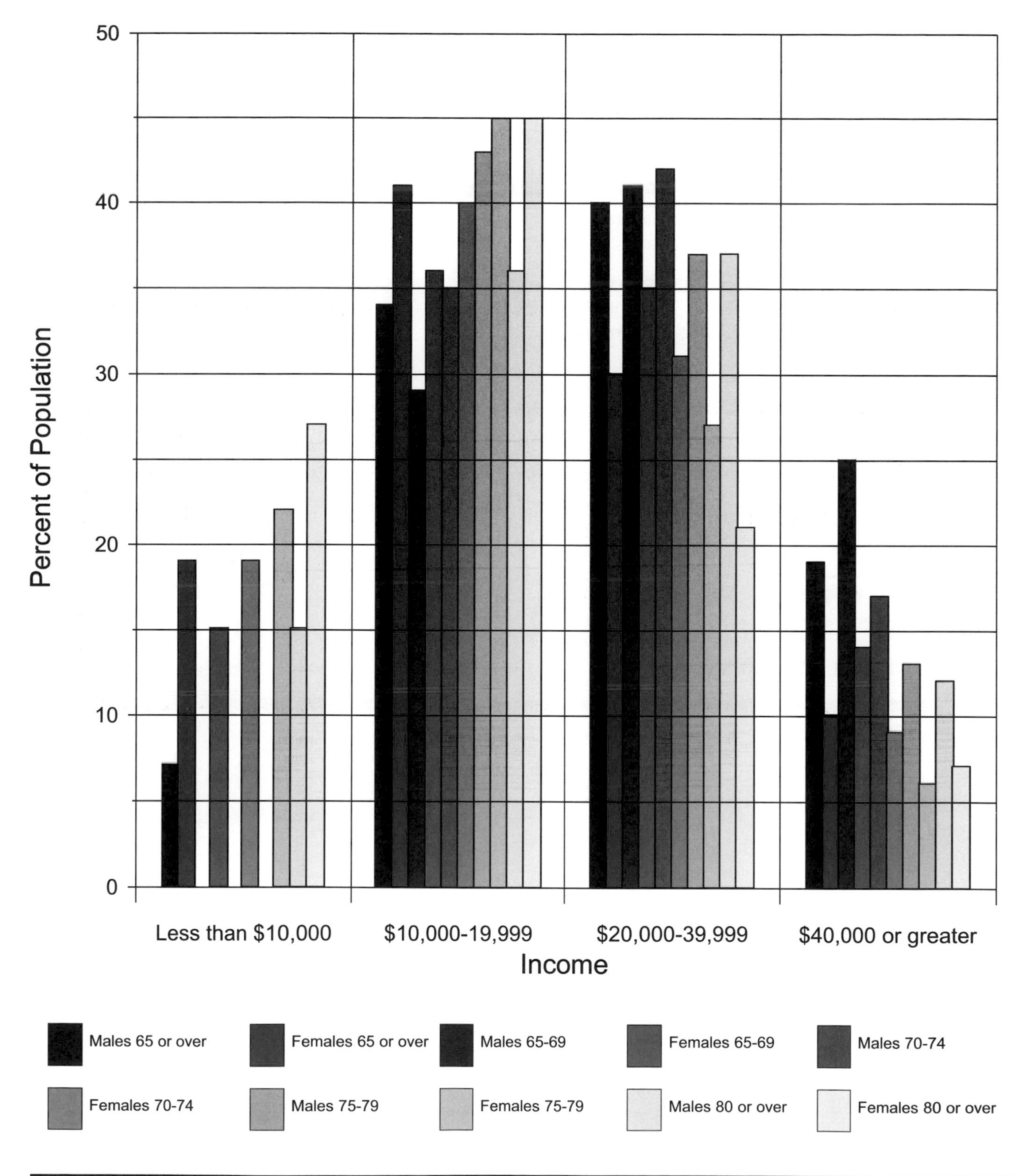

Source: Statistics Canada. Ageing and Independence: Provincial Highlights. Ottawa, 1993.

H.7: Degree to which current income and investments meet needs of Canadians aged 65+, 1991

Degree to which current income meets needs	Males 65+ (%)	Females 65+ (%)
Very well/adequately	82	82
Not very well/totally inadequately	12	13
Not stated/don't know	6	5

Source: Statistics Canada. Ageing and Independence: Provincial Highlights. Ottawa, 1993 (1991 Survey; Table 32-Canada).

Degree to Which Current Income & Investments Meet Needs

Of Canadians 65+, 1991

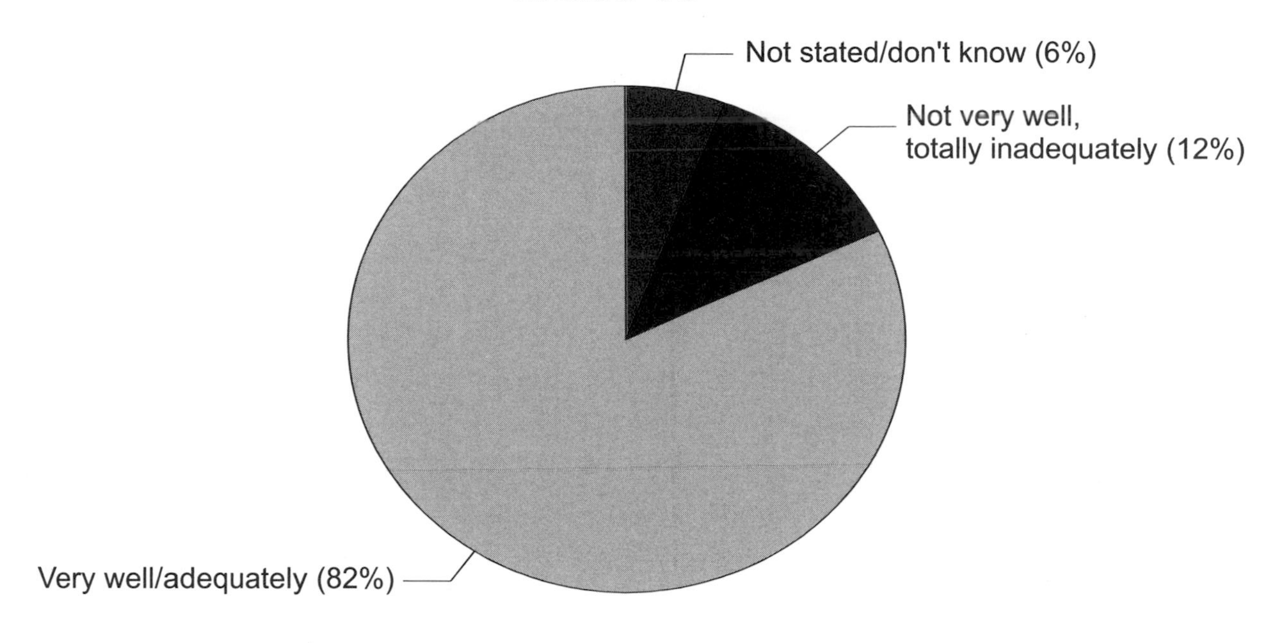

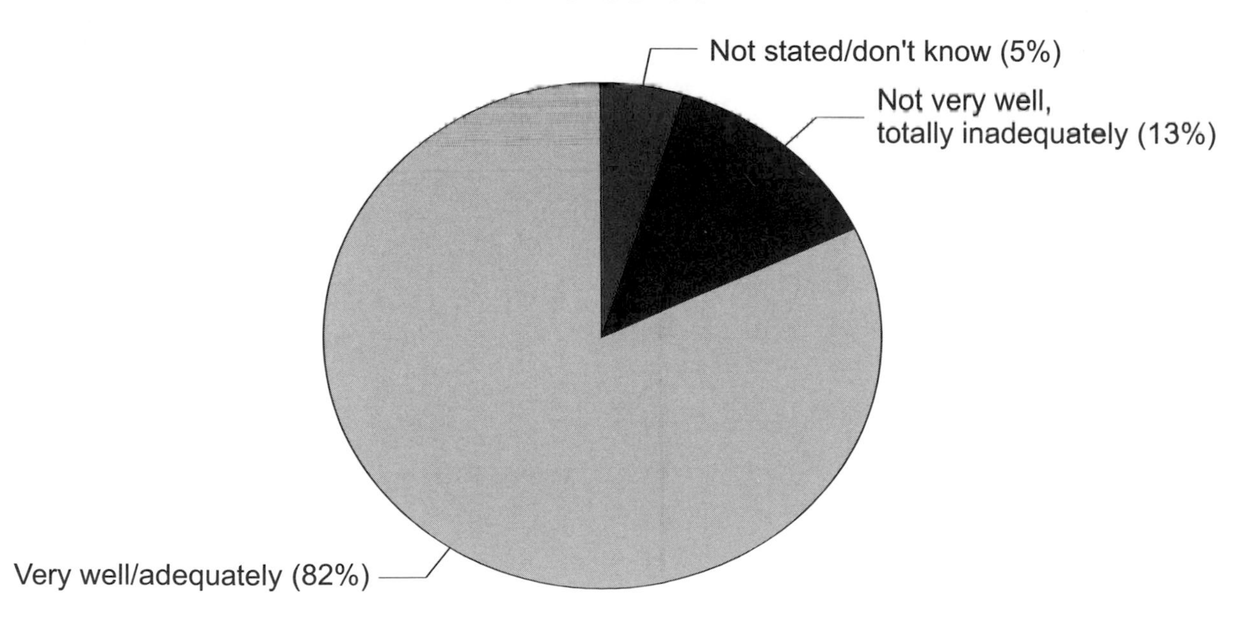

Source: Statistics Canada. Ageing and Independence: Provincial Highlights. Ottawa, 1993.

H.8: Perception of future income adequacy of Canadians 45+, 1991

How well will income satisfy future needs?	Age				
	45-64	65-69	70-74	75-79	80+
Very well/adequately	67	70	72	71	76
Not very well/totally inadequately	21	19	17	15	10

Note: Columns do not sum to 100% due to exclusion of data for people not knowing or not providing information on perception of future income adequacy.

Source: Statistics Canada. Ageing and Independence. Provincial Highlights. Ottawa, 1993 (1991 Survey; Table 28-Canada).

Perception of How Well Future Income Will Meet Needs

Of Canadians 45+, 1991

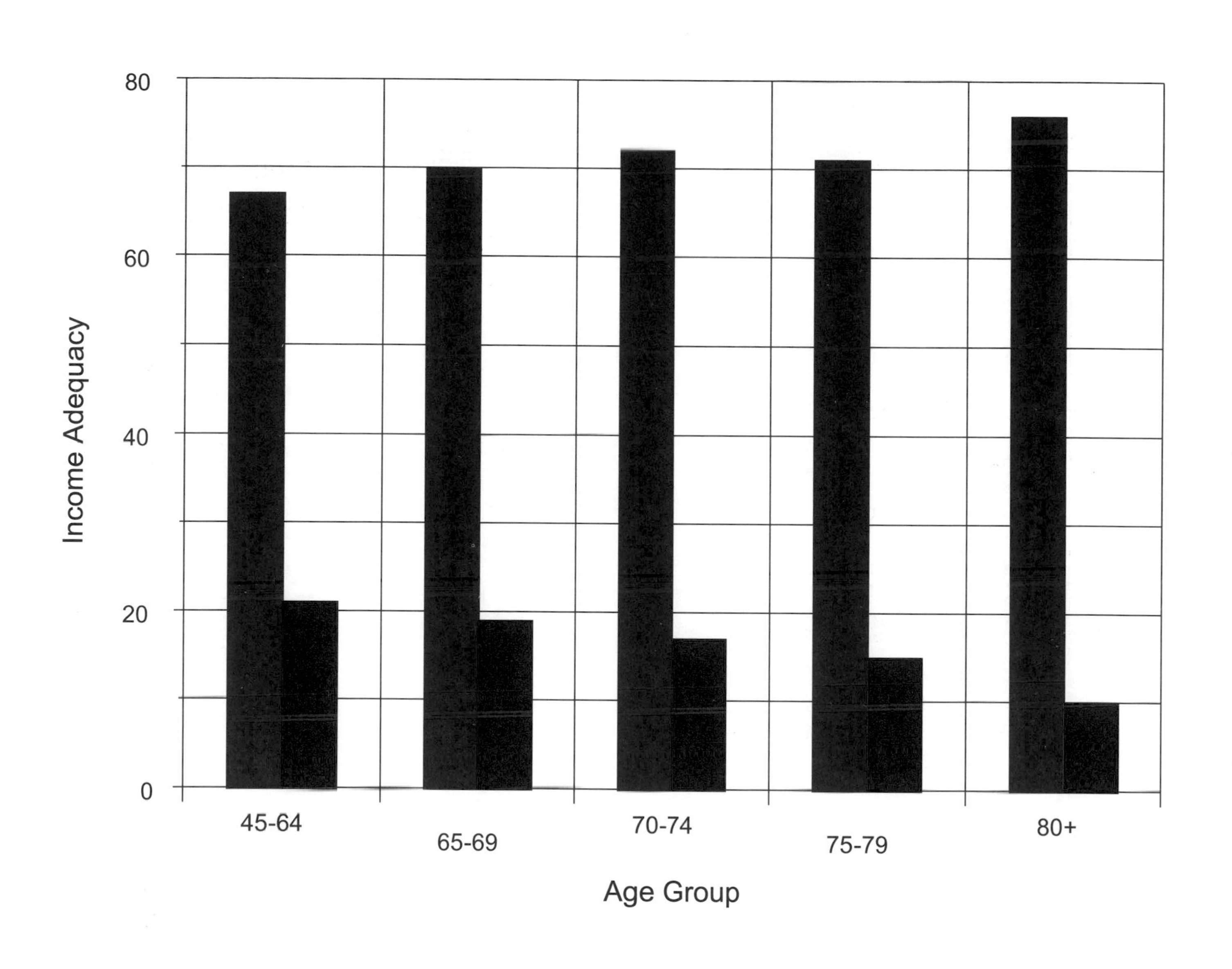

Source: *Statistics Canada. Ageing and Independence: Provincial Highlights. Ottawa, 1993.*

H.9: Canadian household expenditures, 1990

Item of Expenditure	% of Total Expenditures	
	All Households	Senior Households
Food	12.6	13.9
Shelter	17.3	20.8
Household Operation	4.0	3.9
Furnishings and Equipment	3.0	2.7
Clothing	5.5	4.4
Transportation	11.8	9.9
Health Care	1.8	2.4
Personal Care	1.9	2.0
Recreation	5.0	4.6
Reading Materials, Education	4.2	3.4
Tobacco and Alcohol	2.7	2.2
Personal Taxes	22.3	16.8
Security	4.4	2.2
Gifts and Contributions	3.6	10.7

Note: Columns do not sum to 100% due to rounding in source table.

Source: Statistics Canada. J.A. Norland. Focus on Canada - Profile of Canada's Seniors. Ottawa, 1994 (1990 data; p53).

Household Expenditures
Canada, 1990

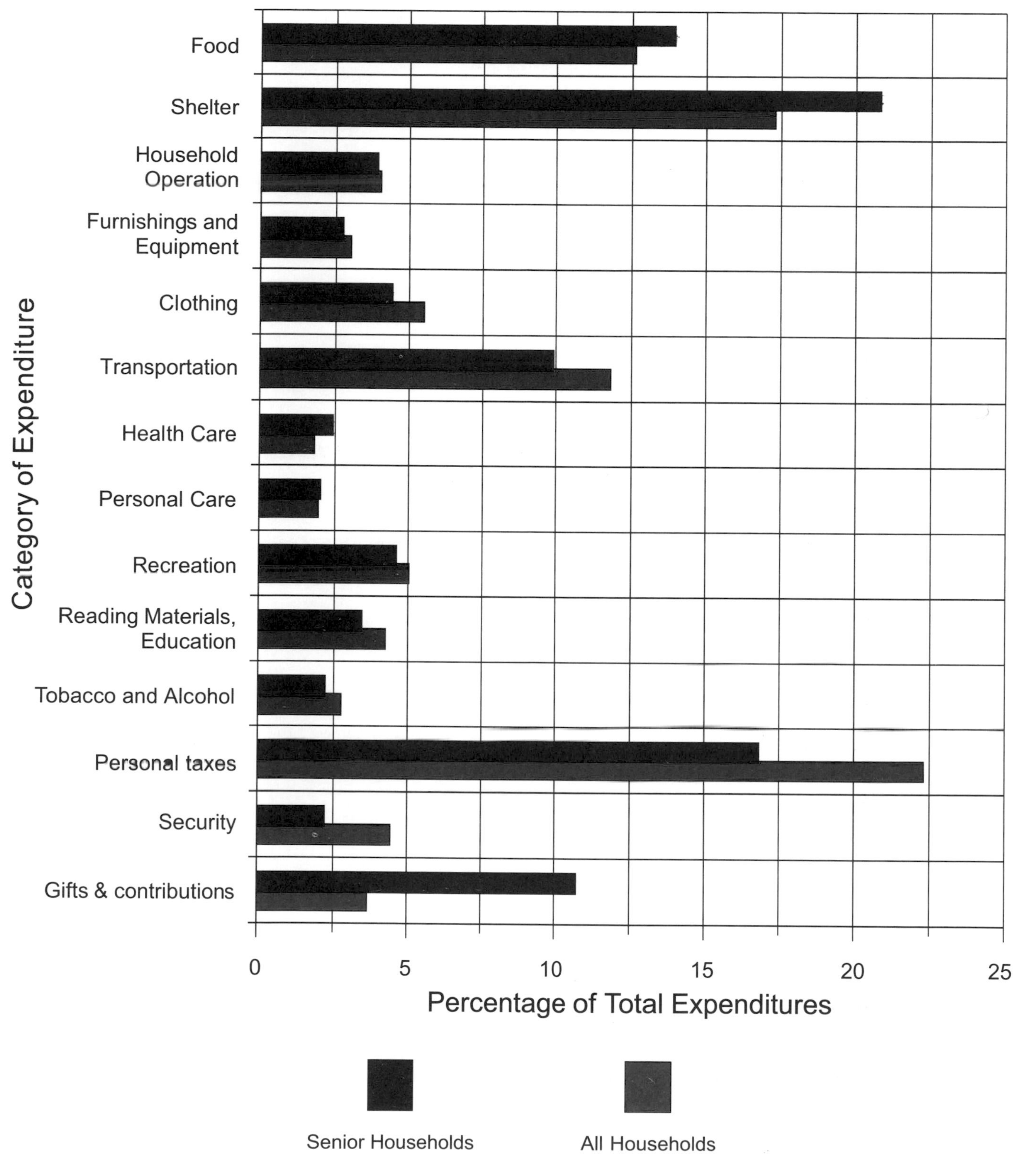

Source: Statistics Canada. J.A. Norland. Focus on Canada - Profile on Canada's Seniors. Ottawa, 1994.

About one-third of all employed Canadians actually expect to retire at the age of 65.

Centre for International Statistics, using Survey on Ageing and Independence microdata, 1991

SECTION I

Retirement

I.1: Percentage of Canadians 55+ who are retired, 1991

Age Group	Men (%)	Women (%)
55-64	22	15
65-74	67	37
75+	79	36

Source: Canadian Council on Social Development. G. Schellenberg. The Road to Retirement: Demographic and Economic Changes in the 90's. Ottawa, 1994 (p14).

Percentage of Canadians 55+ Who Are Retired

By Age Group and Gender, 1991

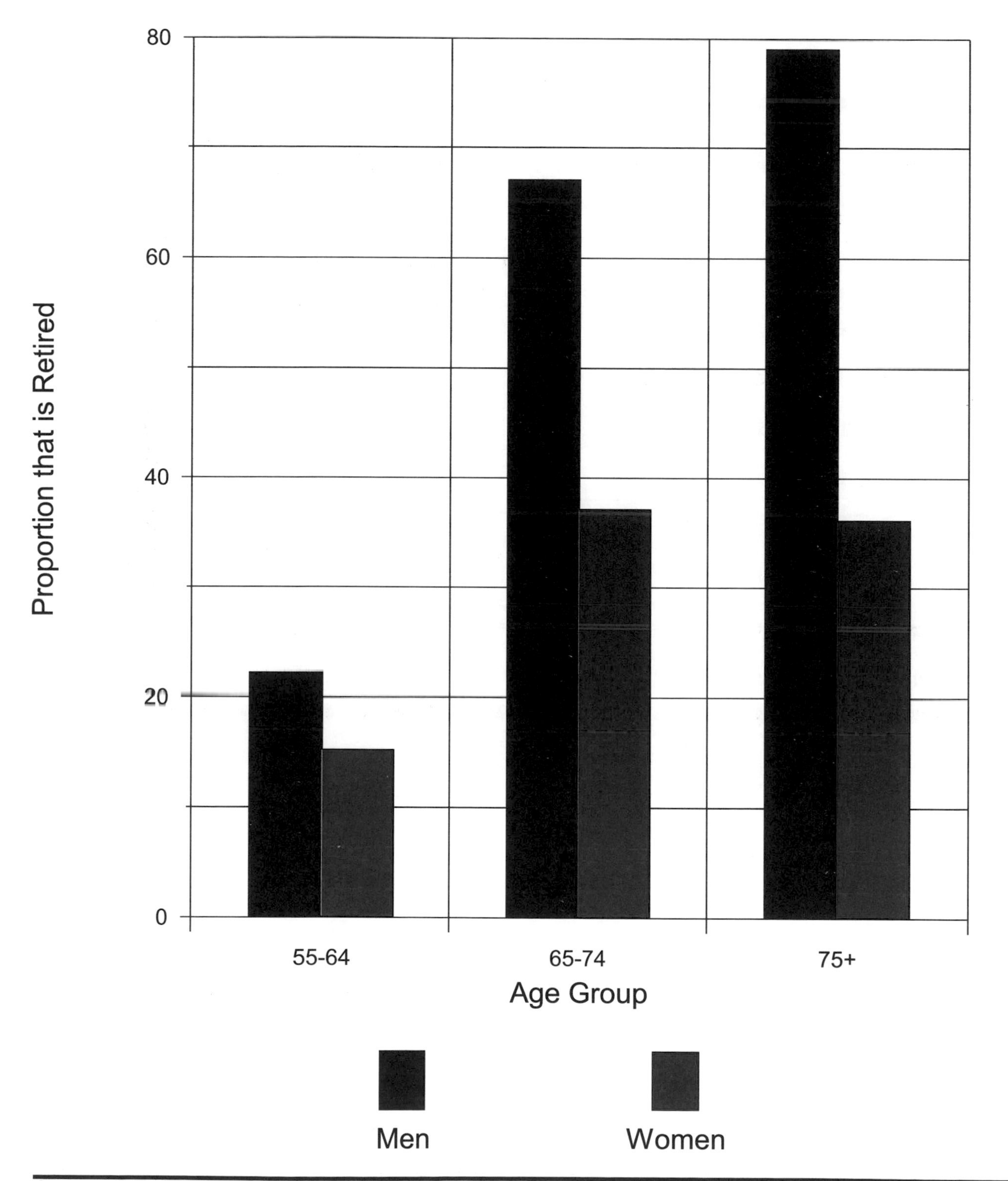

Source: *Canadian Council on Social Development, G. Schellenberg. The Road to Retirement. Ottawa, 1994.*

I.2: Reasons for retirement cited by retired Canadians, 1991

Reasons *	Retired Males (%)	Retired Females (%)
Adequate income	38	27
Mandatory retirement policy	21	13
Early retirement policy	18	7
Provide family care	5	13
Timing of spouse's retirement	2	21
Spouse's health	5	13
Spouse's income	1	12
Pressure from spouse	4	8

* Multiple answers were accepted.

Source: Canadian Council on Social Development: Centre for International Statistics. G. Schellenberg. The Road to Retirement: Demographic and Economic Changes in the 90's. Ottawa, 1994 (p14).

Reasons for Retirement,
By Gender of Retired Canadians, 1991

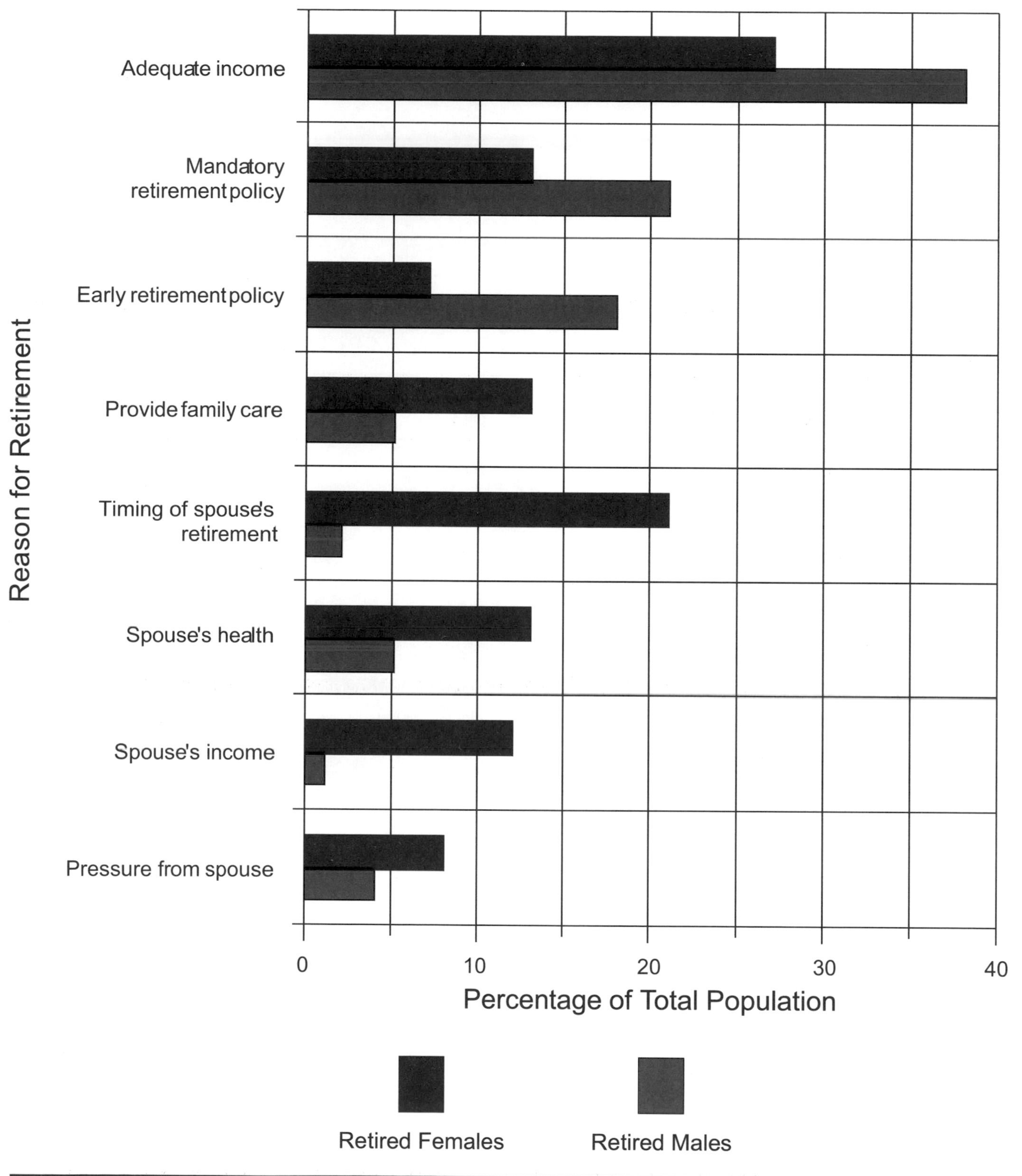

Source: *Canadian Council on Social Development. G. Schellenberg. The Road to Retirement. Ottawa, 1994.*

I.3: Percentage of retired Canadians 60+ who retired involuntarily, 1991

Age Group	Men (%)	Women (%)
60-64	28	19
65-69	28	27
70-74	23	21
75-79	28	24
80+	26	21

Source: Canadian Council on Social Development: Centre for International Statistics. G. Schellenberg. The Road to Retirement: Demographic and Economic Changes in the 90's. Ottawa, 1994 (p66).

Percentage of Canadians Who Retired Involuntarily

By Age and Gender, 1991

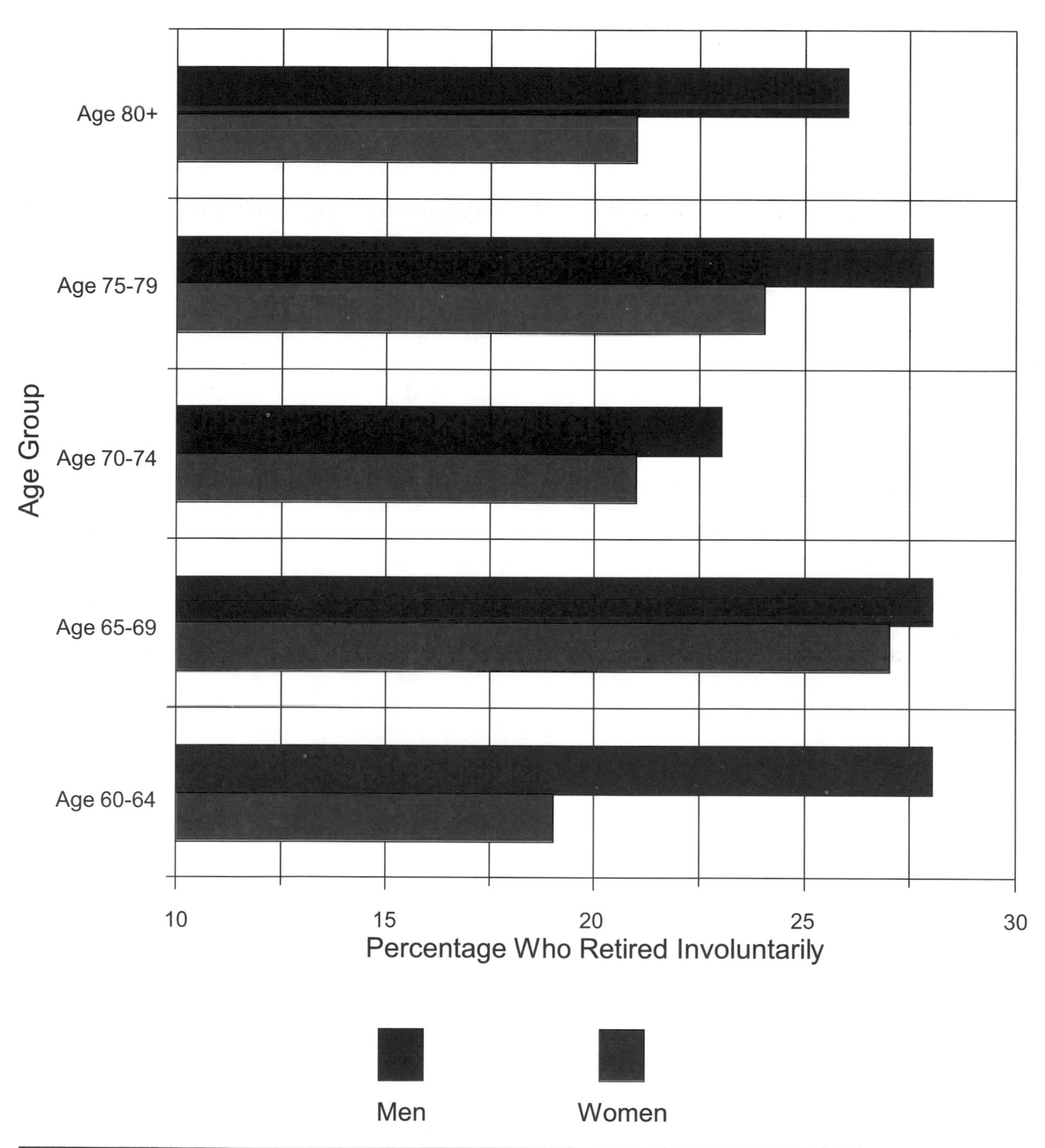

Source: *Canadian Council on Social Development. G. Schellenberg. The Road to Retirement. Ottawa, 1994.*

I.4: Reasons for retirement cited by voluntary and involuntary Canadian retirees, 1991

Reason *	Involuntary retirees (%)	Voluntary retirees (%)
Health	47	25
Mandatory retirement policy	35	12
Lack of work	14	4
Adequate income	11	40
Early retirement policy	9	15

* Multiple answers were accepted.

Source: Canadian Council on Social Development: Centre for International Statistics. G. Schellenberg. The Road to Retirement: Demographic and Economic Changes in the 90's. Ottawa, 1994 (p67).

Reasons for Retirement, Canada, 1991
By Involuntary & Voluntary Retirees

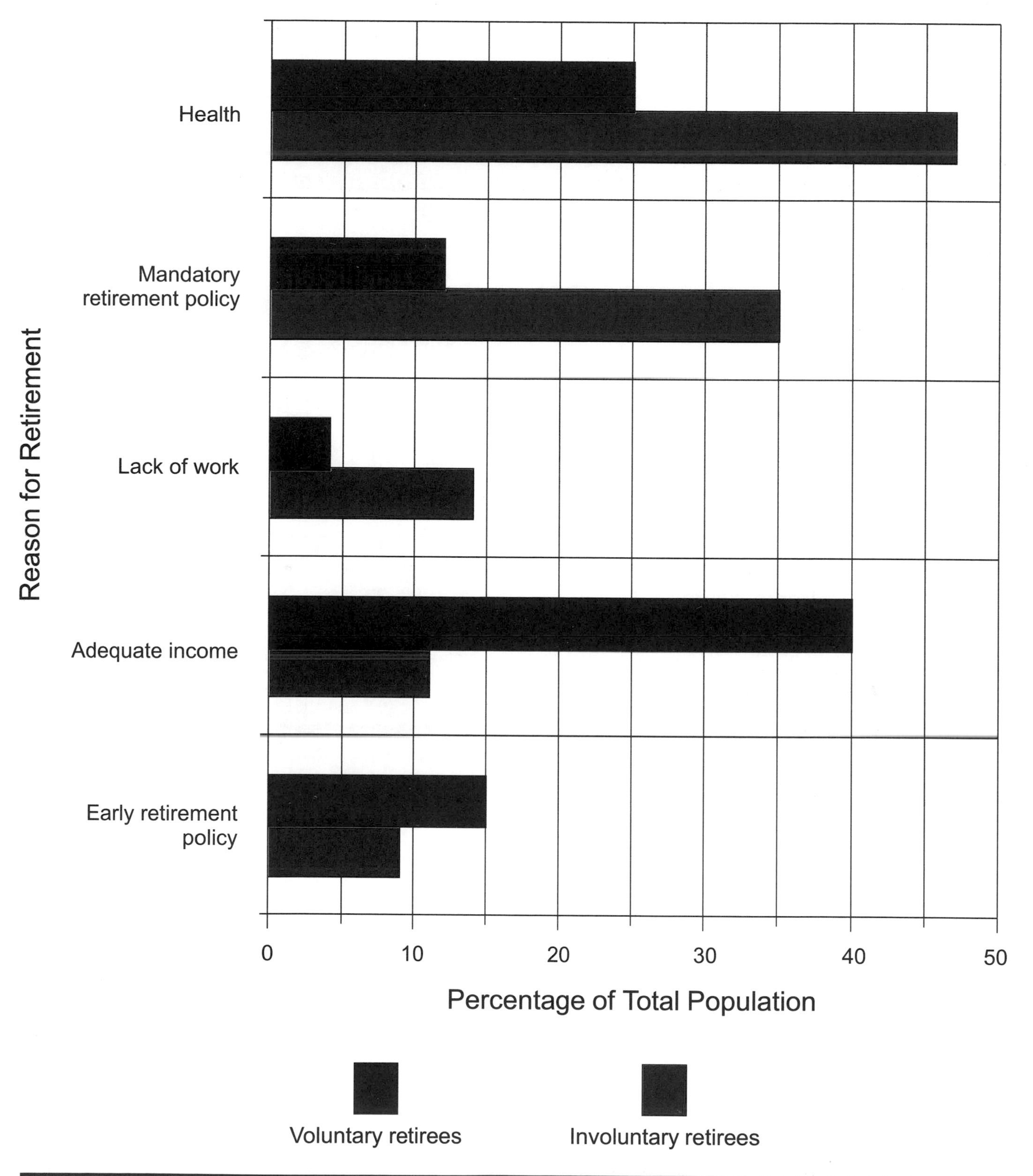

Source: Canadian Council on Social Development. G. Schellenberg. The Road to Retirement. Ottawa, 1994.

I.5: *Retirement planning activities carried out by retired Canadians 45+ in preparation for retirement/future, 1991*

Activity *	Males 45-64 (%)	Females 45-64 (%)	Males 65+ (%)	Females 65+ (%)
Built up savings	66	57	65	59
Contributed to RRSP	66	57	44	36
Paid off/avoided debts	60	54	60	56
Developed hobbies	33	42	34	36
Gathered retirement info	40	27	23	18
Made other investments	32	30	28	21
Developed physical activities	25	26	26	20

* Multiple answers were accepted.

Note: Respondents were retired at the time of the survey and responses were based on what they did previous to the survey with respect to retirement planning.

Source: Health Canada. Ageing and Independence: Overview of a National Study. Ottawa, 1993 (1991 Survey; p116).

Preparation for Retirement/Future
By Retired Canadians 45+ and Gender, 1991

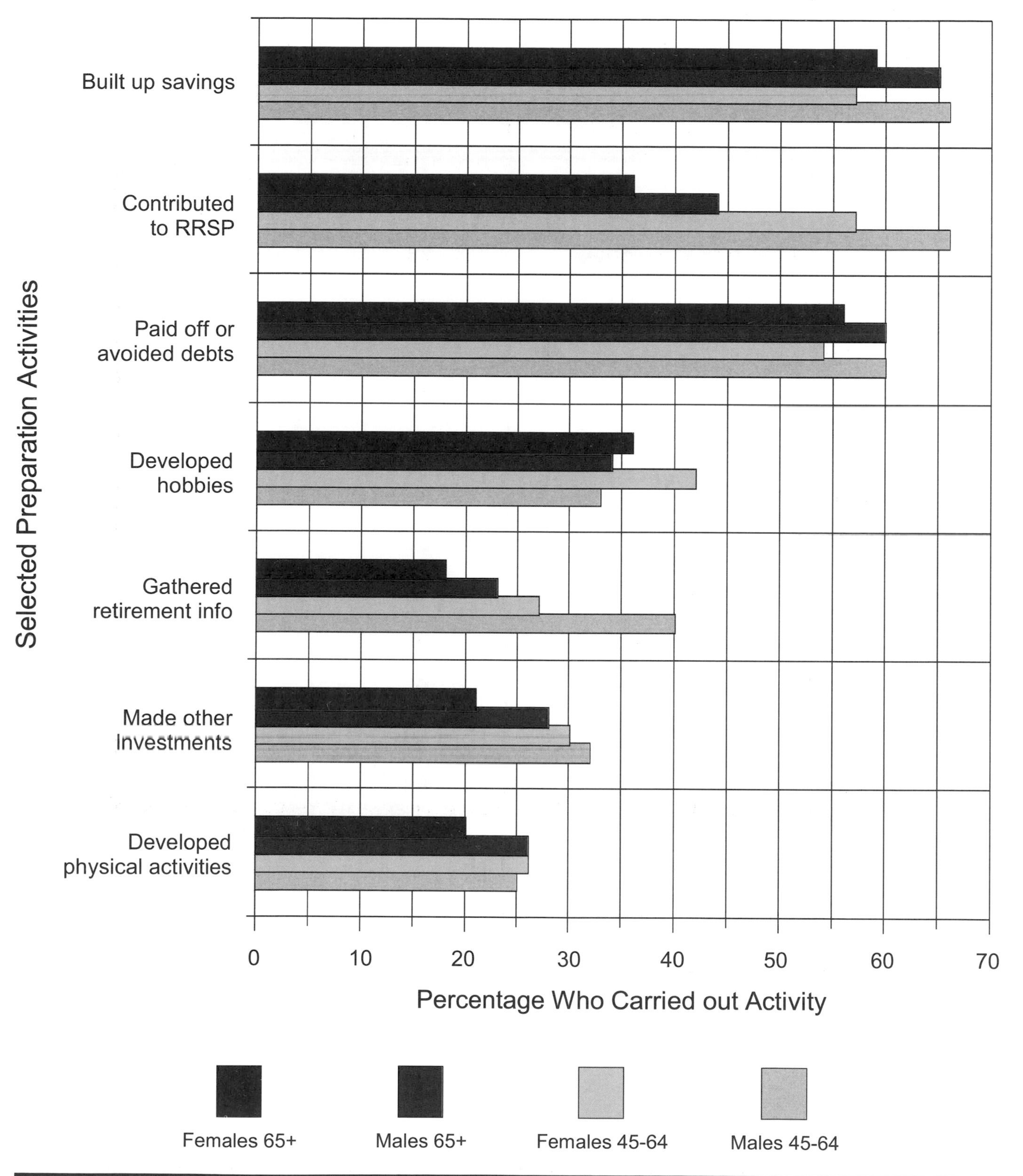

Source: *Health Canada. Ageing and Independence: Overview of a National Study. Ottawa, 1993.*

I.6: Average age at retirement of Canadians, by occupation, 1991

Occupation	Average age	
	Males (years)	Females (years)
Managerial/Administrative	62	57
Science	61	60
Teaching	61	57
Medicine	64	61
Clerical	61	59
Sales	63	60
Service	62	60
Primary Sector	63	61
Processing & Fabricating	62	58
Construction	63	61
Transportation	62	61
Other	64	56

Health Canada Definitions:

Science - includes social and natural sciences.

Other - includes religion, artistic, material handling and other crafts.

Source: Health Canada. Ageing and Independence: Provincial Highlights. Ottawa, 1993 (1991 survey; p108-109).

Average Age at Retirement of Canadians
By Gender & Selected Occupation, 1991

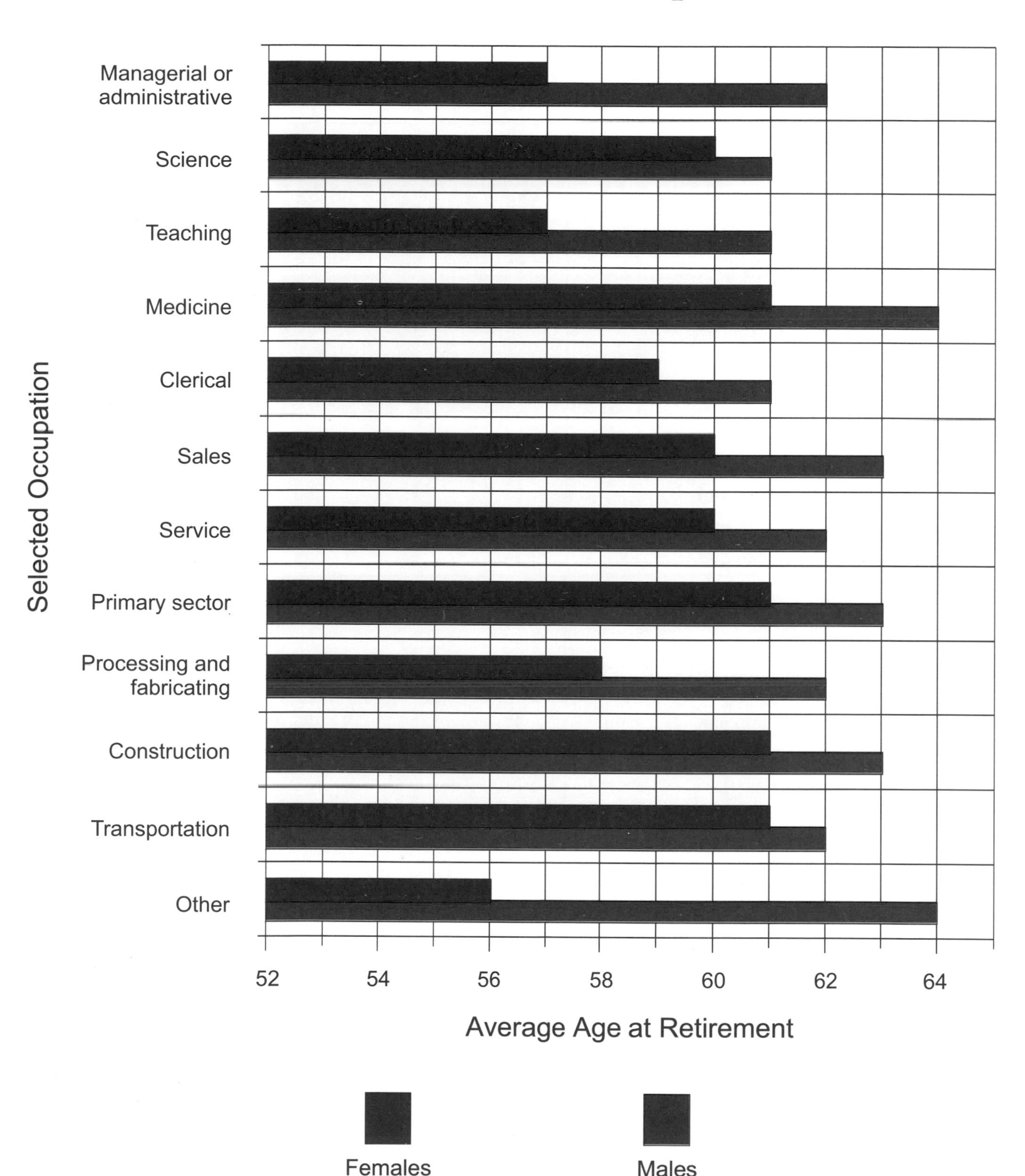

Source: *Health Canada. Ageing and Independence: Provincial Highlights. Ottawa, 1993.*

I.7: Expected age of retirement of employed Canadians by selected characteristics, 1991

	% expecting this age of retirement			
Characteristic	< 59	60-64	65	66+
All Canadians	28	34	34	5
Men	26	33	35	6
Women	30	35	32	3
Labour Force Status - Men				
Working Full-time	28	34	34	5
Working Part-time	( )	( )	( )	( )
Looking for work	11	30	55	4
Labour Force Status - Women				
Working Full-time	33	34	31	2
Working Part-time	26	37	32	5
Looking for work	18	35	43	5
Personal Income - Men				
Less than $10,000	( )	( )	( )	( )
$10,000 to $19,999	14	25	56	5
$20,000 to $39,999	20	34	40	6
$40,000 to $59,999	38	36	23	3
$60,000 or more	33	34	26	8
Personal Income - Women				
Less than $10,000	20	30	47	3
$10,000 to $19,999	26	41	30	3
$20,000 to $39,999	32	36	29	3
$40,000 to $59,999	46	33	18	3
$60,000 or more	( )	( )	( )	( )
Occupation - Men				
Professional/managerial	32	32	32	5
Semi-prof/technical/mid-mgmt	38	30	28	4
Supervisory/skilled	23	39	33	5
Semi-skilled/unskilled	20	30	42	7
Occupation - Women				
Professional/managerial	53	28	15	5
Semi-prof/technical/mid-mgmt	26	36	35	2
Supervisory/skilled	31	39	26	4
Semi-skilled/unskilled	22	34	42	2

Source: Canadian Council on Social Development: Centre for International Statistics. Schellenberg, G. The Road to Retirement. Ottawa, 1994 (1991 data; p 105-107).

I.7: Expected age of retirement of employed Canadians by selected characteristics, 1991 (cont'd)

	% expecting this age of retirement			
Characteristic	< 59	60-64	65	66+
Education - Men				
Less than high school	19	36	39	6
High school graduate	28	34	31	7
Post-secondary graduate	31	30	34	5
Education - Women				
Less than high school	25	38	35	2
High school graduate	27	35	35	2
Post-secondary graduate	37	32	27	4
Employer Pensions - Men				
Has pension	33	34	29	4
Does not have pension	14	31	46	9
Employer Pensions - Women				
Has pension	37	33	28	2
Does not have pension	23	37	36	4
Job Tenure - Men				
Less than one year	17	37	38	9
1 to 10 years	17	31	44	8
11 to 20 years	25	38	33	4
More than 20 years	38	32	26	5
Job Tenure - Women				
Less than one year	22	47	28	3
1 to 10 years	30	34	33	4
11 to 20 years	35	32	31	2
More than 20 years	38	34	24	3

Note: ( ) indicates sample size too small to provide reliable estimate.

Source: Canadian Council on Social Development: Centre for International Statistics. Schellenberg, G. The Road to Retirement. Ottawa, 1994 (1991 data; p105-107).

I.8: Percentage of retired Canadian population reporting dissatisfaction with retirement, 1988

Age Group	Percentage Dissatisfied
Under 60	20.3
60-64	9.5
65-74	4.5
75+	3.9

Source: Statistics Canada: Housing, Family and Social Statistics Division. A Portrait of Seniors in Canada. Ottawa, 1990 (1988 data; Cat. No. 89-519, p53).

Proportion of Retired Canadians Dissatisfied With Retirement
By Age Group, 1988

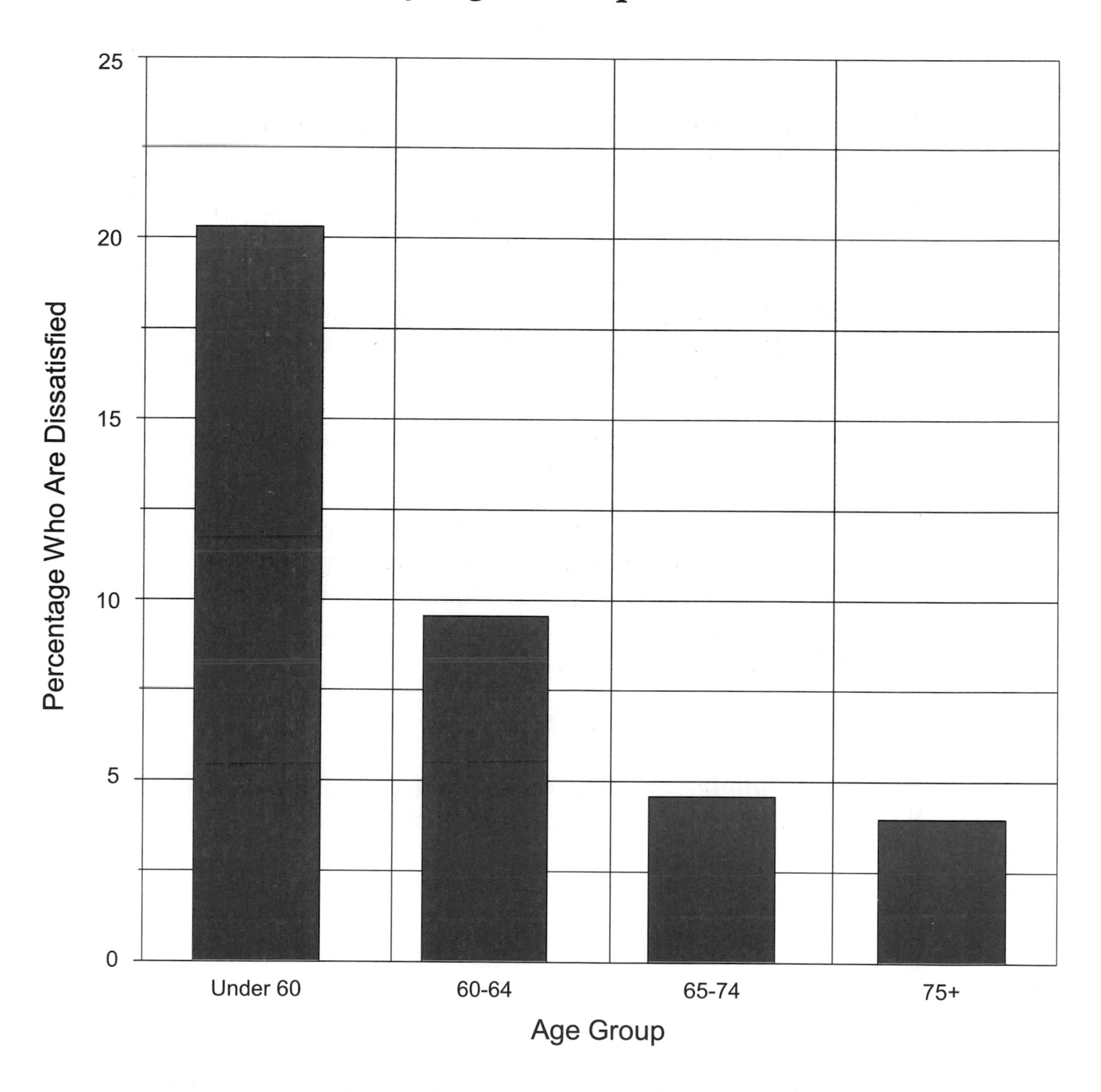

Source: Statistics Canada. Housing, Family and Social Statistics Division. A Portrait of Seniors in Canada. Ottawa, 1990.

Less than half (47%) of seniors check their home water temperature.

Canada's Health Promotion Survey, Health and Welfare Canada, 1990

Just over half (52%) of the 65 and over age group state that they have felt the adverse effects of tobacco smoke.

Canada's Health Promotion Survey, Health and Welfare Canada, 1990

According to the 1985 to 1990 General Social Survey, two-thirds to three-quarters of respondents who were 55 years of age or older reported being in good or excellent health, and over 90% reported being happy or very happy.

Social Trends, Summer 1992

It is estimated that 5.1% of those over the age of 65 meet the criteria for Alzheimer's disease.

Canadian Medical Association Journal, 1994

SECTION J

Health Status & Quality of Life

J.1: Self-rated health status of adult Canadians, 1990

Health Status (Self-rated)	Males 15+ (%)	Females 15+ (%)	Males 65+ (%)	Females 65+ (%)
Poor	3	3	8	7
Fair	10	9	19	19
Good	27	26	31	30
Very Good	35	36	29	27
Excellent	25	26	14	17

Note: Not all columns sum to 100% due to rounding in source table.

Source: Health Canada. Canada's Health Promotion Survey: Technical Report. Ottawa, 1993 (1990 Health Promotion Survey; p32).

Self-rated Health Status
Adult Canadians, 1990

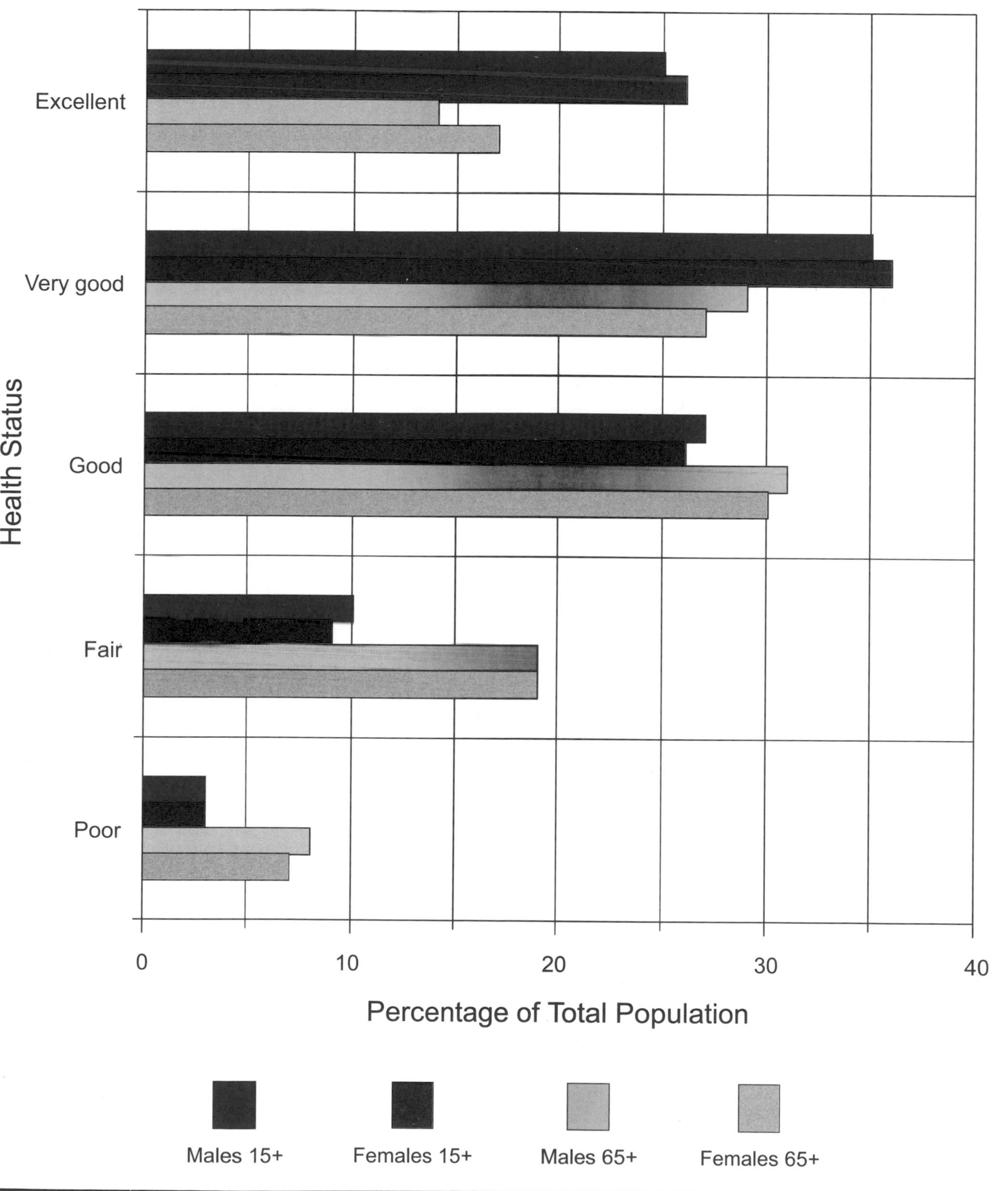

Source: Health Canada. Canada's Health Promotion Survey: Technical Report. Ottawa, 1993.

J.2: Perceived stressfulness of life among Canadian adults, 1990

Perceived stressfulness of life*	Males 15+ (%)	Females 15+ (%)	Males 65+ (%)	Females 65+ (%)
Not at all stressful	12	11	30	30
Not very stressful	27	29	39	37
Somewhat stressful	48	48	24	26
Very stressful	13	12	7	7

*Note: Data are based on a question which asked, "Would you describe your life as... very stressful, somewhat stressful, not very stressful, not at all stressful?"

Source: Health Canada. Canada's Health Promotion Survey: Technical Report. Ottawa, 1993 (1990 Health Promotion Survey; p38).

Perceived Stressfulness of Life
Among Adult Canadians, 1990

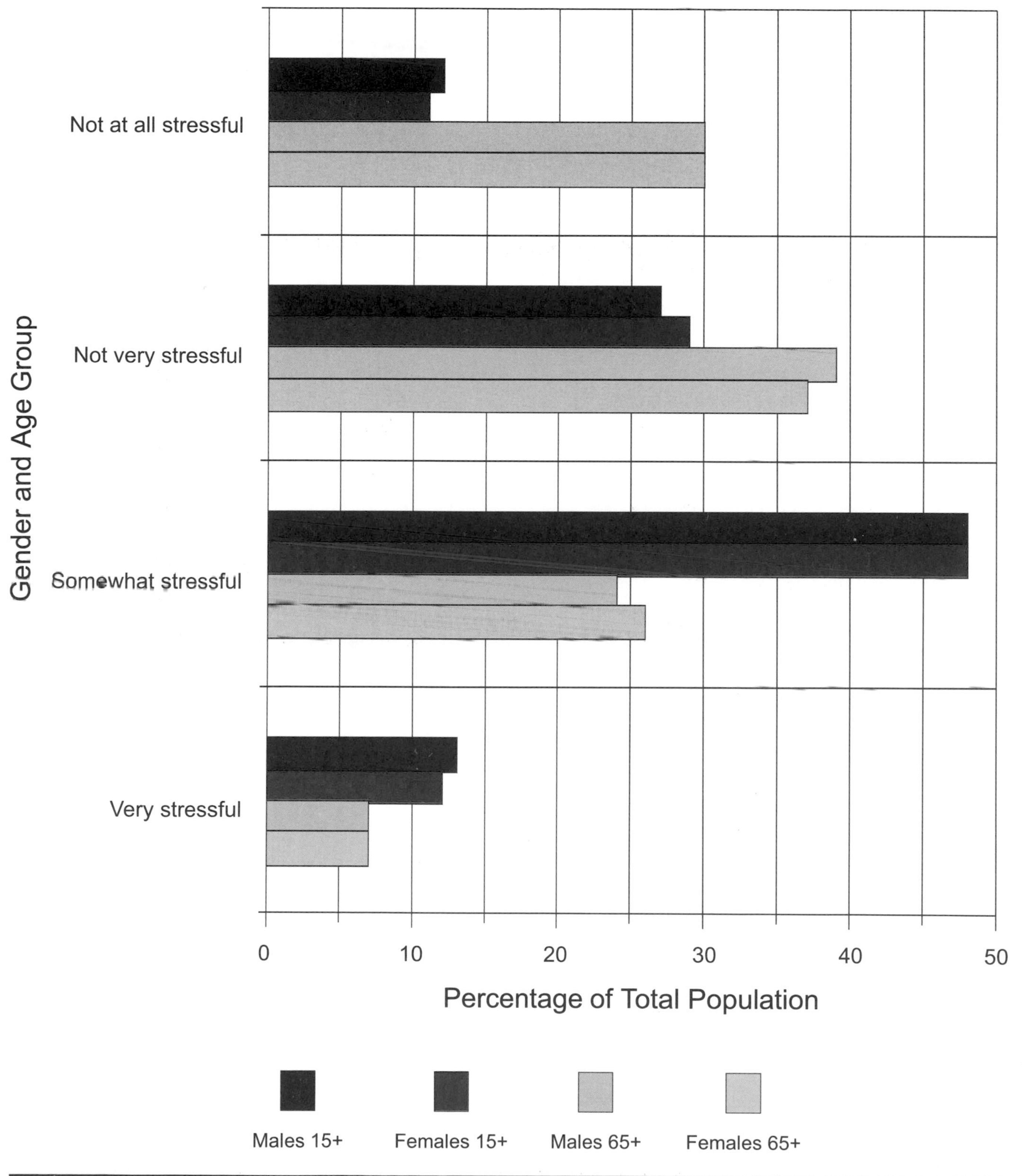

Source: Health Canada. Canada's Health Promotion Survey: Technical Report. Ottawa, 1993.

J.3: Canadians 45+ with self-reported "very stressful" lives, by main source of stress, 1991

Reason for stress	Males 45+* (%)	Females 45+* (%)
Family	11	32
Employment	59	25
Health	16	20
Something Else	13	22

* Data were not available for 65+ age category.

Note: Columns do not sum to 100% due to rounding in source table.

Source: Health Canada. Ageing and Independence: Overview of a National Survey. Ottawa, 1993 (1991 Survey; p59).

Sources of Self-Reported Stress
Canadians Aged 45+, 1991

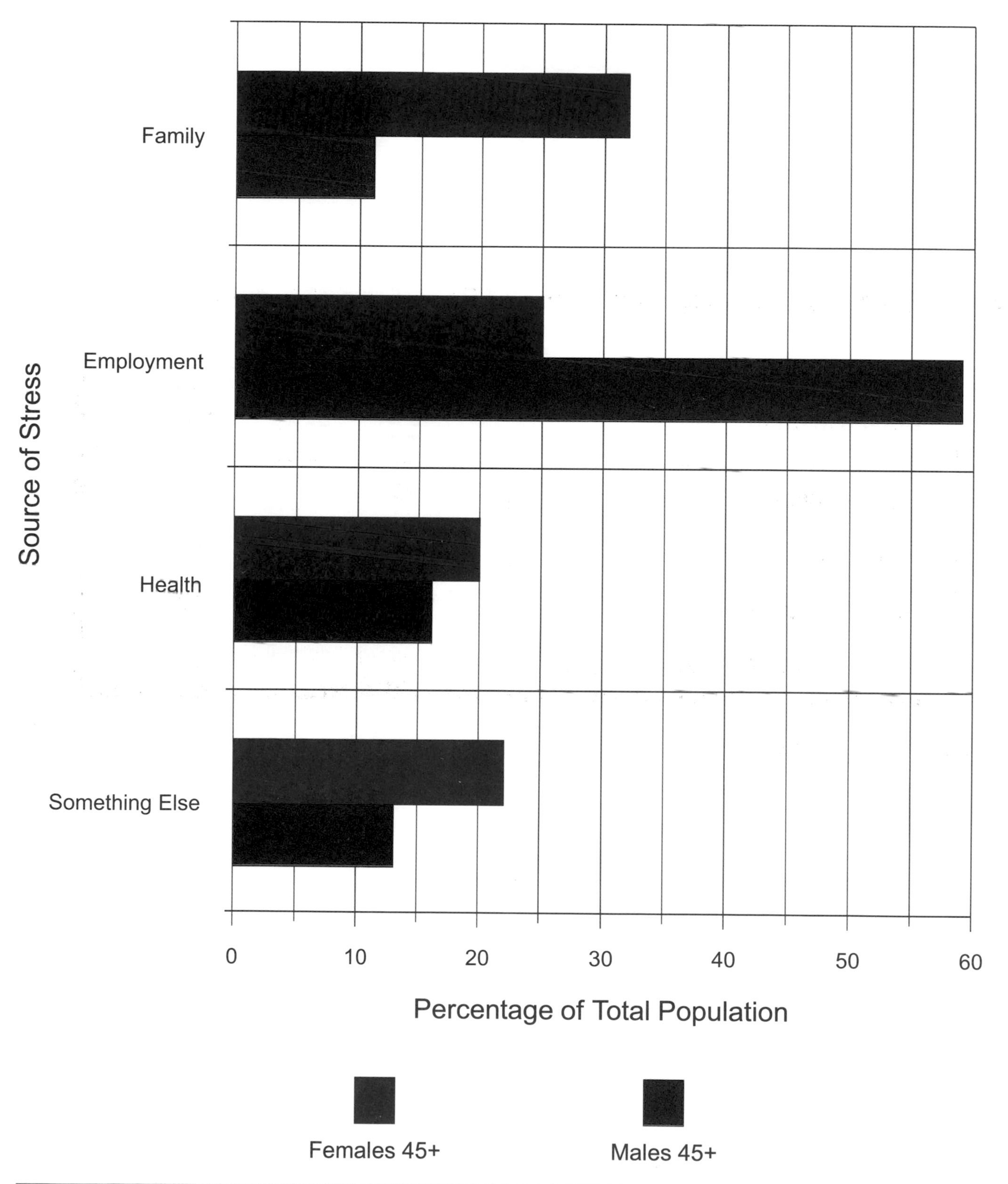

Source: *Health Canada. Ageing and Independence: Overview of a National Survey. Ottawa, 1993.*

J.4: Methods of coping with stress of Canadians 45+, 1991

Coping Method *	Age 45-64 (%)	Age 65+ (%)
Try to accept it	90	90
Keep busy	86	81
Pray or meditate	57	62
Get help from friends or relatives	58	53

* Multiple answers were accepted.

Source: Health Canada. Ageing and Independence: Provincial Highlights. Ottawa, 1993 (1991 Survey; table 16-Canada).

Methods of Coping with Stress
Canadians Aged 45+, 1991

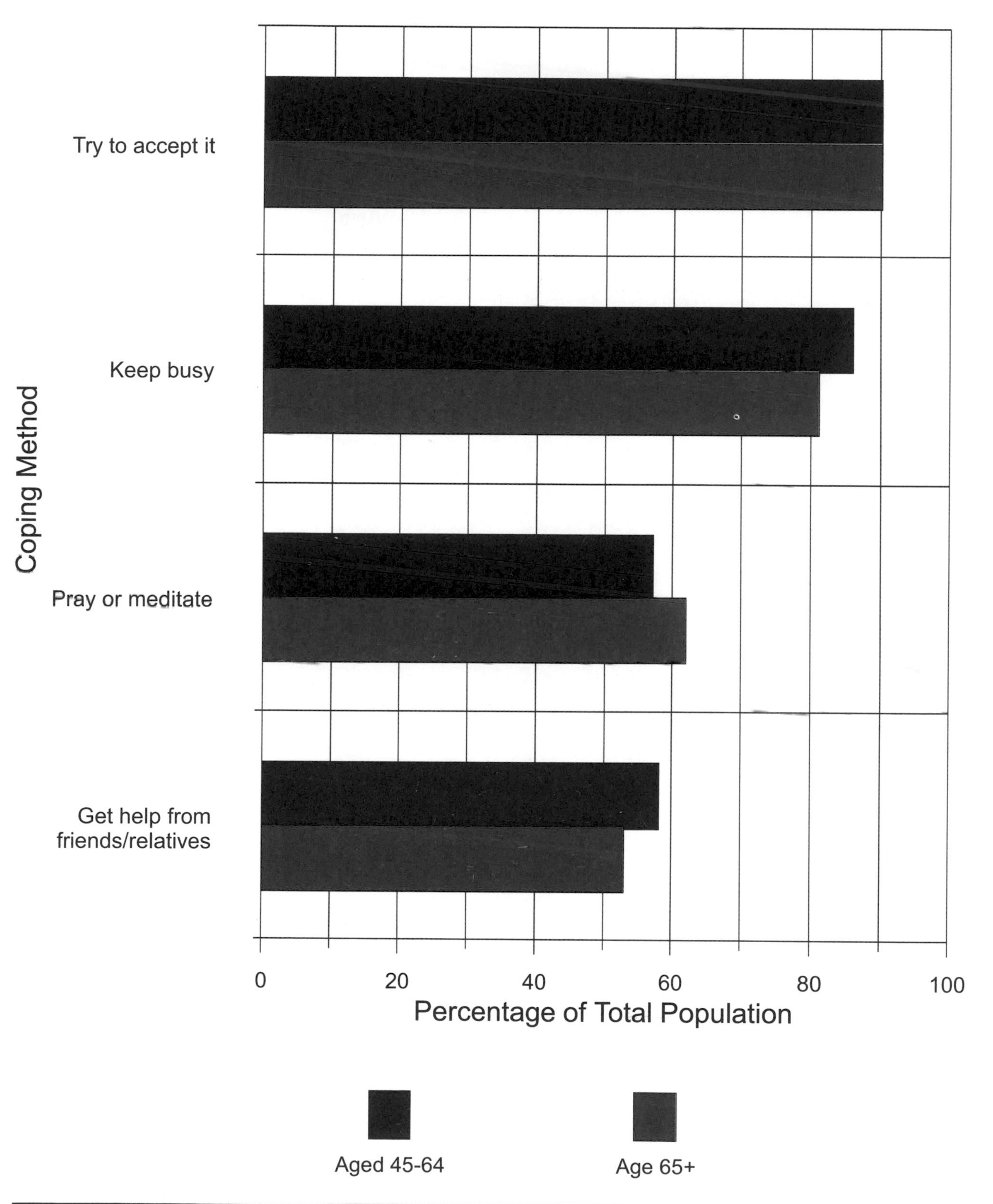

Source: *Health Canada. Ageing and Independence: Provincial Highlights. Ottawa, 1993.*

J.5: Leading causes of deaths, Canada, 1989

CAUSE OF DEATH	Age						
	All ages (%)	65+ (%)	65-69 (%)	70-74 (%)	75-79 (%)	80-84 (%)	85+ (%)
MALES							
Disease of the circulatory system	39.1	44.9	40.9	45.0	46.2	46.2	48.0
Respiratory diseases	8.9	11.6	7.2	9.0	11.6	13.2	16.2
Stroke	5.9	7.4	4.7	5.6	7.6	8.7	10.2
Cancer	27.2	27.1	36.3	32.4	28.1	23.3	16.5
Ischaemic heart disease	24.9	27.6	28.0	29.4	28.1	27.1	25.3
All other causes	24.8	16.4	15.7	14.7	15.3	17.2	19.2
FEMALES							
Disease of the circulatory system	42.6	49.0	34.2	40.2	47.0	51.8	56.3
Respiratory diseases	8.0	9.0	6.0	7.7	8.2	8.6	10.9
Stroke	9.5	11.0	5.7	7.6	9.7	12.5	13.6
Cancer	26.4	22.2	42.7	34.5	25.9	19.5	11.1
Ischaemic heart disease	22.6	26.0	20.8	24.2	26.5	27.6	27.2
All other causes	23.0	19.8	17.1	17.6	18.8	20.2	21.8

Source: Statistics Canada. J.A. Norland. Focus on Canada - Profile of Canada's Seniors. Ottawa, 1994 (1989 data; p109).

Leading Causes of Death
Canada, 1989

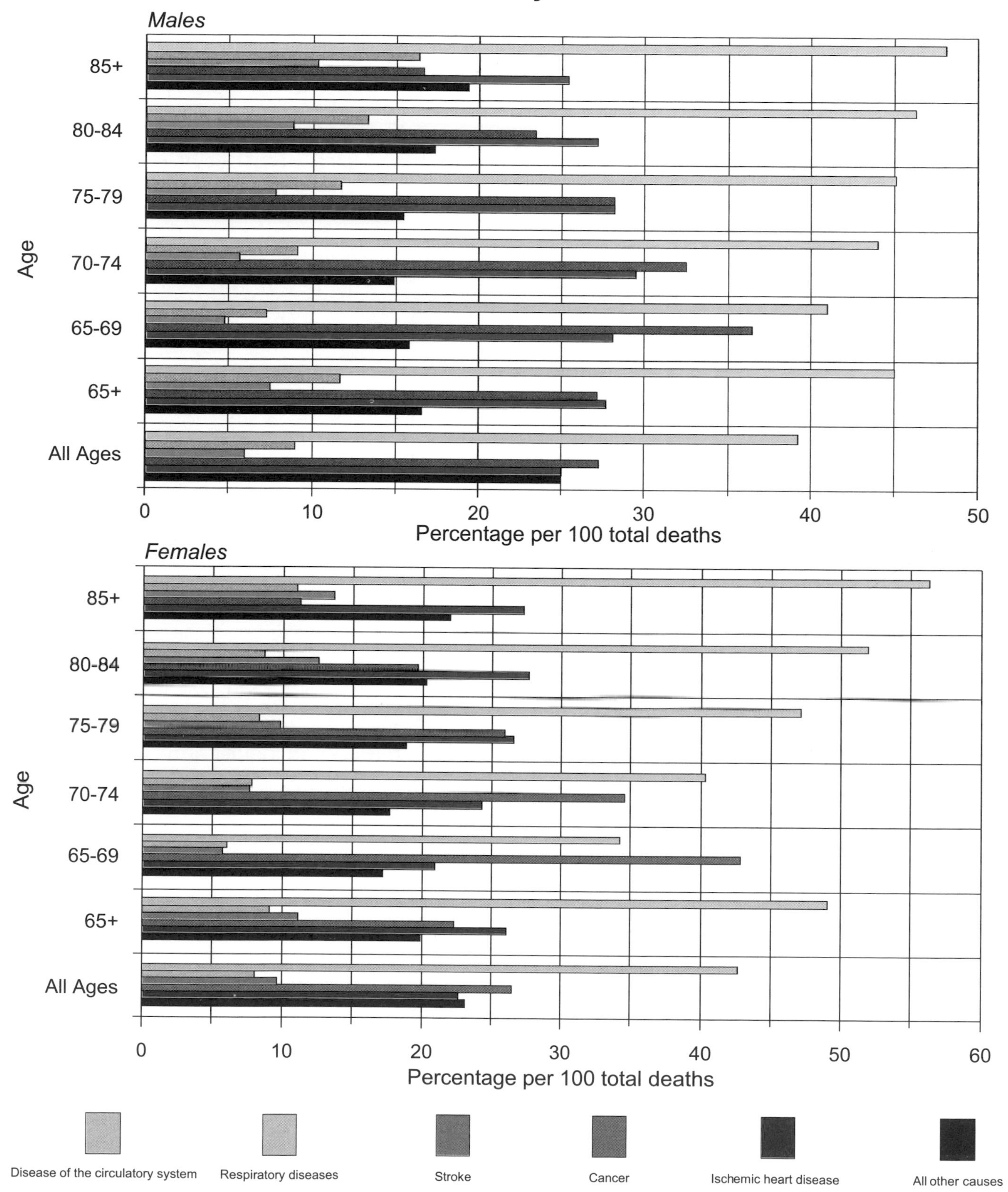

Source: Statistics Canada. J.A. Norland. Focus on Canada - Profile of Canada's Seniors. Ottawa, 1994.

J.6: *Prevalence rates (rate per 1000 elderly in private dwellings) of elder abuse in Canada, 1990*

Type of Abuse	Rate per 1,000
Material Abuse	25
Chronic Verbal Aggression	14
Physical Violence	4
Neglect	4
Multiple Abuse	8

National Survey on Abuse of the Elderly in Canada Definitions:

Material Abuse - includes being tricked or persuaded to give up money or relinquish control over finances; being influenced to change one's will; being made to give up something of value; being persuaded to sign over one's house

Chronic Verbal Aggression - includes being subjected to repeated insults and/or threats.

Physical Violence - includes being pushed, grabbed, shoved, assaulted with knife or guns, etc.

Neglect - includes when help with activities of daily living (e.g. - meal preparation, housework, shopping, dressing, toilet functions) is withheld.

Source: Ryerson Polytechnical Institute. National Survey on Abuse of the Elderly in Canada. Toronto, 1990 (p56).

Prevalence Rates of Elder Abuse, 1990
Canadians 65+ in Private Dwellings

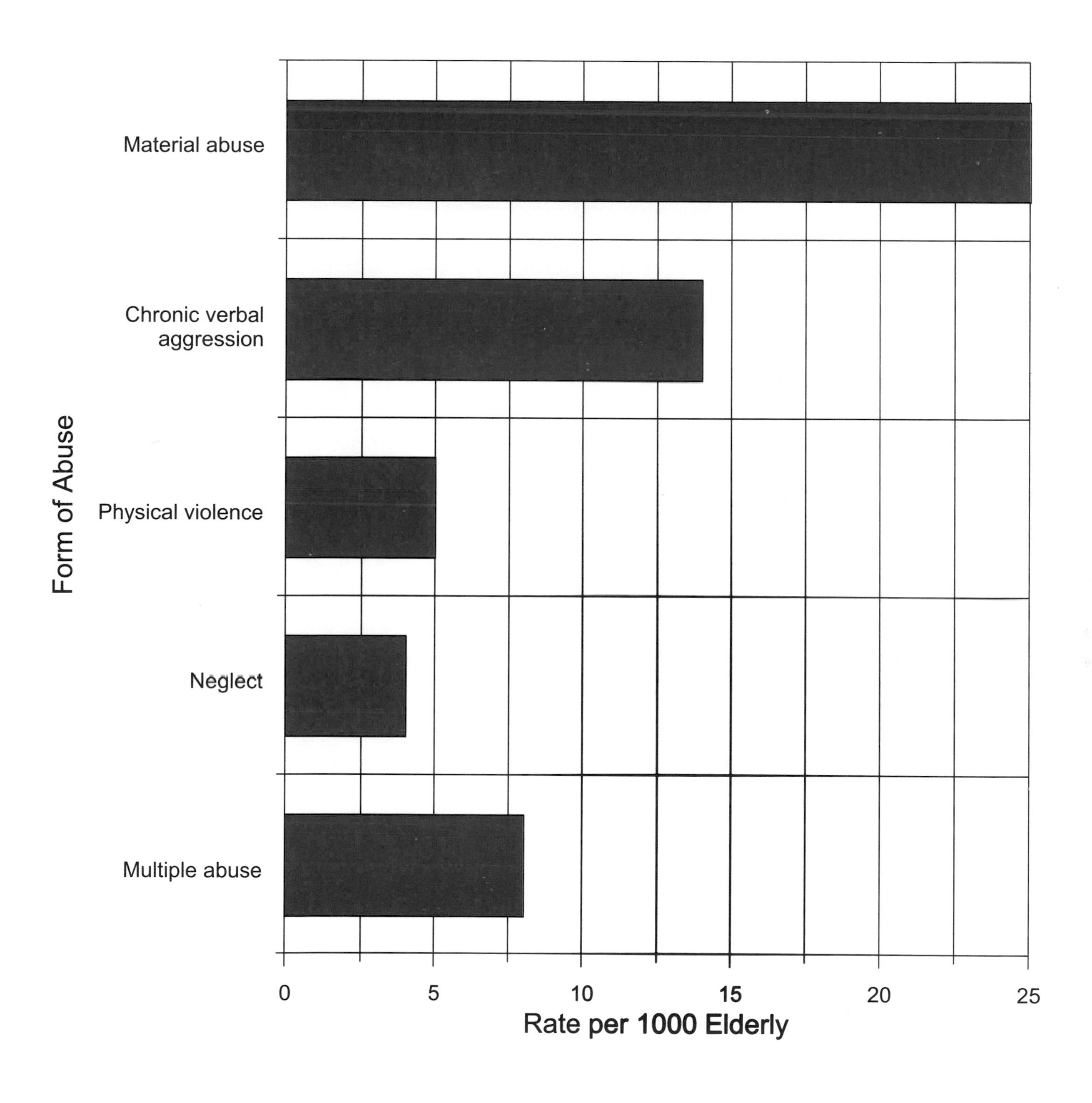

Source: Ryerson Polytechnical Institute. National Survey on **Abuse of the Elderly in Canada**. Toronto, 1990.

J.7: Number of prescription drugs used by Canadian adults in the 30 days prior to survey, 1989

Number of Drugs	Age		
	15-34	35-64	65+
None	31	27	19
One	33	36	33
Two	23	21	24
Three or more	14	16	24

Note: Not all columns sum to 100% due to rounding in source table.

Source: Statistics Canada. M. Bergob. Drug Use Among Senior Canadians, Canadian Social Trends. Ottawa, 1994 (1989 data; Summer, p25-29).

Number of Prescription Drugs Used
By Canadians, 1989

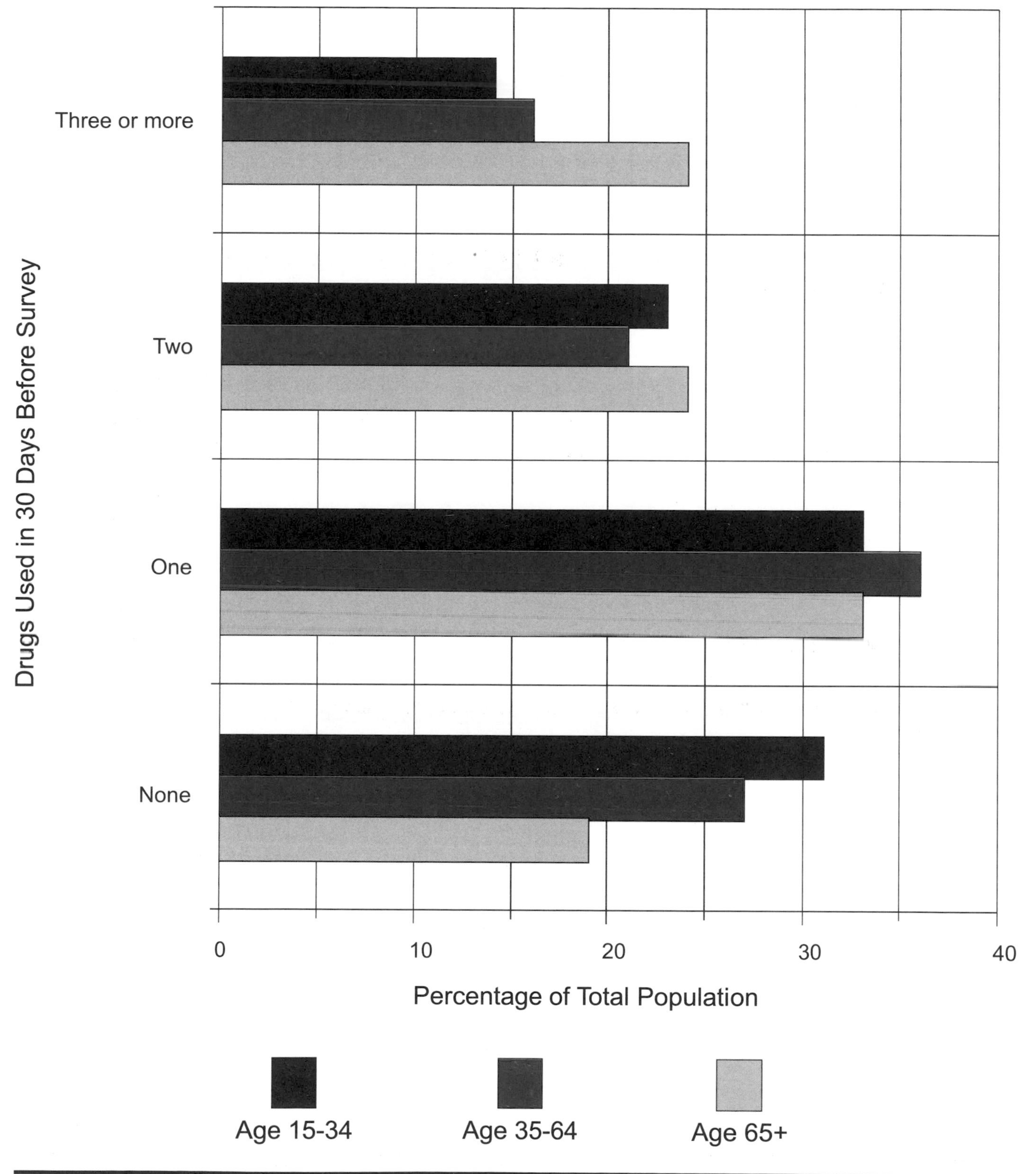

Source: *Statistics Canada. M. Bergob. Drug Use Amoung Senior Canadians, Canadian Social Trends. Ottawa, 1994.*

J.8: Proportion of seniors using top five prescription drugs, Canada, 1989

Type of Drug	Males 65+ (%)	Females 65+ (%)
Heart/blood pressure medication	35	45
Pain relievers	30	33
Stomach remedies/laxatives	9	14
Sleeping pills	10	11
Cough/cold medications	7	9

Source: Statistics Canada. M. Bergob. Drug Use Among Senior Canadians, Canadian Social Trends. Ottawa, 1994 (1989 data; Summer, p26).

Top Five Prescription Drugs Used
By Canadians 65+, 1989

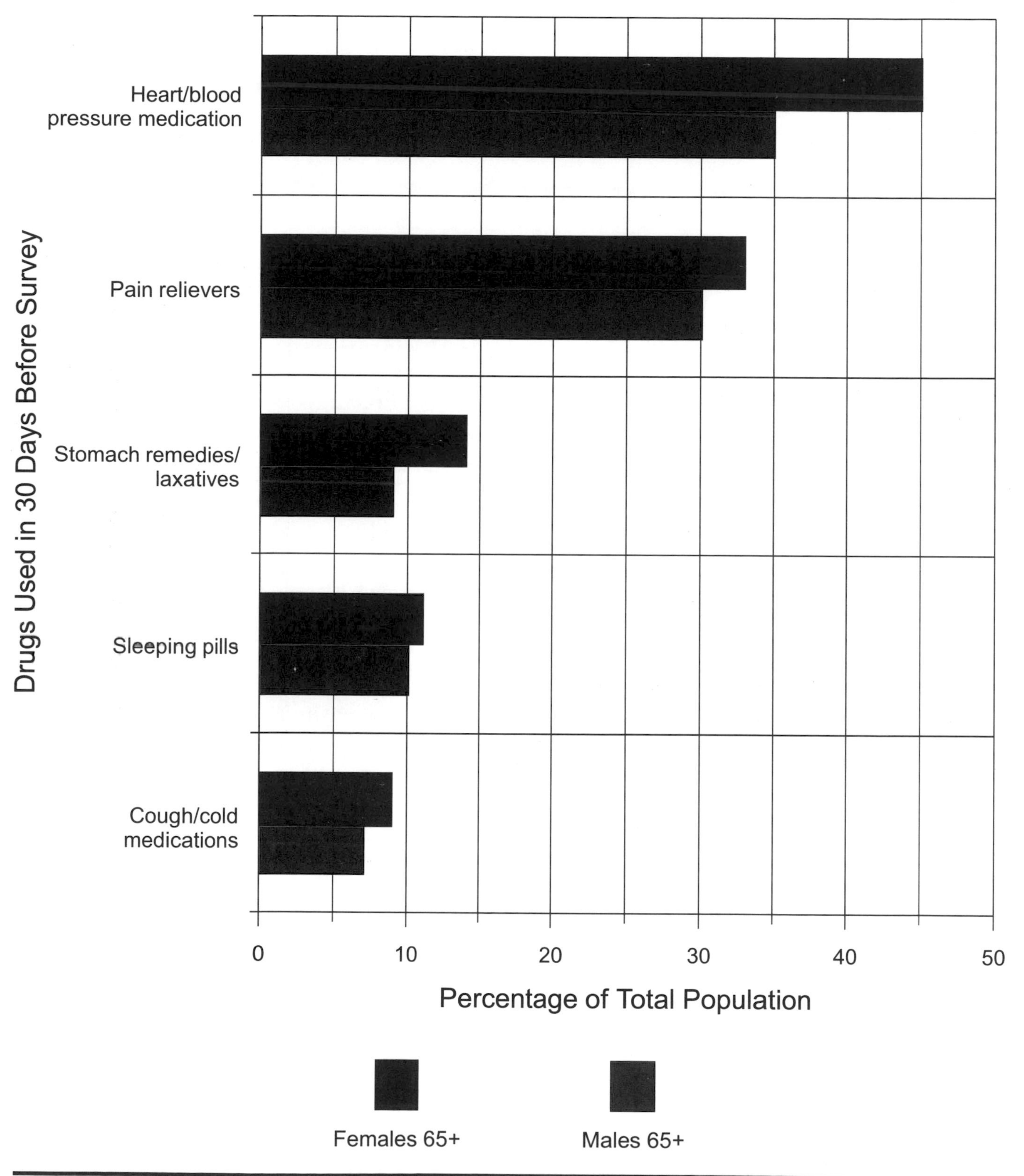

Source: Statistics Canada. M. Bergob. Drug Use Amoung Senior Canadians, Canadian Social Trends. Ottawa, 1994.

J.9: *Percentage of Canadians who are satisfied with various aspects of life, 1990*

Satisfaction With:	Age 15+	Age 65+
Spouse/partner/single status	90	89
Immediate family	93	93
Distribution of housework	85	81
Job or main activity	86	83
Balance between job and family	81	76
Time for other interests	74	87
Relationships with friends	93	91
Accommodation/housing	90	93

Source: Statistics Canada. Family and Friends. Ottawa, 1994 (1990 General Social Survey; Cat. No. 11-612, p61).

Percentage of Canadians Satisfied
With Selected Aspects of Life, 1990

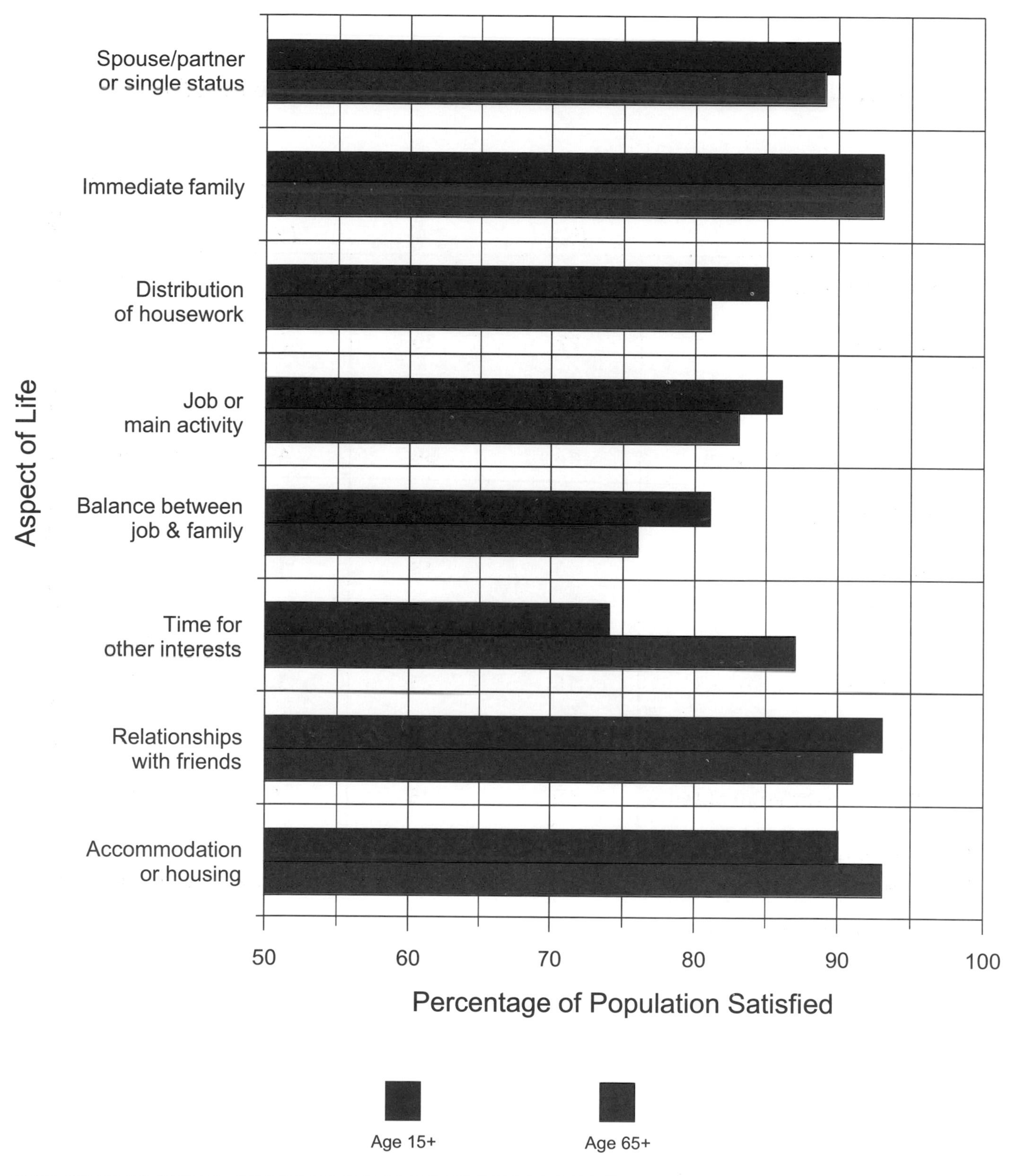

Source: *Statistics Canada. Family and Friends. Ottawa, 1994.*

J.10: Prevalence of selected health problems of Canadians 65+, 1991

Health Problem *	Males 65-74 (%)	Females 65-74 (%)	Males 75+ (%)	Females 75+ (%)
Hypertension	33	40	27	42
Heart trouble	22	20	30	30
Diabetes	10	9	13	9
Arthritis/rheumatism	44	56	49	65
Asthma	7	7	6	7
Emphysema	19	16	19	21
Hay fever	8	9	8	7
Allergies	15	23	13	19
Stomach ulcer	7	6	10	5
Other digestive problems	10	15	5	16
High blood cholesterol	10	20	9	10

* Multiple responses were accepted.

Source: Health Priorities Analysis Unit. McMaster University. Hamilton, 1995 (1991 General Social Survey).

Prevalence of Selected Health Problems
Canadians Aged 65+, 1991

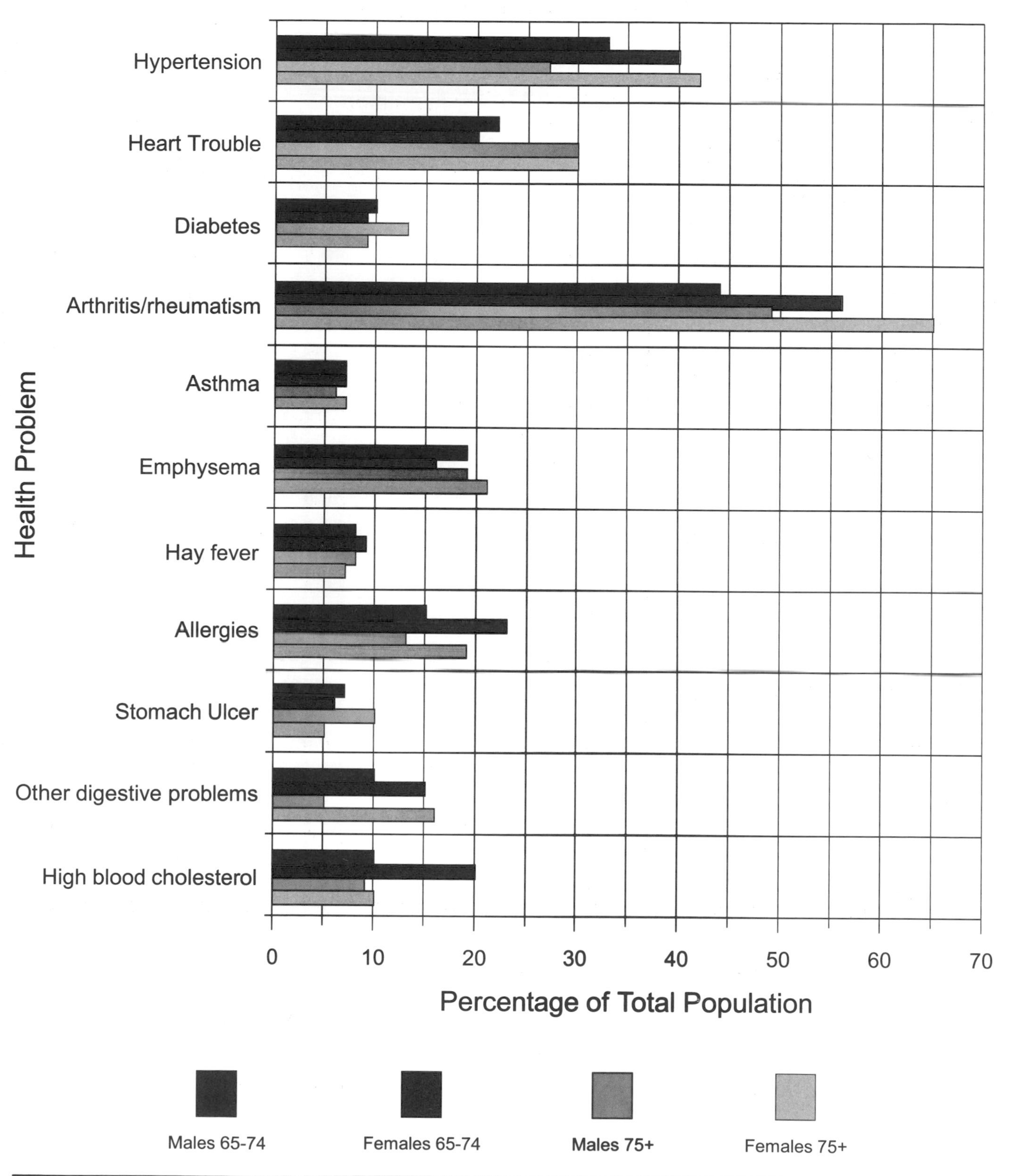

Source: *Health Priorities Analysis Unit. McMaster University. Hamilton, 1995.*

J.11: Prevalence of dementia (all types) in the population 65+, by gender and region, Canada, 1991 (showing numbers of cases, in thousands, and percentages of the population in that regional and residential group)

Region	Residence					
	Community		Institution		Total	
	Estimated # in 1000's	%	Estimated # in 1000's	%	Estimated # in 1000's	%
Atlantic Provinces						
Male	5.7	5.3	3.3	60.8	9.0	8.2
Female	8.0	5.0	6.6	56.5	14.6	8.4
Total	13.7	5.1	9.8	59.4	23.6	8.4
Quebec						
Male	13.7	5.3	8.1	47.6	21.8	8.3
Female	21.0	4.9	19.2	44.0	40.2	8.4
Total	34.7	5.2	27.4	44.8	62.0	8.4
Ontario						
Male	8.9*	2.2	11.5	53.2	20.4	5.0
Female	33.3	5.1	36.5	59.9	69.8	9.3
Total	42.2	3.8	48.0	58.0	90.2	7.7
Prairies						
Male	10.1	4.8	8.6	69.4	18.7	8.6
Female	8.2	2.9	18.2	66.0	26.4	7.9
Total	18.3	3.7	26.8	67.9	45.1	8.3
British Columbia						
Male	7.2	4.3	4.1	56.4	11.3	6.7
Female	7.8	3.4	12.6	66.0	20.4	7.9
Total	15.0	3.7	16.7	63.4	31.7	7.5
All						
Male	45.6	3.9	35.6	55.5	81.2	6.9
Female	78.3	4.5	93.1	57.2	171.4	8.6
Total	123.9	4.2	128.7	56.9	252.6	8.0

Canadian Study of Health and Aging Definition:

Dementia - the diagnostic criteria of dementia for this study followed the 3rd revision of the Diagnostic and Statistical Manual of Mental Disorders (DSM - III - R).

*Note: This number was questioned by the investigators of this study and should thus be used with caution.

Source: Canadian Study of Health and Aging Working Group. Canadian Study of Health and Aging: study methods and prevalence of dementia. Canadian Medical Association Journal. 1994: 150:899-913.

Percentage of Persons 65+ in the Community Who Have Dementia (All Types)

By Region, Canada, 1991

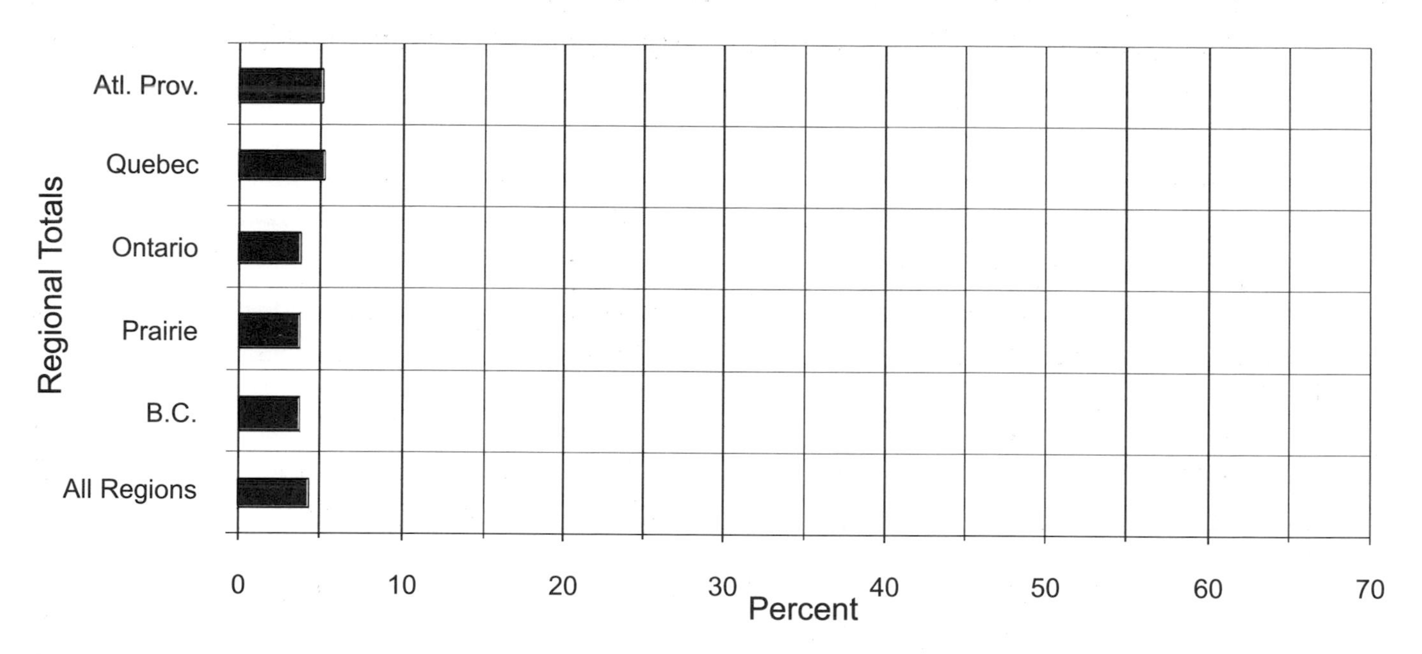

Percentage of Persons 65+ in Institutions Who Have Dementia (All Types)

By Region, Canada, 1991

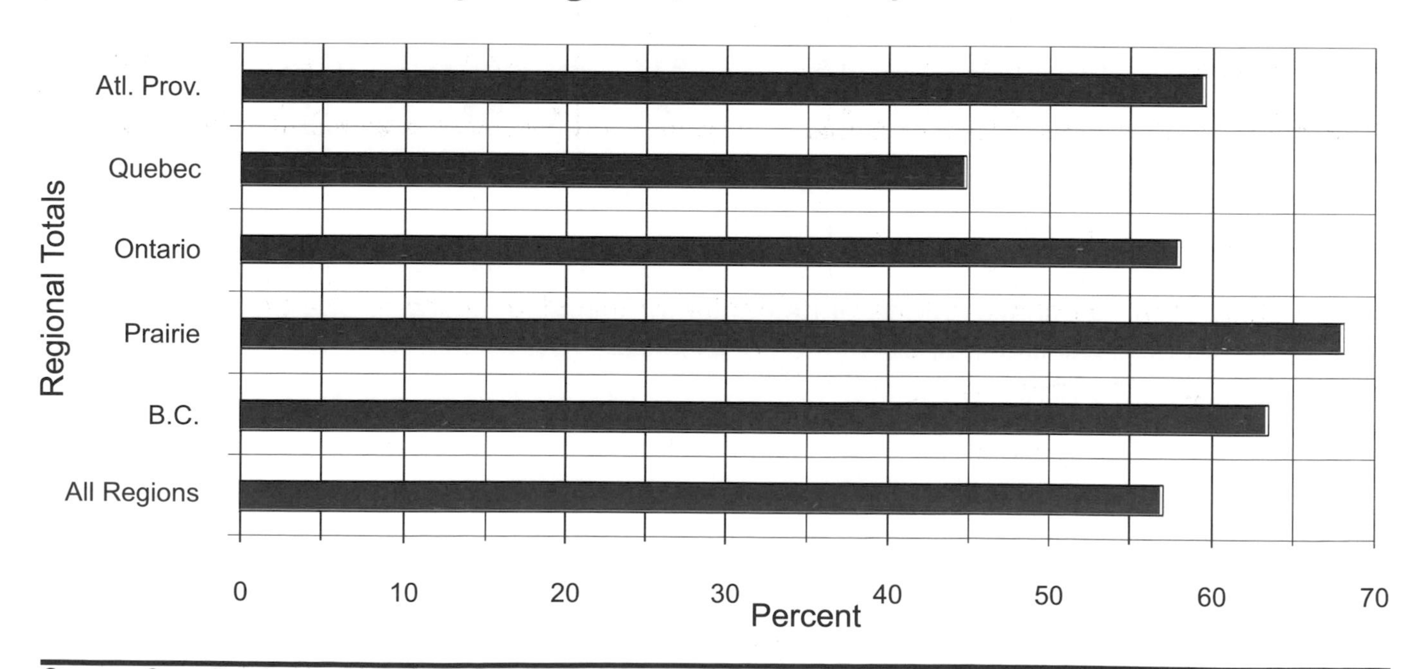

Source: Canadian Study of Health and Aging Working Group. Canadian Study of Health and Aging. CMA Journal 1994.

J.12: *Estimated number, in thousands, and percentage of dementia cases (all types) in the 65+ population, by age, gender and residential group, Canada, 1991*

Age Group	Residence					
	Community		Institution		Total	
	Estimated # in 1000's	%	Estimated # in 1000's	%	Estimated # in 1000's	%
65-74						
Male	8.6	1.0	7.2	43.7	15.8	1.9
Female	20.2	2.0	8.7	40.6	28.9	2.8
Total	28.8	1.6	15.8	41.9	44.7	2.4
75-84						
Male	25.8	7.1	14.8	53.6	40.6	10.4
Female	36.4	6.8	33.2	53.2	69.6	11.6
Total	62.2	6.9	48.0	53.3	110.2	11.1
85 and over						
Male	11.1	17.3	13.6	61.8	24.8	28.7
Female	21.7	18.0	51.2	67.3	72.9	37.1
Total	32.9	17.8	64.9	66.0	97.7	34.5
All Ages						
Male	45.6	3.9	35.6	55.5	81.2	6.9
Female	78.3	4.5	93.1	57.2	171.4	8.6
Total	123.9	4.2	128.7	56.9	252.6	8.0

Canadian Study of Health and Aging Definition:

Dementia - the diagnostic criteria of dementia for this study followed the 3rd revision of the Diagnostic and Statistical Manual of Mental Disorders (DSM - III - R).

Source: Canadian Study of Health and Aging Working Group. Canadian Study of Health and Aging: study methods and prevalence of dementia. Canadian Medical Association Journal. 1994; 150: 899-913.

Percentage of Persons 65+ in the Community Who Have Dementia (All Types)

By Age Group, Canada, 1991

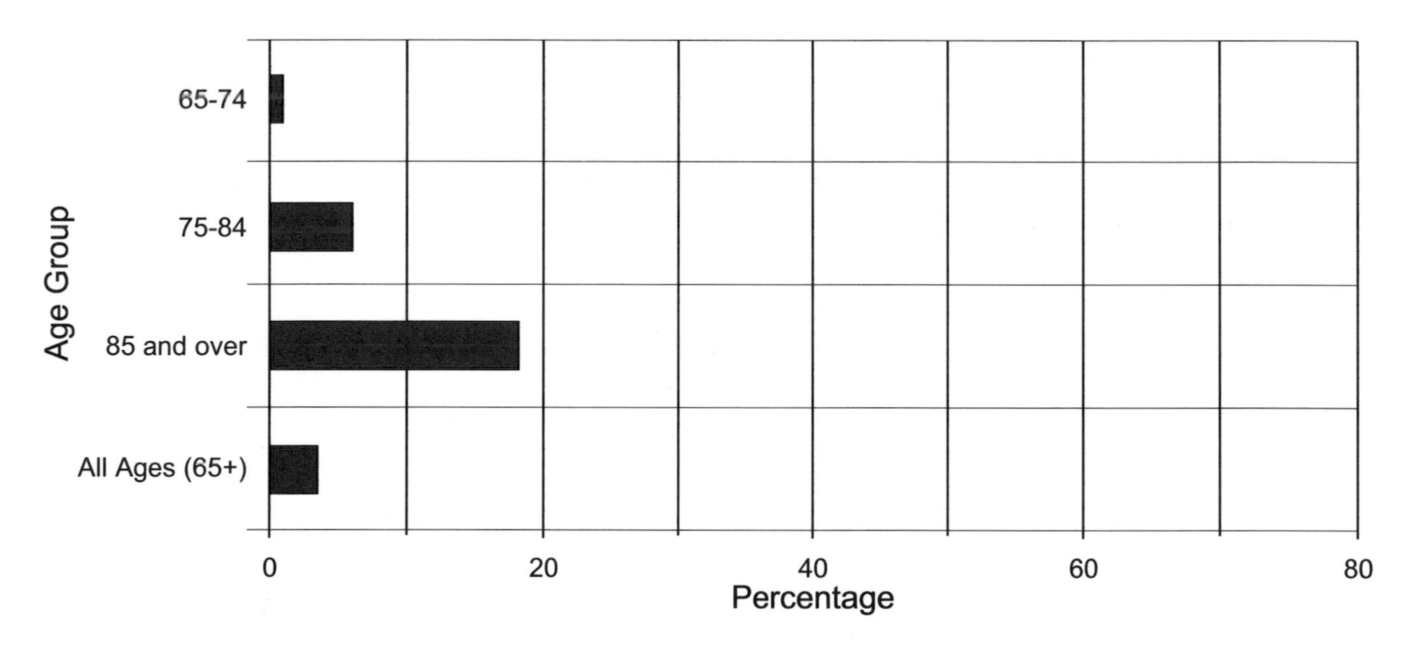

Percentage of Persons 65+ in Institutions Who Have Dementia (All Types)

By Age Group, Canada, 1991

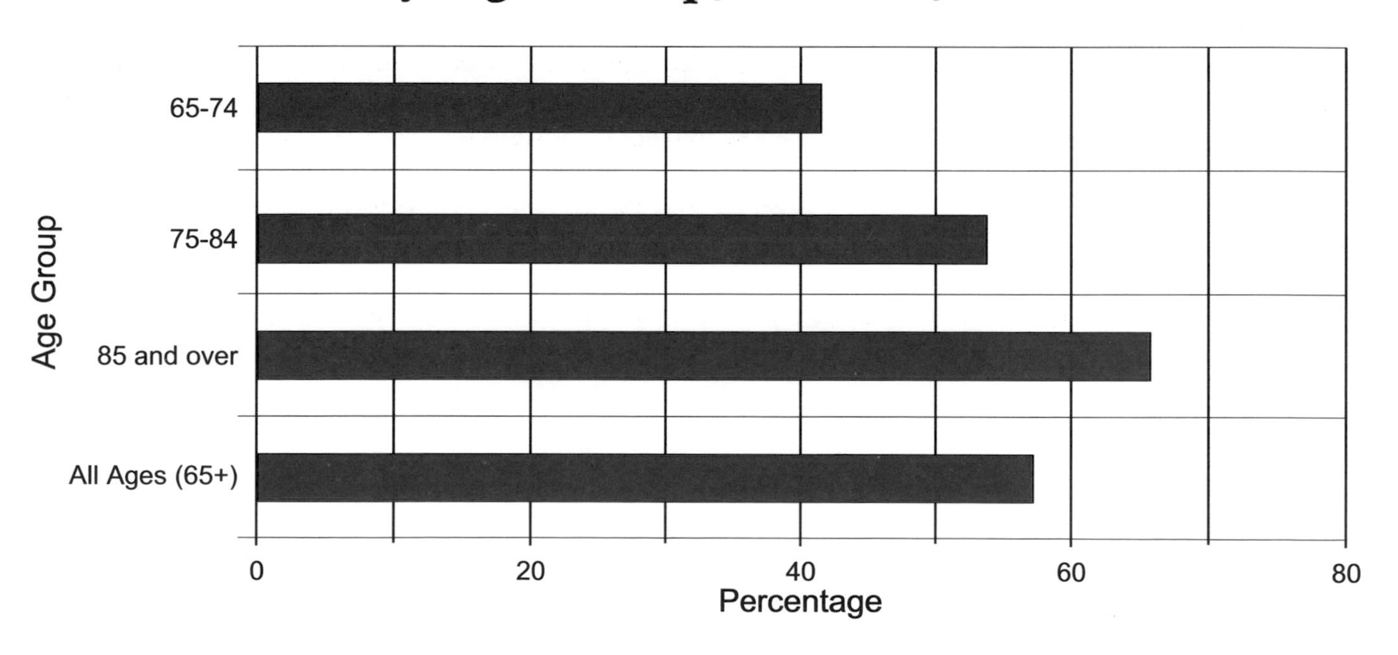

Source: Canadian Study of Health and Aging Working Group. Canadian Study of Health and Aging. CMA Journal 1994.

J.13: Projected prevalence of dementia cases in Canada, age 65+, by dementia type, 1991 - 2031

Year	Type of Dementia no. of cases X 1000		
	All	Alzheimer's Disease	Vascular dementia
1991	253	161	49
2001	364	238	68
2011	475	314	86
2021	592	387	109
2031	778	509	144

Canadian Study of Health and Aging Definition:

Alzheimer's disease - the diagnostic criteria for this study were based on the criteria of the National Institute of Neurological and Communicative Disorders and Stroke and the Alzheimer's Disease and Related Disorders Association (NINCDS & ADRA).

Vascular dementia - this study used a draft of the 10th revision of the International Classification of Diseases which was used to define the subcategories of vascular dementias.

Source: Canadian Study of Health and Aging Working Group. Canadian Study of Health and Aging: study methods and prevalence of dementia. Canadian Medical Association Journal. Ottawa, 1994: 150: 899-913.

Projected Prevalence of Dementia Cases, 65+
By Dementia Type, Canada, 1991-2031

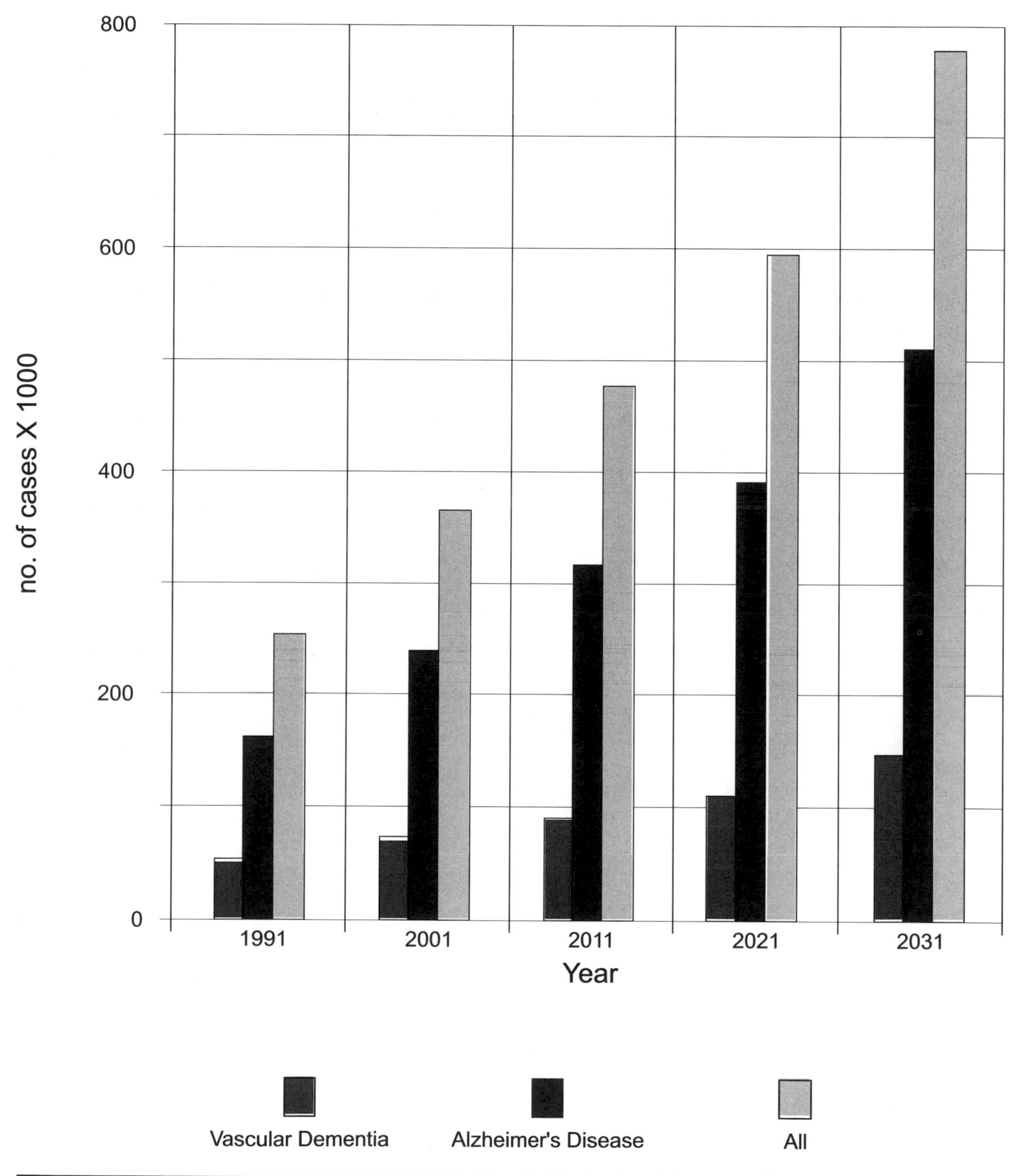

Source: *Canadian Study of Health and Aging Working Group. Canadian Study of Health and Aging. CMA Journal 1994.*

J.14: Estimated number, in thousands, and percentage of cases of Alzheimer's disease in the 65+ population, by region and residential group, Canada, 1991

Region	Residence					
	Community		Institution		Total	
	Estimated # in 1000's	%	Estimated # in 1000's	%	Estimated # in 1000's	%
Atlantic Provinces						
Male	3.3	3.1	2.0	39.8	5.3	5.0
Female	6.2	3.9	5.5	46.7	11.7	6.7
Total	9.5	3.5	7.5	45.1	17.0	6.0
Quebec						
Male	8.4	3.4	3.3	21.4	11.7	4.6
Female	15.2	3.6	14.9	33.9	30.1	6.3
Total	23.6	3.5	18.2	30.3	41.8	5.7
Ontario						
Male	3.8	1.0	5.4	27.3	9.2	2.4
Female	20.4	3.1	23.7	37.6	44.0	5.8
Total	24.2	2.2	29.1	34.6	53.2	4.5
Prairies						
Male	5.3	2.5	4.9	41.1	10.2	4.8
Female	6.3	2.2	13.8	49.0	20.1	5.9
Total	11.6	2.3	18.7	46.9	30.3	5.5
British Columbia						
Male	4.1	2.5	2.2	31.6	6.3	3.9
Female	5.3	2.2	7.1	36.8	12.4	4.7
Total	9.4	2.3	9.3	35.1	18.7	4.4
All						
Male	24.9	2.2	17.8	30.0	42.7	3.8
Female	53.4	3.0	65.0	39.4	118.3	5.8
Total	78.3	2.7	82.8	36.7	161.0	5.1

Canadian Study of Health and Aging Definitions:

Alzheimer's Disease - the diagnostic criteria for this study were based on the criteria of the National Institute of Neurological and Communicative Disorders and Stroke and the Alzheimer's Disease and Related Disorders Association (NINCDS & ADRA).

Source: Canadian Study of Health and Aging Working Group. Canadian Study of Health and Aging: study methods and prevalence of dementia. Canadian Medical Association Journal. Ottawa, 1994; 150: 899-913.

Percentage of Persons 65+ in the Community Who Have Alzheimer.s Disease

By Region, Canada, 1991

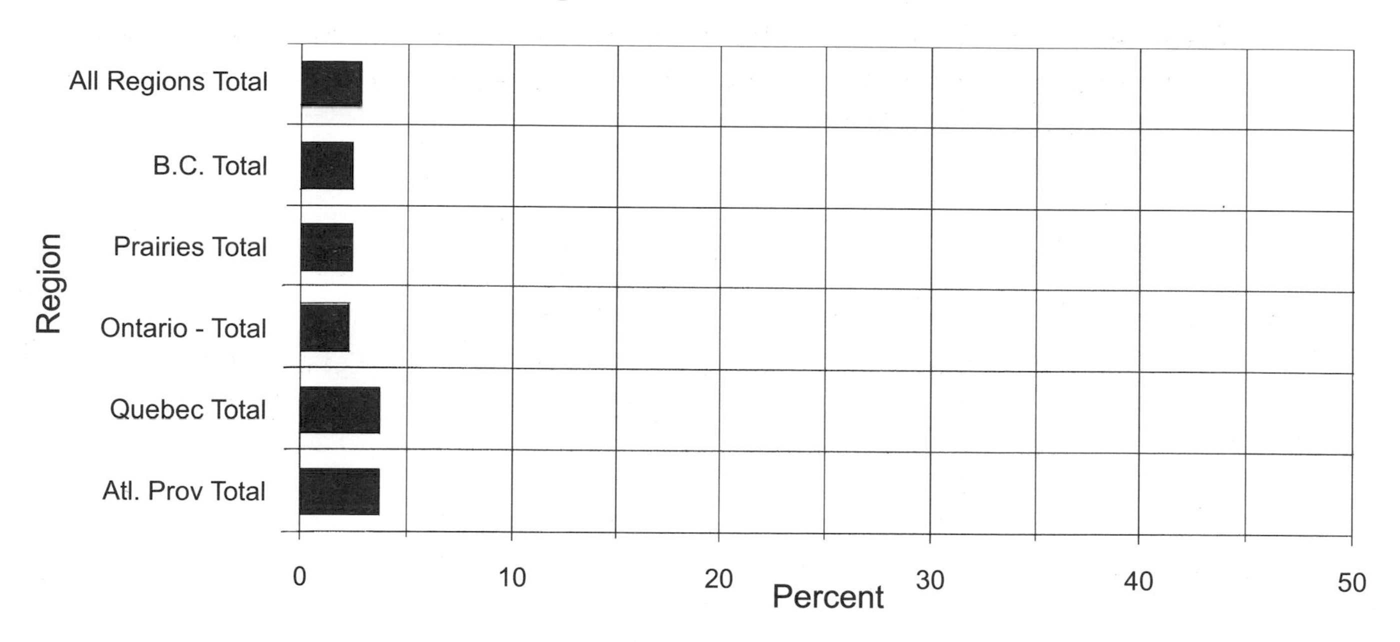

Percentage of Persons 65+ in Institutions Who Have Alzheimer.s Disease

By Region, Canada, 1991

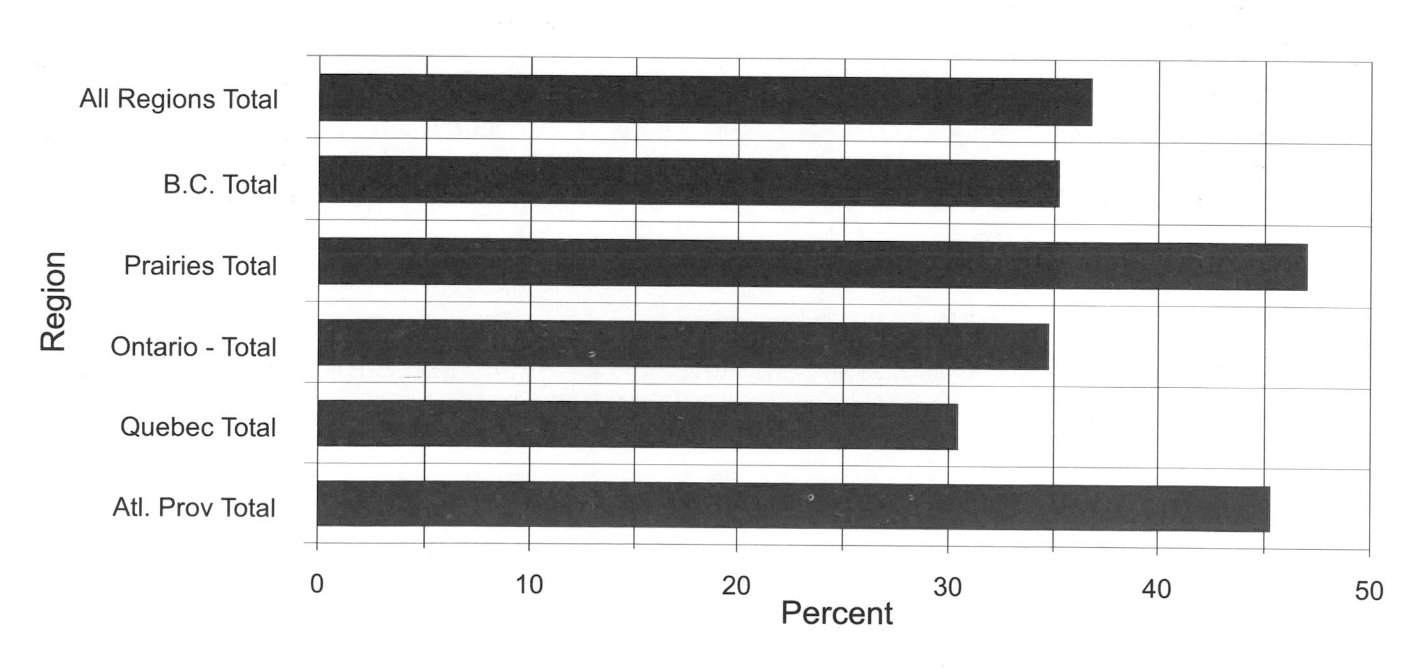

Source: Canadian Study of Health and Aging Working Group. Canadian Study of Health and Aging. CMA Journal 1994.

J.15: Estimated number, in thousands, and percentage of cases of Alzheimer's disease in the 65+ population, by age, gender and residential group, Canada, 1991

Age Group	Residence					
	Community		Institution		Total	
	Estimated # in 1000's	%	Estimated # in 1000's	%	Estimated # in 1000's	%
65-74						
Male	3.0	0.4	1.3	8.1	4.3	0.5
Female	11.2	1.1	3.6	16.9	14.7	1.4
Total	14.1	0.8	4.9	13.1	19.0	1.0
75-84						
Male	14.2	3.9	7.3	26.4	21.5	5.5
Female	24.5	4.6	22.5	36.0	47.0	7.8
Total	38.7	4.3	29.8	33.1	68.5	6.9
85 and over						
Male	7.7	12.1	9.2	41.7	16.9	19.6
Female	17.7	14.7	38.9	51.1	56.6	28.8
Total	25.5	13.8	48.1	49.0	73.5	26.0
All Ages (65+)						
Male	24.9	2.2	17.8	30.0	42.7	3.8
Female	53.4	3.0	65.0	39.4	118.3	5.8
Total	78.3	2.7	82.8	36.7	161.0	5.1

Canadian Study of Health and Aging Definition:

Alzheimer's disease - the diagnostic criteria for this study was based on the criteria of the National Institute of Neurological and Communicative Disorders and Stroke and the Alzheimer's Disease and Related Disorders Association (NINCDS & ADRA).

Source: Canadian Study of Health and Aging Working Group. Canadian Study of Health and Aging: study methods and prevalence of dementia. Canadian Medical Association Journal. Ottawa, 1994; 150: 899-913.

Percentage of Persons 65+ in the Community Who Have Alzheimer.s Disease

By Age Group, Canada, 1991

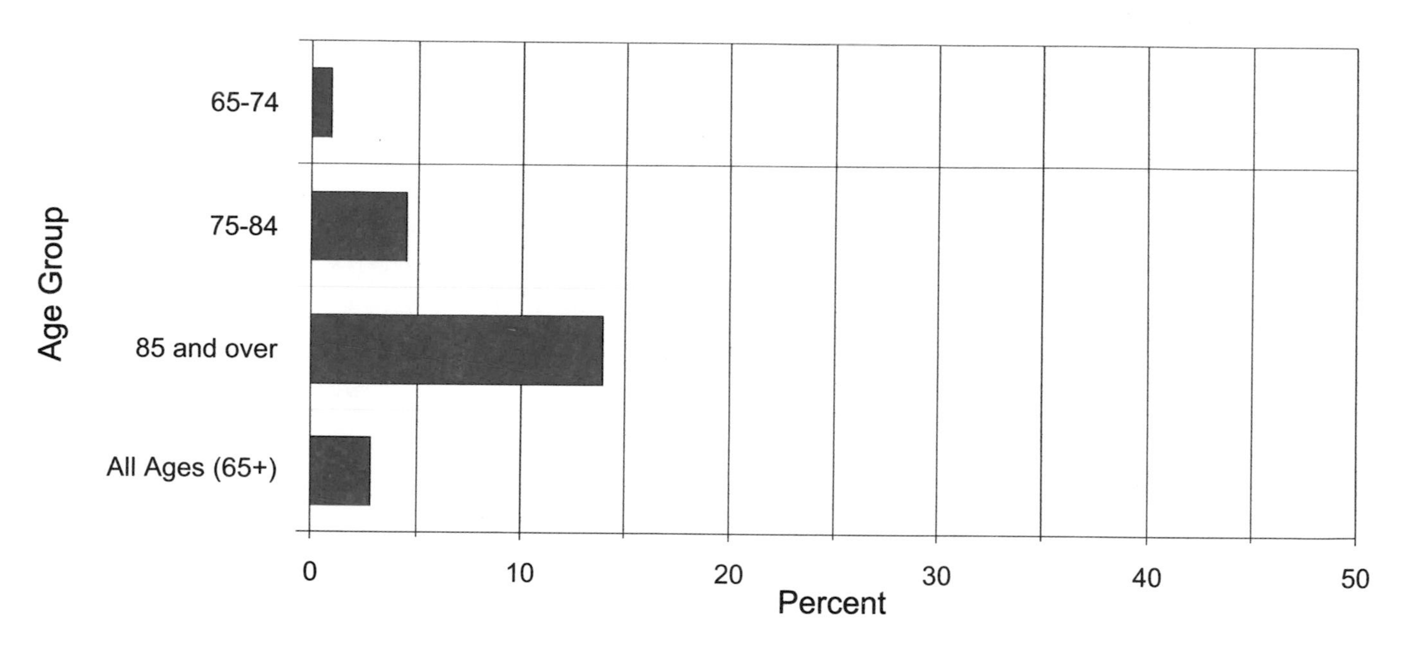

Percentage of Persons 65+ in Institutions Who Have Alzheimer.s Disease

By Age Group, Canada, 1991

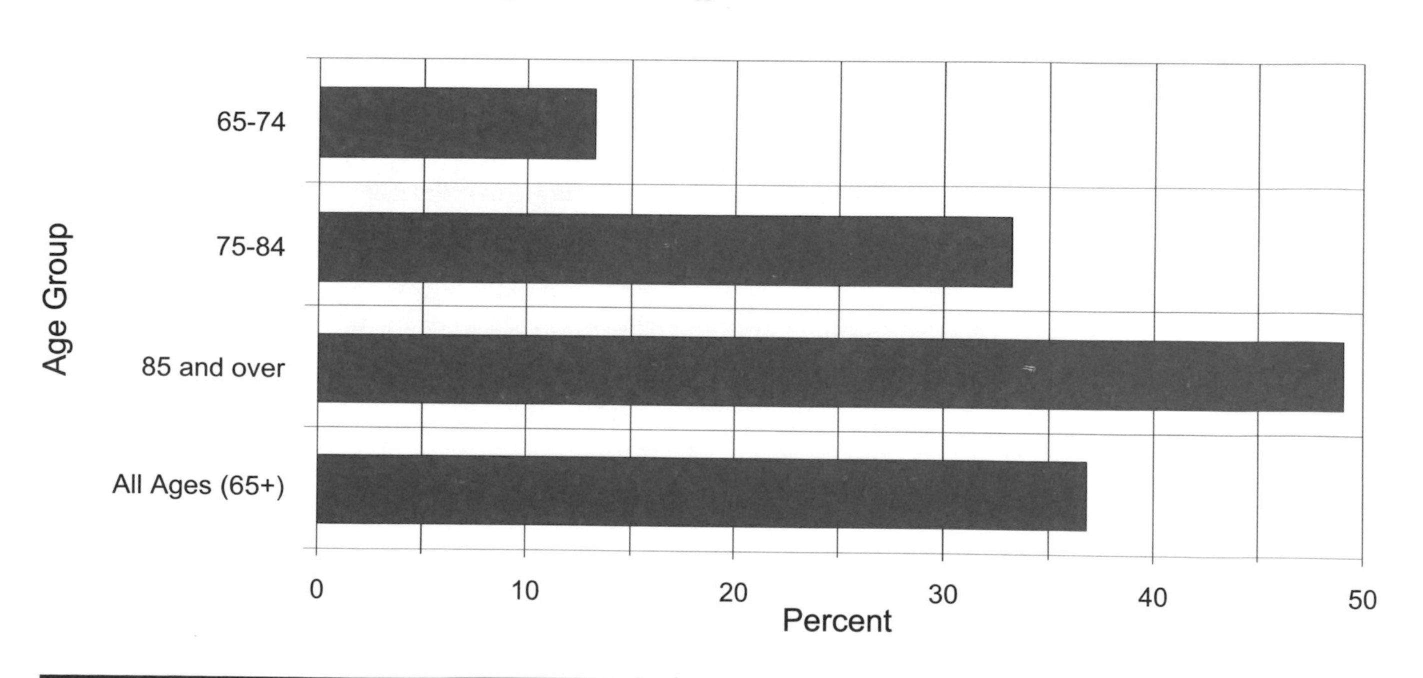

Source: Canadian Study of Health and Aging Working Group. Canadian Study of Health and Aging. CMA Journal 1994.

J.16: *Estimated number, in thousands, and percentage of cases of vascular dementia in the 65+ population, by age, gender and residential group, Canada, 1991*

Age Group	Residence					
	Community		Institution		Total	
	Estimated # in 1000's	%	Estimated # in 1000's	%	Estimated # in 1000's	%
65-74						
Male	3.8	0.5	3.4	20.7	7.2	0.8
Female	2.3	0.2	1.8	8.4	4.1	0.4
Total	6.1	0.3	5.2	13.7	11.2	0.6
75-84						
Male	7.6	2.1	4.8	17.3	12.3	3.1
Female	4.5	0.8	6.9	11.0	11.4	1.9
Total	12.1	1.3	11.7	12.9	23.8	2.4
85 and over						
Male	1.7	2.7	2.7	12.4	4.5	5.2
Female	2.7	2.3	6.4	8.4	9.1	4.6
Total	4.5	2.4	9.1	9.3	13.6	4.8
All Ages (65+)						
Male	13.1	1.1	10.9	15.7	24.0	1.9
Female	9.5	0.5	15.1	9.4	24.6	1.2
Total	22.7	0.7	26.0	11.5	48.6	1.5

Canadian Study of Health and Aging Definition:

Vascular Dementia - this study used a draft of the 10th revision of the International Classification of Diseases which was used to define the subcategories of vascular dementias.

Source: Canadian Study of Health and Aging Working Group. Canadian Study of Health and Aging: study methods and prevalence of dementia. Canadian Medical Association Journal. Ottawa, 1994; 150: 899-913.

Percentage of Persons 65+ in the Community Who Have Vascular Dementia

By Age Group, Canada, 1991

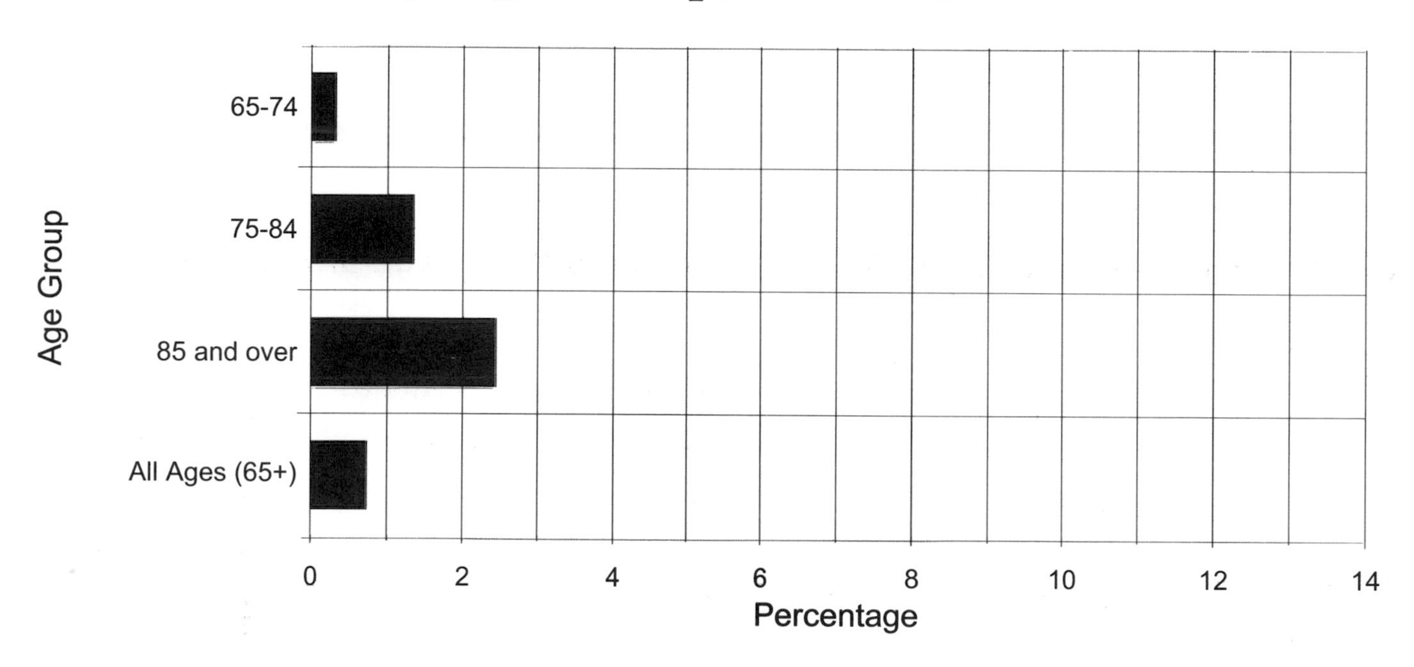

Percentage of Persons 65+ in Institutions Who Have Vascular Dementia

By Age Group, Canada, 1991

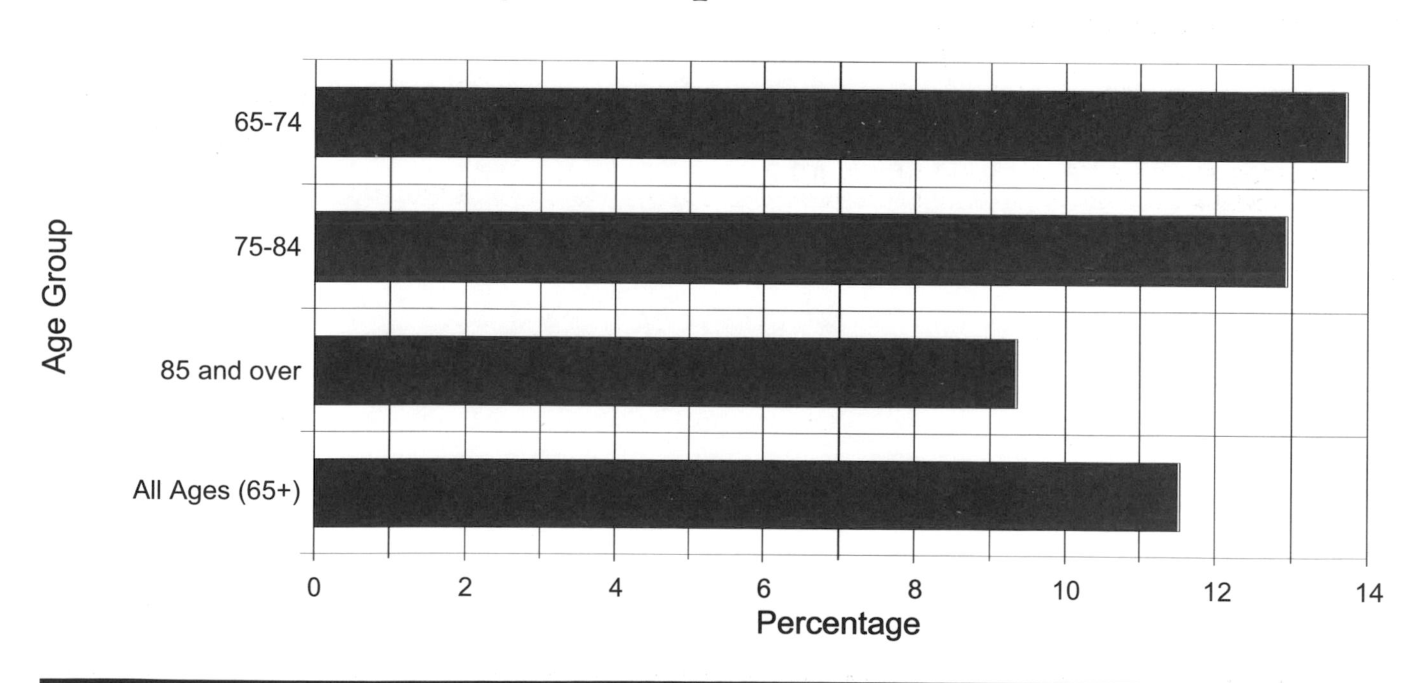

Source: Canadian Study of Health and Aging Working Group. Canadian Study of Health and Aging. CMA Journal 1994.

J.17: Percentage of Canadians with a disability, by age and gender, 1991

Age Group	Males (%)	Females (%)
15-64	12.8	12.9
65-74	43.4	37.0
75-84	53.3	59.0
85+	79.6	85.5

Statistics Canada Definition:

Respondents with disabilities include those who "report some level of disability or long-term health condition that limits the kind or amount of activity at home, work, school or in other activities such as travel, sport or leisure."

Source: Statistics Canada. Selected Characteristics of Persons with Disabilities Residing in Households. Ottawa, 1993 (1991 Health and Activity Limitation Survey; Cat. No. 82-555, p2-4).

Canadians with a Disability
By Age and Gender, 1991

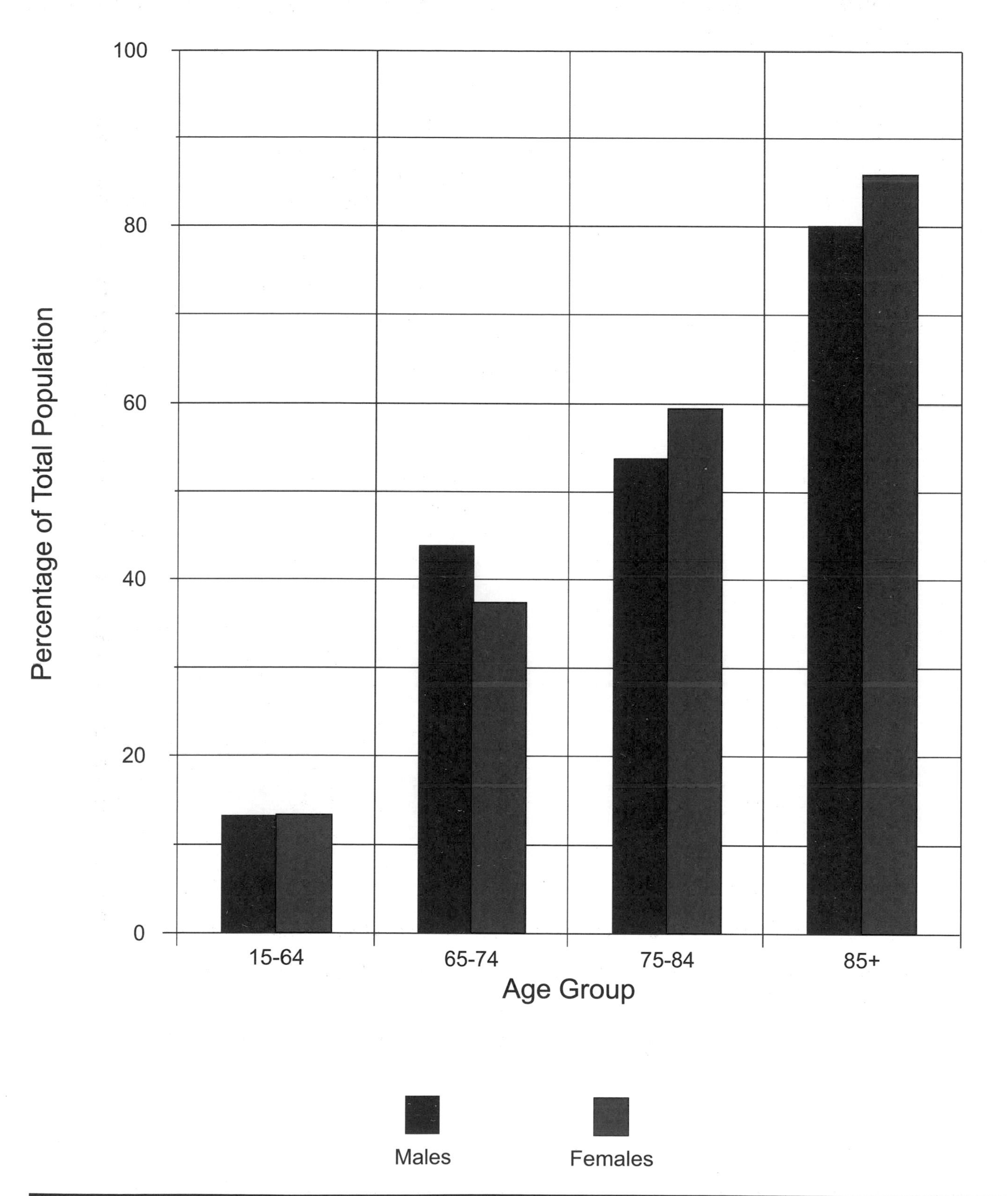

Source: Statistics Canada. Selected Characteristics of Persons With Disabilities Residing in Households. Ottawa, 1993.

J.18: Selected characteristics of Canadians 65+ with disabilities who reside in households, 1991

Characteristic †	%	Characteristic †	%
Marital Status		*Barriers Preventing Greater Participation in Leisure*	
Married & Common-Law	53.2	Physically unable to do so	18.8
Separated	1.3	Cost too high	6.5
Divorced	2.7	Lack of nearby facilities	8.4
Widowed	33.1	Need someone's assistance	7.7
Never Married	9.7	Inadequate transportation	6.3
Severity of Disability		Not accessible	2.9
Mild	39.4	Need special aids	1.3
Moderate	35.2	Lack of support from family or friends	1.2
Severe	25.4		
Nature of Disability		*Overall Feeling at Present*	
Mobility	71.7	Very Happy	21.0
Agility	60.7	Pretty Happy	59.6
Seeing	24.1	Not too happy	10.8
Legally Blind	1.6	Not specified	8.6
Hearing	41.1		
Speaking	5.1		
Other	25.7		
People Reporting Barriers to Receiving Health or Social Services	3.8		
Too costly	0.3*		
Require assistance	0.9*		
Inadequate transportation	0.8*		
Location too far	0.6*		
Facilities Not accessible	0.4*		
Physically unable to go	0.6*		

† Characteristics do not sum to 100% due to rounding and the exclusion of those responses not providing information or not knowing.

Note: * "Data to be used with caution. The standard deviation of the estimate is between 17.7% and 33.39%."

Source: Statistics Canada. Selected Characteristics of Persons with Disabilities Residing in Households. Ottawa 1994 (1991 Health and Activity Limitation Survey; Cat. No. 82-555, p148-205).

Section K

Health Care

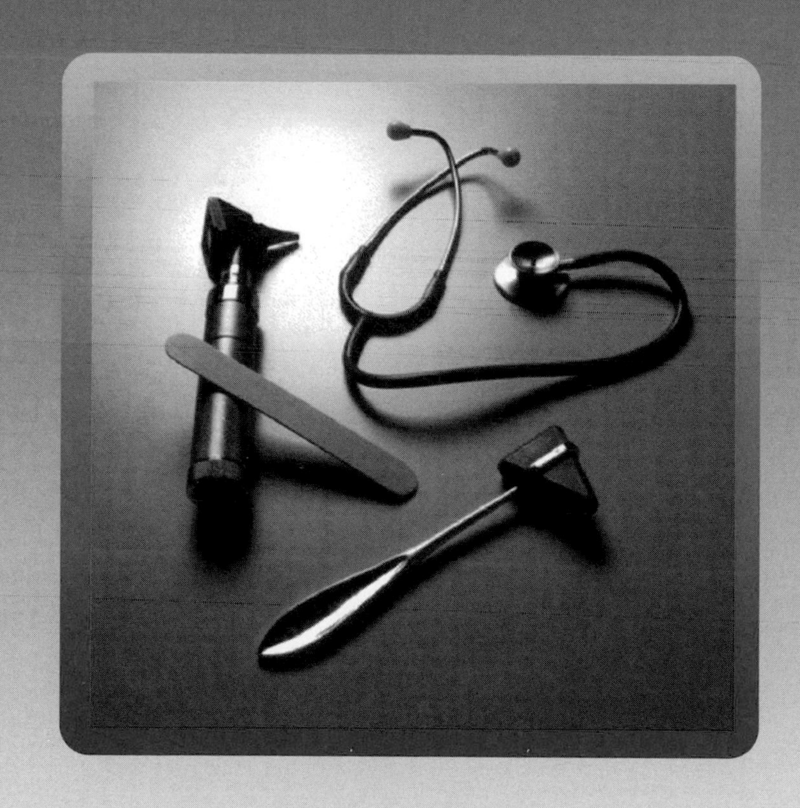

K.1: Selected causes of hospitalization* of Canadians, 1989/90

Cause of Hospitalization	Males All Ages (%)	Females All Ages (%)	Males 65+ (%)	Females 65+ (%)
Diseases of circulatory system	21.3	17.8	28.0	26.7
Diseases of nervous system	8.2	7.8	8.5	8.4
Mental disorders	11.2	12.3	8.6	11.8
Respiratory diseases	9.0	6.0	9.9	6.5
Cancer	9.7	7.8	11.4	7.5
All other causes	40.6	48.4	33.6	39.1

Note: Not all columns sum to 100% due to rounding in source table.

* Based on total number of hospitalizations in Canada in 1989/90.

Source: Statistics Canada. J.A. Norland. Focus on Canada - Profile of Canada's Seniors. Ottawa, 1994 (Cat. No. 96-312E, p111).

Selected Causes of Hospitalization
Canadians, 1989/90

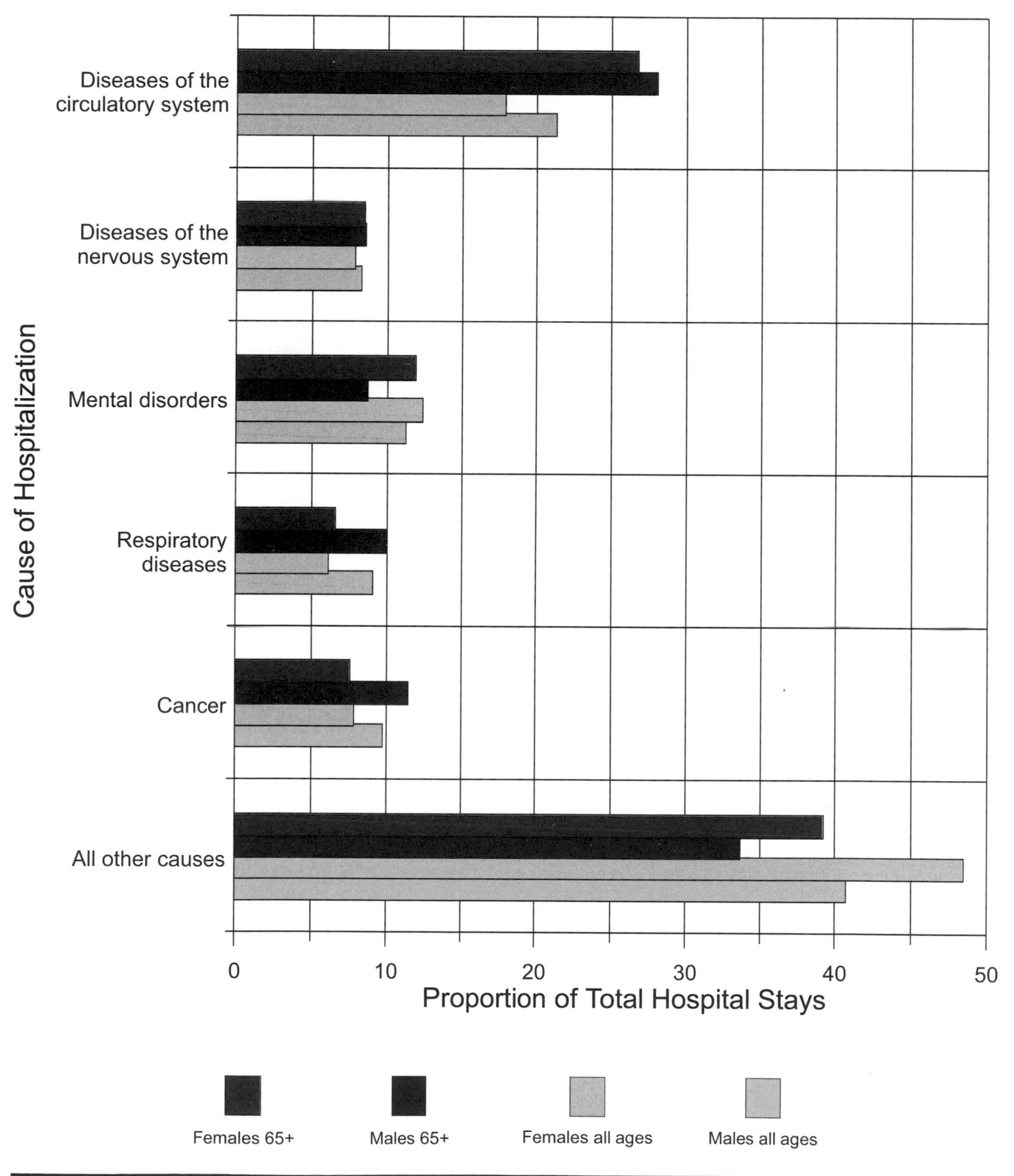

Source: *Statistics Canada. J.A. Norland. Focus on Canada - Profile of Canada's Seniors. Ottawa, 1994.*

K.2: Type of health care professional consulted by Canadians 65+ in year preceding survey, 1991

Type of Professional	Males 65-74 (%)	Females 65-74 (%)	Males 75+ (%)	Females 75+ (%)
Medical doctor	87	92	92	92
Specialist	37	35	43	35
Dentist	39	39	26	20
Nurse	10	11	16	17
Optometrist	32	39	39	41

Source: Health Priorities Analysis Unit. McMaster University. Hamilton, 1995 (1991 General Social Survey)

Health Care Professionals Consulted
By Canadian Patients Aged 65+, 1991

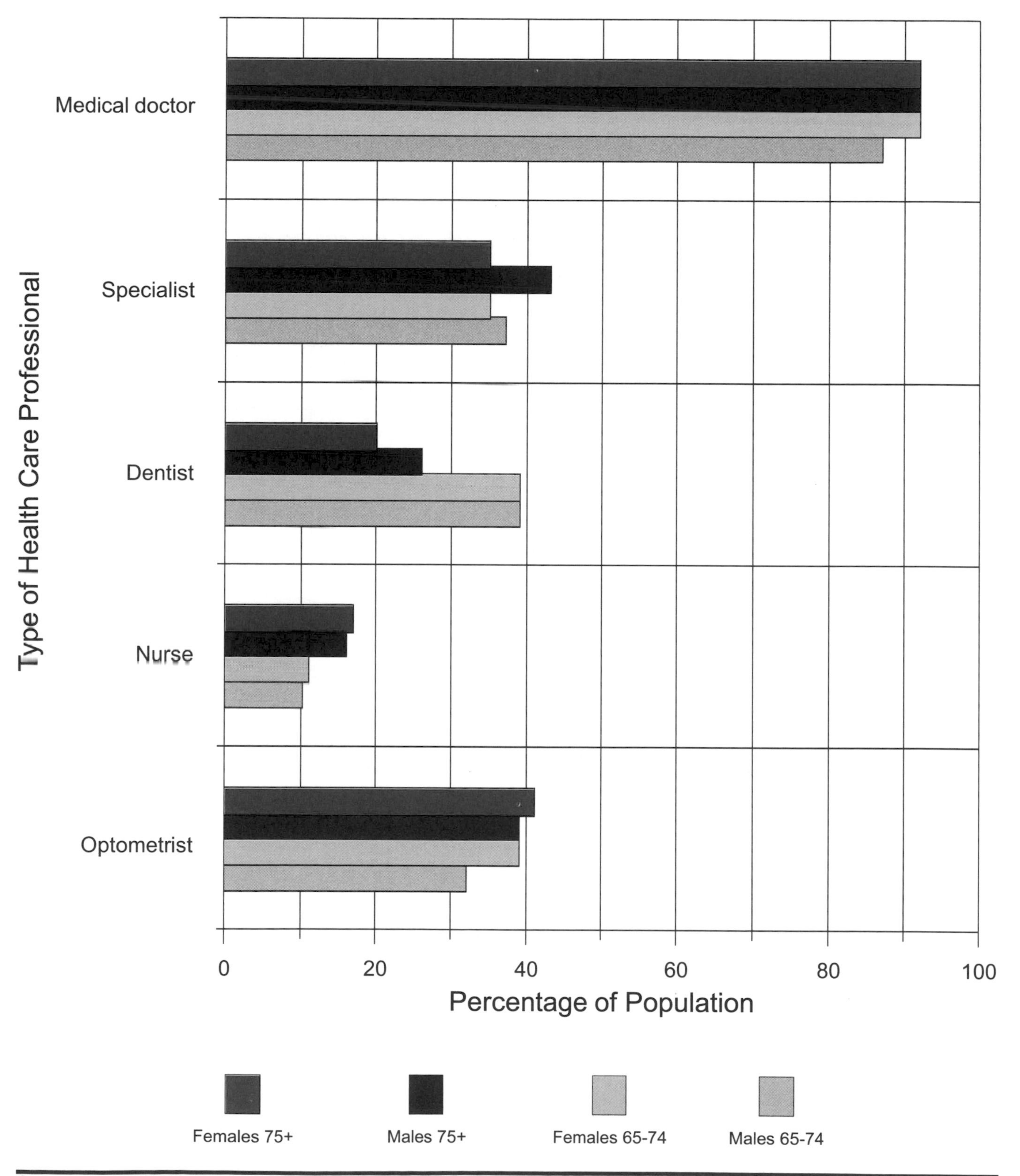

Source: *Health Priorities Analysis Unit. McMaster University. Hamilton, 1995*

K.3: Number of medical doctor consultations made by Canadians 65+ in year preceding survey, 1991

Number of Consultations	Males 65-74 (%)	Females 65-74 (%)	Males 75+ (%)	Females 75+ (%)
None	11	7	7	6
One to Two	29	27	23	20
Three to Nine	42	44	46	42
Ten or More	17	21	23	29

Note: Columns do not sum to 100% due to the exclusion of results of people who did not provide information regarding number of medical doctor consultations.

Source: Health Priorities Analysis Unit. McMaster University. Hamilton, 1995 (1991 General Social Survey)

Number of Contacts With Medical Doctor
By Canadian Patients Aged 65+, 1991

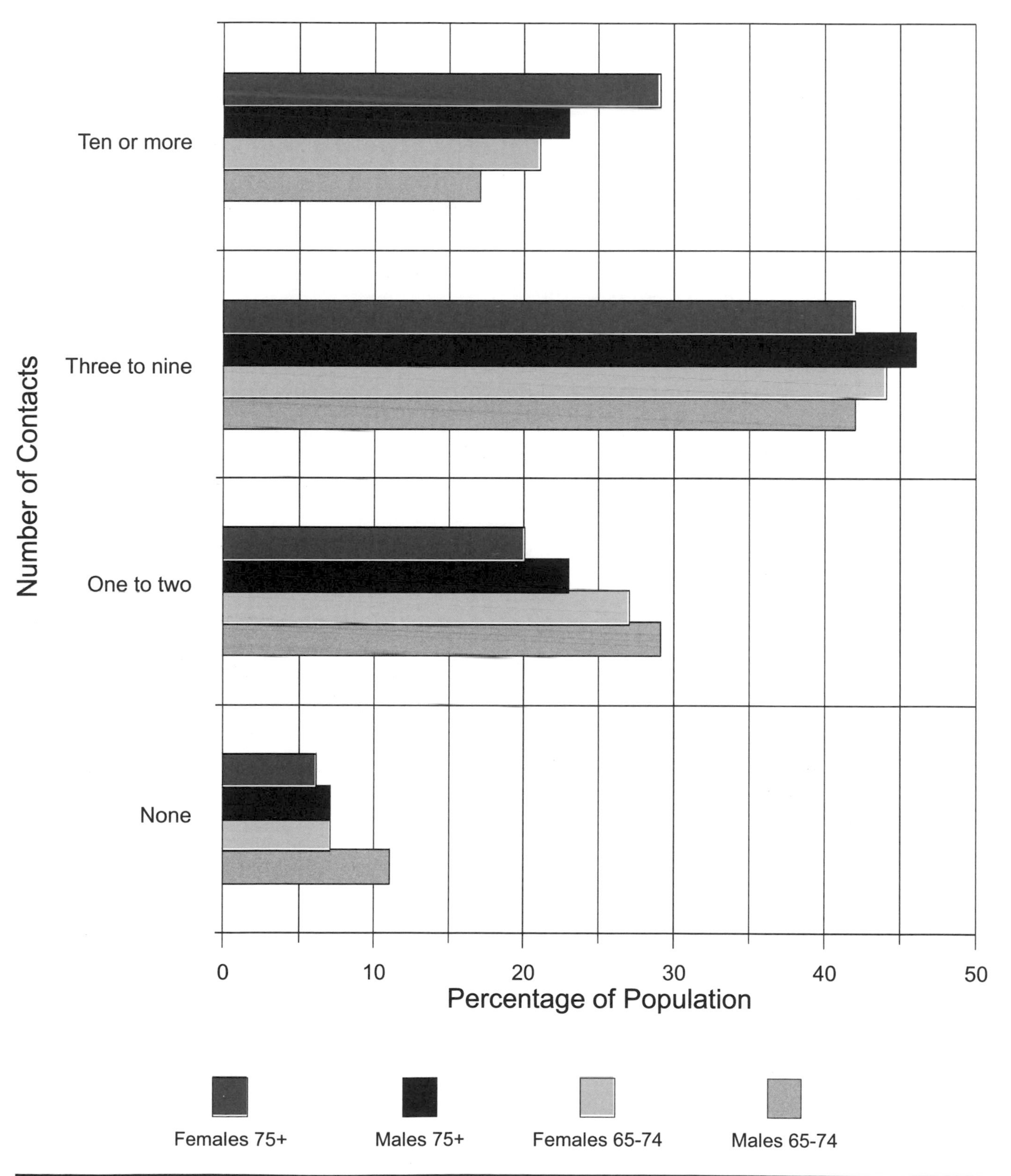

Source: Health Priorities Analysis Unit. McMaster University. Hamilton, 1995

Canadian drinking patterns indicate that adults consume less alcohol with age, and the population drank less in 1991 than it did in 1978-1979.

Health Status of Canadians, General Social Survey, 1991

The percentage of daily smokers over the age of 65 is lower than it is for all younger age groups, and fewer people reported being daily smokers, in all groups, in 1991 than in 1985.

Health Status of Canadians, General Social Survey, 1991

Sleep difficulties are reported more often by women than men in all age groups of the population 15 years of age and older, and the prevalence tends to increase with age for both males and females.

Health Status of Canadians, General Social Survey, 1991

Bibliography

Canadian Council on Social Development, G. Schellenberg (Centre for National Statistics). The Road to Retirement: Demographic and Economic changes in the 90's. Ottawa, 1994.

Canadian Study of Health and Aging Working Group. "Canadian Study of Health and Aging: Study methods and prevalence of dementia," Canadian Medical Association Journal. Ottawa, 1994: 150 (6) (1991 data).

Health Canada. Ageing and Independence: Overview of a National Survey. Ottawa, 1993 (1991 Survey).

Health Canada. Ageing and Independence: Provincial Highlights. Ottawa, 1993 (1991 Survey).

Health Canada. Canada's Health Promotion Survey 1990: Technical Report. Ottawa, 1993 (1990 Health Promotion Survey).

Health Priorities Analysis Unit, McMaster University. Hamilton, 1995 (1991 General Social Survey).

Ryerson Polytechnical Institute. National Survey on Abuse of the Elderly in Canada. Toronto, 1990.

Statistics Canada. Ethnic Origin: The Nation. Ottawa, 1992 (1991 Census of Canada; Cat. No. 91-315).

Statistics Canada. Family and Friends. Ottawa, 1994 (1990 General Social Survey; Cat. No. 11-612).

Statistics Canada. Health Status of Canadians. Ottawa, 1994 (1991 General Social Survey; Cat. No. 11-612E).

Statistics Canada. Immigration and Citizenship: The Nation. Ottawa, 1993 (1991 Census of Canada;Cat No. 93-316).

Statistics Canada. Mother Tongue: The Nation. Ottawa, 1992 (1991 Census of Canada; Cat. No. 93-313).

Statistics Canada. Pension Plans in Canada. Ottawa, 1992 (1991 Census of Canada; Cat. No. 74-401).

Statistics Canada. "Employer-sponsored pension plans -- who is covered?", Perspectives on Labour and Income. Ottawa, 1992 (1989 data; Cat. No. 75-001).

Bibliography (cont'd)

Statistics Canada. Population Ageing and the Elderly. Ottawa, 1993 (1991 Census of Canada; Cat. No. 91-533E).

Statistics Canada. Religions in Canada: The Nation. Ottawa, 1993 (1991 Census of Canada; Cat. No. 93-319).

Statistics Canada. Selected Characteristics of Persons with Disabilities Residing in Households. Ottawa, 1993 (1991 Health and Activity Limitation Survey; Cat. No. 82-555).

Statistics Canada - Demography Division, B. Desjardins. Population, Ageing and the Elderly. Ottawa, 1993 (1986 Census of Canada; Cat. No. 91-533E).

Statistics Canada - Housing, Family and Social Statistics Division. A Portrait of Seniors in Canada. Ottawa, 1990 (1988 data; Cata. No. 89-519).

Statistics Canada, D. Kerr and B. Ram. Focus on Canada -- Population Dynamics in Canada. Ottawa, 1994 (1991 Census of Canada, Cat. No. 96-305E).

Statistics Canada, J.A. Norland. Focus on Canada -- Profile of Canada's Seniors. Ottawa, 1994 (Cat. No. 96-312E).

Statistics Canada, M. Bergob. "Drug Use Among Senior Canadians," Canadian Social Trends. Ottawa, 1994 (1989 data; Summer).

Woodruff, D., and Birren, J. Aging: Scientific Perspectives and Social Issues, Second Edition. Brooks/Cole Publishing Company, California, 1983.